Major Corrections

Tom Geue teaches classical studies at the Australian National University. He has written about the mysteries of anonymous writing in the ancient world, including the books *Author Unknown: The Power of Anonymity in Ancient Rome* and *Juvenal and the Poetics of Anonymity*. He has also written Marxist criticism of classical Latin poetry. In 2021, his original research won him a Philip Leverhulme Prize.

Major Corrections

An Intellectual Biography
of Sebastiano Timpanaro

Tom Geue

VERSO

London • New York

First published by Verso 2025
© Tom Geue 2025

1 3 5 7 9 10 8 6 4 2

Verso
UK: 6 Meard Street, London W1F 0EG
US: 207 East 32nd Street, New York, NY 10016
versobooks.com

Verso is the imprint of New Left Books

ISBN-13: 978-1-80429-377-5
ISBN-13: 978-1-80429-378-2 (UK EBK)
ISBN-13: 978-1-80429-379-9 (US EBK)

British Library Cataloguing in Publication Data
A catalogue record for this book is available from the British Library

Library of Congress Cataloging-in-Publication Data

Names: Geue, Tom, author.
Title: Major corrections : an intellectual biography of Sebastiano
    Timpanaro / Tom Geue.
Description: First edition. | London ; New York : Verso, 2025. | Includes
    bibliographical references and index.
Identifier s: LCCN 2024034378 (print) | LCCN 2024034379 (ebook) | ISBN
    9781804293775 (trade paperback) | ISBN 9781804293799 (US ebook) | ISBN
    9781804293782 (UK ebook)
Subjects: LCSH: Timpanaro, Sebastiano. | Philologists—Italy—Biography.
Classifica tion: LCC PC1064.T56 G48 2025 (print) | LCC PC1064.T56 (ebook)
    | DDC 409.2 [B]—dc23/eng/20240918
LC record available at https://lccn.loc.gov/2024034378
LC ebook record available at https://lccn.loc.gov/2024034379

Typeset in Minion by Hewer Text UK Ltd, Edinburgh

To the people of Livorno, whose youth still drink
a cocktail called 'Violence of the Proletariat'.

And to my mother, Vania Pittioni (b. 1948 Asiago,
d. 2022 Sydney), who is sipping it somewhere.

'In the end we also will be dead, and our own lives will lie inert within the finished process, our intentions assimilated within a past event which we never intended. What we may hope is that the men and women of the future will reach back to us, will affirm and renew our meanings, and make our history intelligible within their own present tense. They alone will have the power to select from the many meanings offered by our quarrelling present, and to transmute some part of our process into their progress.'

E. P. Thompson, *The Poverty of Theory*

'And the most rewarding of all projects, they say, is to restore to its earlier lustre some relic from the history of ideas. No matter what uses you find for it, or what coruscations you bring to light in its long-obscured surface, you may always enjoy a pleasant mistrust of your estimation of it. The insights you would like to cherish for their completeness may one day be newly enlarged by the merest footnote found in some outdated text. And even though you delight in your possession of neglected notions and discarded ideas, you must acknowledge that someone before your time has considered them in a different light.'

Gerald Murnane, *The Plains*

'Humanism, I think, is the means, perhaps the consciousness we have for providing that kind of finally antinomian or oppositional analysis between the space of words and their various origins and deployments in physical and social place, from text to actualized site of either appropriation or resistance, to transmission, to reading and interpretation, from private to public, from silence to explication and utterance, and back again, as we encounter our own silence and mortality – all of it occurring in the world, on the ground of daily life and history and hopes, and the search for knowledge and justice, and then perhaps also for liberation.'

Edward Said, *Humanism and Democratic Criticism*

Contents

Preface

It is a strange feeling to write a whole book on someone who would have surely despised your work. But here we are. I was originally attracted to Sebastiano Timpanaro for the obvious synergy of our interests: both of us trained in classical philology, both with ties and sympathies to the radical left. But, the more I read of Timpanaro's work, the more I became attuned with his mode of seeing the world, the more I realised that he would have scoffed at my own contributions to the field of Latin literature as superficial, sophistic, and too 'clever' to be *true*. My own training in an intellectual tradition basking in the long afterglow of post-structuralism, of which the Cambridge Faculty of Classics (my PhD institution) remained particularly enamoured in the 1990s and 2000s, was anathema to Timpanaro, the product of a very different culture and historical moment. Timpanaro was a technical philologist committed to truth, science, and objectivity. The kind of things I have written in my life, by contrast, are probably closer to the unhinged interpretations of the Freudian skewered by Timpanaro (see chapter 5) than to Timpanaro himself. If the subject of this book had been able to appoint his intellectual synthesiser and exegete, one thing is for sure: he would not have chosen me.

I first came to Timpanaro through good mentoring. With the final exams of my undergraduate degree at the University of Sydney over, I availed myself of the carnival space of the end of the year to have some frank chats with my beloved supervisor, the classical and renaissance

Latinist Frances Muecke. After four years' hard slog in Latin and Greek, I lived more than ever to read classical literature and literary scholarship on it. What I could not abide – I moaned to Frances – was textual criticism: the dry and dusty art of consulting manuscripts and emending texts. It just did not interest me. Frances asked me if I had read Timpanaro's *The Freudian Slip*. No? Well, then, I should.

I took the book out of the library and imbibed it in a single sitting. It was unlike anything I had ever read in classical scholarship: sharp, funny, lucid, scathing. And on many points it felt . . . true. It connected what I saw at that time to be a disturbingly esoteric, marginal, and hermetically sealed universe – classical scholarship – to some of the most important currents of twentieth-century intellectual history: to Marx and Freud and their afterlives. It opened a portal between the small things of philology and the big things of politics; it made philology *matter*. This was the spark that fired my love for Timpanaro. Sixteen years later, at the end of a project which has seen me go over this thinker with a fine-toothed comb – a workaday domestication perhaps not conducive to keeping that spark alive – I am happy to report the flame burns brighter than ever. The histories of philology and of the left have few figures in their number more eccentric, more compelling, or more penetrating than Sebastiano Timpanaro. He is due some serious attention.

While my admiration for Timpanaro is clear, I should also come clean on my relationship to certain parts of his thought-world. I remain sceptical of the strand of positivism running through his work, which seems determined to discount some of the most important continental critical traditions of the twentieth century, from the Frankfurt school to post-structuralism. I do not subscribe to these dismissals. But making this book has been an exercise, for me, in the salutary process of writing across a divide. As Timpanaro well knew, great thinkers deserve to be read on their own terms, with sympathy and depth, even if we do not agree with everything they say. While I have much more respect than Timpanaro did for the theoretical currents informing Western Marxism in the 1960s and '70s, and also for what came after, I think that Timpanaro's challenges to Freud et al. are fascinating and generative pieces of countercultural criticism, deserving of sustained treatment. What is more, his call for a restored materialism, and a profound marriage between the sciences (especially the physical and biological) and Marxism, has refreshed resonance in the wake of a global pandemic that has shown us all too sharply the biological limits of which Timpanaro warned, but also the disastrous impact of the cosiness between science and global capital. After writing this book, I have decided that merely issuing critiques of science is not the best way forward for the left. We should be taking back what is ours, rather than leaving it warily to the market or the venture capitalists; and we should be advancing socialism as, among other things, the best vector for scientific progress imaginable. We should be courting, not alienating, the scientists. While I began this project somewhat sceptical of Timpanaro's blunt and (at times seemingly) naive celebrations of science, I end it a partial convert: a properly scientific, properly materialist Marxism remains the only way forward.

Having said that, I would still emphasise that my approach in this book is one of patient and 'sympathetic' explanation, which should not be confused with across-the-board, ringing endorsement. I do think that Timpanaro misses important elements in arguing with his various bugbears, from psychoanalysis to literary criticism; and it is often a case of discursive systems simply being unable to find any productive common ground because they begin from such different premises. But what I have privileged in this book is the goal not of resistant criticism, or active antagonism towards the object of study, but of understanding a particular way of thinking, and of presenting the most important aspects of that system in as generous a manner as possible. In other words, I try to treat Timpanaro the way he treated his favourite poet, Giacomo Leopardi, rather than the way he treated his nemesis, Freud. This has resulted, at times, in a strange merging of voices, a kind of free indirect discourse, where my attempts to ventriloquise Timpanaro sometimes take me dangerously close to fully identifying with his way of thinking. Perhaps not all the way though: Timpanaro would be quick to write off my disclaimer as psychobabble. While I have come to identify with my subject over time, this is the fruit of many years' work. Particularly at the beginning, it was not always easy to treat even-handedly a thinker who represents precisely the kind of philological nitpicker I have spent a lifetime forming myself against (and with whom I have often had unpleasant dealings). But I still believe, taking after Timpanaro, that reading and conversing seriously with those who might disagree with us is one of the most important intellectual activities in which one can partake. Historical research can be powered by such fruitful tensions.

The problem of treating a 'renaissance' thinker such as Timpanaro – versed in so many fields – as a 'whole' is that you quickly butt up against the hard barriers of your own very circumscribed expertise. I come to Timpanaro from a proper métier in literary criticism on Latin literature, with a general knowledge of the Marxist tradition (but mainly filtered through Marxist literary criticism), and with a smattering of occasional and desultory political activity on the left. As such, I have no hope of pulling off a satisfactory critical evaluation of Timpanaro's intellectual historiography in all of his various fields beyond classical philology: nineteenth-century Italian culture and literature, the philosophical history of materialism versus idealism, psychoanalysis, and linguistics, to name the main subjects of this book. In order to make such judgements, I would have had to acquaint myself with an unmanageable amount of bibliography in alien fields. Even were such a thing possible (Timpanaro himself, inhumanly productive as he was, arguably showed it is not), you would need a lifetime to accrue such knowledge – and probably a job less demanding and time consuming than that of a modern university lecturer. But, I hope I do not risk accusations of ex post justification when I say that this task of evaluation was never my main objective. I set out to show the interrelations within Timpanaro's thought, the particular profile of attractions and repulsions that forms his intellectual universe and system – and for that, I do not think it necessary to issue authoritative opinions on whether Timpanaro was right or wrong about the contributions of Franz Bopp to nineteenth-century linguistics.

What I lack in preparation in all these various fields, I hope to make up in the extensive *Timpanaro* research on which the book is based. This is, I think, the first work on Timpanaro to combine a broad reading of his major published works with a long and laborious sifting of almost all of his correspondence, which was positively Victorian in volume. The Timpanaro archive at the Scuola Normale Superiore in Pisa contains 10,738 letters shared with 1,515 separate correspondents. By my calculations, this equates to about one letter either sent or received every day for about thirty years – in other words, a lot. I worked solidly for six months at this archive to mine some enlightening nuggets from these letters, and I hope their presence sheds new light on the published content (and vice versa). But, even here, I should admit that my methods have been singularly un-Timpanaran in the way I have combined pieces of evidence. Firstly, Timpanaro, when evaluating a given thinker, believed in a fairly strict ontological hierarchy of the published over the unpublished, whereas in this book I treat these forms of evidence almost interchangeably. Secondly, Timpanaro's use of correspondence in his intellectual historiography usually served a sensitive reconstruction of the granular evolution of a given thinker's thought on a particular subject, *over time*. While this book follows a rough chronological order through Timpanaro's major works and topics – from philology, to the nineteenth century, to materialism, to Freud, to linguistics, to 'literary criticism' – I have not concerned myself with reconstructing subtle historical arcs showing the 'evolution' of Timpanaro's thought in these camps. Rather, I have tried to point out the most striking 'common denominators' which endure in his thought over several years. Timpanaro, again, would have accused me of ahistoricism here, or worse, of being an overly synchronic structuralist neglecting the dimension of diachrony. But I have chosen this broader-brush, temporal-leaping approach for two reasons: first because it helps focus attention on the wood, with some marginal loss of a sense of precisely how the trees within it have grown; and second because Timpanaro, despite constant acts of self-revision, remained substantially consistent on many of the subjects most important to him (see the conclusion of this volume). What is more, the benefit of wide consultation across the entirety of a thinker's published and unpublished output is that the most important habits of thought start to emerge, becoming visible as they cut across contexts, addressees, genres, venues, formats, and years. If I have forfeited some of the history for the sake of the system, I ask for my subject's forgiveness.

I have tried to answer most of the very helpful comments on the manuscript given by a range of readers, from literary critics to philologists to cultural and political historians. The one piece of feedback I have felt shamefully unable to answer is the issue of 'citational justice' – the fact that the book's core material turns on the written word of (mostly) white men. This is in part a reflection of the make-up of Timpanaro's social and cultural world. Academia and politics in post–World War II Italy were spheres dominated by men – ethnically homogeneous men at that. This has had flow-on effects in the work done on Timpanaro since his death. For diversity of age and profile at least, I have tried to show-case some of the work of a younger generation of brilliant Italian schol-ars (particularly Luca Bufarale and Anna Maria Cimino) who are employed outside the academy and may not ordinarily have gained much exposure in the anglophone world. But this is a poor compensa-tion for a very skewed citational base. I can only hope to do better in the future.

Finally, a note on the form of the book. In addition to the dotting of *i*'s and crossing of *t*'s in the introduction and conclusion, the bulk is divided into seven chapters, each of which focusses on a different segment of Timpanaro's intellectual output. As such, they are mainly concerned with Timpanaro's life on the page. The chapters are punctu-ated, however, by occasional snapshots of particularly charged and interesting affairs in Timpanaro's life, points of controversy which throw certain parts of his complex personality into relief. I hope these detailed episodes give some body and colour to the otherwise-cerebral Timpanaro of this decidedly 'intellectual' biography. As we shall see, few thinkers of the twentieth century did more to remind us that we are stuff as much as mind – so it is good to see Timpanaro as a body working in the world.

Timpanaro always thought of himself as prematurely old. But his central field, philology, was cut to treat problems that never go out of date. I write this in full faith and hope that not so much will be said for the biggest problem Timpanaro once confronted, and the problem we still now confront: capitalism. If only it could one day be corrected away, a blip to be removed from the manuscript of history by the philological collective of the future. Timpanaro would have said: *that is a stupid metaphor; stop the wishful thinking; let us get to the real work of it.* We can still feel his corrections acting upon us.

Abbreviations

Sources by Sebastiano Timpanaro

AF	*Aspetti e figure della cultura ottocentesca*, Pisa, 1980
AN	*Antileopardiani e neomoderati nella sinistra italiana*, Pisa, 1982
CF	*Contributi di filologia e di storia della lingua latina*, Rome, 1978
CI	*Classicismo e illuminismo nell'Ottocento italiano*, 2nd ed., Pisa, 1969
FGL	*La filologia di Giacomo Leopardi*, 2nd ed., Rome, 1978
FR	*La 'fobia romana' e altri scritti su Freud e Meringer*, Pisa, 1992
FS	*The Freudian Slip: Psychoanalysis and Textual Criticism*, trans. Kate Coper, London, 1985
GLM	*The Genesis of Lachmann's Method*, trans. Glenn Most, Chicago, 2006
LF	*Il lapsus freudiano. Psicanalisi e critica testuale*, 2nd ed., ed. Fabio Stok, Turin, 2002
NC	*Nuovi contributi di filologia e storia della lingua Latina*, Bologna, 1994
NS	*Nuovi studi sul nostro Ottocento*, Pisa, 1995
OM	*On Materialism*, trans. Lawrence Garner, London, 1975.
PLS	*Per la storia della filologia virgiliana antica*, Rome, 1986
SED	*Il socialismo di Edmondo De Amicis. Lettura del 'Primo Maggio'*, Verona, 1984.
SLO	*Sulla linguistica dell'Ottocento*, Bologna, 2005
SM	*Sul materialismo*, 3rd ed., Milan, 1997

VA   *Virgilianisti antichi e tradizione indiretta*, Florence, 2001
VR   *Il verde e il rosso. Scritti militanti (1966–2000)*, ed. Luigi Cortesi,
        Rome, 2001

Sources by other authors
BS   Paul H. T. d'Holbach, *Il buon senso* (*Good Sense*), trans. and ed.
        Sebastiano Timpanaro, Milan, 1985
DD   Marco Tullio Cicerone, *Della divinazione* (*On Divination*),
        trans. and ed. Sebastiano Timpanaro, Milan, 1988
SF   *Giacomo Leopardi: Scritti filologici (1817–1832)*, ed. Giuseppe
        Pacella and Sebastiano Timpanaro, Florence, 1969

For detailed notes on the bibliography, see Appendix 2.

Introduction

Bit Parts

Sebastiano Timpanaro was bad at coping with praise. Whenever he felt fawning in his direction, he shut it down. He immediately poured cold water over his interlocutor's enthused panegyric, rattling off a litany of reasons why, on the contrary, he was in fact a worthless nothing. In March 1981, a young aspiring intellectual by the name of Antonio Perin sent Timpanaro some fan mail expressing unbounded admiration for him as a thinker and militant. But Timpanaro would have none of the folly of youth, whose distorted field of vision rendered figures bigger than they actually were. With age, Perin would undoubtedly cut him down to the size he deserved:

> With the passing of time and with the advancement of your studies and your human experience, without doubt you will 'resize' me: you will realise that I don't have the stature of a 'leader', neither cultural nor 'moral' nor political, and that therefore, unfortunately, it's impossible to hope for direction from me, in this society in which I am ever more directionless and to which I feel myself ever more alien, without having the capacity to point to new ways.[1]

Timpanaro denied himself any status as moral or political figurehead. He was not one to look up to. He could offer no guidance to the new

---

1 S.T. to Antonio Perin, 28 March 1981. Translations from Italian are my own throughout the book, unless marked otherwise.

generation. Someone as disoriented as he could be no source of direction. Our young student would only be disappointed by this old prophet
past his prime, now isolated, exhausted, and out of ideas.

Despite prematurely sabotaging the value of any further wisdom that
might come from his pen, Timpanaro responded to Perin's request for
more details about his life. But there is a problem with content here:
even if Timpanaro had managed to write an autobiography, there would
be precious little of interest to the next generation. He had lived 'an
honest but mediocre life, lacking material that might interest others'.[2]
What to mention, if pressed? Timpanaro lost his father young, in 1949,
when he was only twenty-six. He got married – one of the few successful
experiences of his life. He never had children; he was not sure whether
for good or for ill. He had had feelings, strong ones, but of a 'traditional
type' – nothing particularly interesting. None of this material could
serve to help the younger generation address the problems of their
private and public lives. Timpanaro swore to having lived a life of nothing, a biography without note or value – none of it usable to assist future
generations to reinvent themselves.

The only way Timpanaro could stomach writing autobiographically[3]
– he went on to explain to his mentee Perin – would be if he could make
the story about the political climate and personalities in which he was
immersed throughout the 1940s, '50s, and '60s. At this point in the
letter, as soon as there was scope for escaping the self and inhabiting a
context bigger than it, Timpanaro's prose relaxed, unwound. From the
clammed-up denial of an interesting life, he finally settled in his chosen
position. He took the bit part, that of the secondary opera singer, not
shining enough to attract riotous applause but someone who was there
on stage, who had seen it and had something to say about it:

> But I'd want to do it [i.e., write autobiographically], indeed, speaking
> as little as possible – almost not at all – of myself: not for modesty
> (which would be false modesty), but because I've observed many
> things and people, I've participated in many discussions and confron-
> tations, but always taking a part not of protagonist and not even of

---

2   Ibid.
3   Cf. Timpanaro's comments on the ideal autobiographical mode (S.T. to Giorgio
Voghera, 15 April 1968).

important actor: only of an 'extra' or something just above it: as one of those singers in the opera theatre who have always been entrusted only with secondary or even the most minor parts, and who for that reason have never had the applause nor the boos of the audience, but, living in the theatre environment, have seen up close the great singers and great orchestra conductors and the entire 'world of the theatre', and they have something to say about them.[4]

An argument could be made that this statement, in 1981, was penned by one of the most prominent leftist intellectuals in Italy.[5] Timpanaro had by then published a host of books and articles in all of his fields of expertise – classical philology (i.e., the close study of the Latin and Greek languages, and reconstruction and interpretation of the classical texts written in them), nineteenth-century Italian culture (including literature and linguistics), the philosophy of materialism, psychoanalysis and its discontents. Two of these books had been translated into English and won extensive plaudits in the Anglophone world. Timpanaro was a famed and respected classical philologist whose reputation resonated both in Italy and abroad. He was already elected as a corresponding fellow of the British Academy in 1975, at the age of fifty-two (young for this group of the predominantly silver haired). So how could the extreme self-minimisation of the above letter not be a form of false modesty? Perhaps it was: it is a known rhetorical trope of a particular form of male intellectual to disavow authority and thirst for validation in the very same gesture. But we could also try to cast out a suspicious reading and trust this verdict on himself. Timpanaro, eminent philologist and committed materialist, Enlightenment thinker and militant Marxist, believed that the human self, the ego, subjectivity itself, were not worthy of discussion. His attention was always turned to the world outside them. If that ego could earn a place in the opera of life, it could never be

---

4   S.T. to Antonio Perin, 28 March 1981.

5   Timpanaro's 'fame' within Italy was mainly restricted to the Tuscan leftist intelligentsia. Most of his written output was with academic presses and had limited circulation (with the exception of the *LF* and *SM*); and he did not tend to write for the mainstream Italian press. For an at-a-glance yet comprehensive overview of Timpanaro's oeuvre (incl. a full bibliography) and accolades, see Giorgio Piras's entry 'Sebastiano Timpanaro' in *Dizionario biografico degli Italiani*, vol. 95, ed. Raffaele Romanelli, Rome, 2019, 688–92.

as the showy tenor showered in roses at the curtain call. It would have to be the part you barely notice because the whole, everything else, is just that much more interesting.

There was more to Timpanaro than his denial of the autobiographical mode would have us think. He remains, in fact, a singularly interesting figure of the post-war Italian left and its intellectual groups based in and around Pisa and Florence in the second half of the twentieth century. Born in Parma in 1923 to a historian of ancient Greek science for a mother and a physicist for a father, the young Timpanaro's family life was entwined with and imprinted by fascism from earliest childhood. Timpanaro's father, Sebastiano Sr, ended up teaching in a Catholic school to dodge the Fascist Party card requirement in public *licei* (Italian second-ary 'grammar' schools).[6] But after these havens were cracked down on, in 1942 he was forced, by financial necessity, to take a job as director of the Domus Galilaeana in Pisa, a cultural institute for the history of science. He was appointed specially by none other than Giovanni Gentile (1875–1944) himself, the Hegelian idealist philosopher who provided the crucial intellectual scaffolding for Italian Fascism. While the decision sat quea-sily with Timpanaro Sr, the family made the move to Pisa, and the subse-quent mild colouring of shame and guilt shadowed both Timpanaro Sr and Jr for the rest of their lives. In the ratcheting up of the politics of past scrutiny after the end of Italian Fascism, the question would become inescapable: What were your family doing during the *ventennio*, the twenty-year Fascist interregnum? Timpanaro Jr would always declare, with full and uncompromising honesty, that his family were 'reluctant' (*renitente*) but not 'resistant' (*resistente*), unwilling non-collaborators, but not all-out partisan heroes.[7] Such guilt at not being in a family at the vanguard of resistance perhaps underlay Timpanaro's locked and unswerving commitment to revolutionary socialism for the rest of his life. At the same time, it set the tone for his self-definition as someone who could never quite be *truly* on the front lines.[8]

---

6 See also Luca Bufarale, *Sebastiano Timpanaro: L'inquietudine della ricerca*, Pistoia, 2022, 20.

7 S.T. to Antonio Russi (numbered 3 in the Timpanaro archive), n.d.; cf. Bufarale, *Sebastiano Timpanaro*, 23.

8 S.T. to Luca Baranelli, 6 July 1962; S.T. to Giorgio Voghera, 3 September 1965; S.T. to Luciano Della Mea, 30 June 1976.

Timpanaro was remarkably close to both his parents, and they loom large as figures in his intellectual formation (and beyond). His father died in 1949, when Timpanaro was not yet thirty, and well before he had become a name on the Tuscan left. But Timpanaro Jr would later talk of the influence exercised by early discussions with Timpanaro Sr over his political and intellectual awakening in youth. All three members of the Timpanaro clan joined the Italian Socialist Party (PSI), then a revolutionary party,[9] immediately after World War II. Timpanaro's mother had been involved with the PSI through the multi-party anti-fascist organisation, the Comitato di Liberazione Nazionale (National Liberation Committee), in which she had been active from the moment of Pisa's liberation in 1944; the father and son Timpanaro eventually followed suit by registering as members of the PSI in 1947.[10] Politically, both Timpanaro generations were more or less on the same page. But Timpanaro's father was of a completely different philosophical orientation: he was a scientific idealist at heart, sympathising with the Hegelian strand of Italian philosophy then dominating through its authoritative representatives Gentile and Benedetto Croce (1866–1952), although he dissented vigorously from their contempt for science.[11] You might say that, though Timpanaro Sr resisted the political conclusions of Gentile, he was receptive to the philosophical. Timpanaro Jr, meanwhile, cut himself from very different cloth. His incipient materialism was hammered out largely in spirited debates with his father – and he would spread this private discussion well beyond the bounds of his household for all his later life, taking the fight against Hegelian idealism so hard that he would even deny the value, for Marxism, of intellectual institutions like the 'dialectic'. Hegel's absolute idealism posited that the world was a kind of unity of subject and object, thought and being. His notion of dialectics, the apprehension of that world through the constant interaction of opposites, extended the logic of the individual human mind to the course of history, where each stage was marked by a tension of

---

9   On the political tenor and composition of the PSI at this time, see Bufarale, *Sebastiano Timpanaro*, 31. Things began to change drastically in the late 1950s (ibid., 36). See also chapter 1.
10   Bufarale, *Sebastiano Timpanaro*, 30.
11   Although Timpanaro's father also, importantly, resisted the artificial separation between the sciences and the humanities beloved by neoidealist culture (ibid., 19). On Timpanaro Sr's idealism, see also *VR*, 185, 208.

opposites eventually overcome and subsumed in the next stage within a more encompassing unity. For Timpanaro, this identification of mind and world was rebarbative. The essence of Marxism, in his view, had to be always and ever protected from the corrupting influence of Hegel. Timpanaro's father thus served as a force for Timpanaro's philosophical radicalisation towards an immovable materialism – by conflict, rather than imitation.[12]

Timpanaro's mother was, arguably, an even more outsize (and ongoing) presence in his intellectual landscape. Maria Timpanaro Cardini (1890–1978) was a trained philologist who wrote weighty tomes on the history of ancient philosophy and science. Her party allegiance was more or less directly aligned with Timpanaro's, progressing through the splintering of the Italian radical left as the mainstream socialist and communist parties became increasingly reformist. Timpanaro Cardini shared both philological discussion and party meetings with her son – but also lived with him for the whole of her life, even after Timpanaro married Maria Augusta Morelli (1938–2021; a Tuscan archivist, historian of eighteenth-century culture, and fellow early-Leopardi expert) in 1968. It is hard to overestimate the depth of Timpanaro and his mother's enmeshment. Even if the correspondence in the Timpanaro archive does not reflect the full extent of their relationship (you do not tend to send letters to your mother living in the next room), the outburst of paralysing grief Timpanaro suffered and wrote about after her death in 1978 testifies to the deep bond. In addition to their common interests in philology and leftist politics, as well as their constant proximity, the other important inheritance passed from mother to son was a staunch atheism and a withering contempt for the Catholic Church. For Timpanaro, this was a key part of his intellectual make-up, making him gravitate to many atheist or anti-religious thinkers (such as the poet Giacomo Leopardi [1798–1837]) and the Enlightenment philosopher Paul-Henri Thiry, Baron d'Holbach [1723–1789]). But for his mother, it was almost a way of life. Timpanaro said, on several occasions, that he suspected his mother's real enemy was not so much capitalism as the Catholic Church in cahoots with it.

Timpanaro Cardini's life progression also provides an interesting template for explaining Timpanaro's long-standing investment in the

---

12   Cf. *VR*, 185–6.

empirical sciences as the only means of phasing into truth about the world. Such an investment would later come to define Timpanaro's battle against the science-sceptical culture of the New Left, inflected by the currents of anti-empiricism in works such as Althusser's *For Marx* (1965) and *Reading Capital* (1965). This strand, of course, came from both mother and father: Timpanaro Cardini was a historian of early Greek science, and Timpanaro Sr a physicist by trade. As Glenn Most points out in the introduction to his translation of Timpanaro's *Genesis of Lachmann's Method*, the Timpanaro family shelves would have been stacked with history of science bibliography, which explains the strange complexion of Timpanaro's most famous work in the history of philology – that is, its greater debt to methods taken from the history of science than from philology.[13] But the imprint of science on Timpanaro did not just come from the general domestic climate favouring all things scientific (itself a rare thing in Italian humanistic culture of the mid-twentieth century, skewed as it was away from the sciences). It was also that Timpanaro Cardini's biography seemed to model a disavowal of certain intellectual activity in favour of scientific philology. As a young woman, Timpanaro's mother had been heavily involved in the avant-garde poetry scene in Naples, around the time of World War I.[14] She later absolutely refused to talk about that moment in her life, both because, so Timpanaro thought, she was ashamed of the nationalist and pro-war politics attached to that scene, but also because she was embarrassed to have fiddled around with what were (to her) the trivialities and indulgences of poetry. The life of Timpanaro's mother – according to Timpanaro's interpretation, at least – was structured around a disowning of the 'soft' creative arts and the embrace of a 'harder' scientific philology. It was, in its own way, a version of the founding Timpanaran gesture with which we opened: an elimination of the self and a move towards the world. Timpanaro would have problems with the alleged narcissism of certain poets and artists, hacks of idealist creativity, for the rest of his life (see chapter 7).

The other significant figure in Timpanaro's domestic life was surely his wife, Maria Augusta Morelli Timpanaro. The two met in the mid-60s

---

13   See Glenn Most, introduction to Sebastiano Timpanaro, *The Genesis of Lachmann's Method*, Chicago, 2006, 18.
14   Cf. Bufarale, *Sebastiano Timpanaro*, 21.

(their correspondence begins in 1965) and married in 1968, the year after Timpanaro and his mother moved to Florence. Though the age difference was marked (she was fifteen years Timpanaro's junior), Morelli was already showing herself to be a brilliant young scholar by the late 1960s. She and Timpanaro committed to some promising collaborative work editing and commenting on the early dissertations of Leopardi – but the prospect fell away for political reasons (to be explained in chapter 3). They also collaborated on an interesting biography of the partisan hero of the Tuscan resistance Aligi Barducci (1913–1944), better known as 'Potente'.[15] Morelli went on to distinguish herself as a scholar of eighteenth-century Italian (particularly Tuscan) history, becoming an expert on the free-thinker and poet Tommaso Crudeli (1702–1745), a victim of the Holy Inquisition in Florence in 1739.[16] Morelli's day job was as an archivist working, at various stages, for the ministry of 'cultural goods' (*beni culturali*), for the regional board of archives for Tuscany (an official government body responsible for managing the entire region's vast swathe of historical records), and for the state archives of both Florence and Pisa. Morelli was an established scholar in her own right. But she was also remarkably devoted to the memory of her husband, leveraging her skills and network as an archivist to put together the exhaustive and impeccably organised Timpanaro archive at the Scuola Normale in Pisa, on which much of the research behind this book depends. If it were not for Morelli's tireless pursuit of Timpanaro's correspondents after his death, her disciplined work requesting copies of his letters, we would be infinitely poorer in writing this chapter of intellectual history.

Timpanaro's family, particularly his mother, was especially important in his formation partly because he suffered from a brutal 'neurosis' (Timpanaro's own word for it) which compromised his ability to travel. This neurosis, never professionally diagnosed, was more manageable in the earlier part of his life. While it influenced his career decisions, it did

---

15   Gino and Emirene Varlecchi, *Potente: Aligi Barducci, comandante della divisione Garibaldi 'Arno'*, ed. Maria Augusta Morelli Timpanaro and Sebastiano Timpanaro, Florence, 1975.

16   Maria Augusta Morelli Timpanaro, *Per Tommaso Crudeli nel 255o anniversario della morte, 1745-2000*, Florence, 2000; Maria Augusta Timpanaro Morelli, *Tommaso Crudeli. Poppi (1702-1745). Contributo per uno studio sulla Inquizione a Firenze nella prima metà secolo XVIII*, Florence, 2003.

not affect his ability to participate fully in political life (party meetings, etc.). It was only later in life that a kind of agoraphobia, if it was that, kicked in and, in periods of greatest intensity, made it difficult for him to cross the piazza or the street.[17] This long-standing neurosis, combined with Timpanaro's almost textbook Oedipal situation – a competitive philosophical rivalry with his father and a deep enmeshment with his mother – make his lifelong resistance to psychoanalysis (chapter 5) almost comical. Timpanaro himself admitted he expressed a classic hyperdefensiveness against psychoanalysis – and that those defences were not exactly born from rude psychological health.[18] In this book, I shall abstain from armchair analysis (were I even qualified to perform it), but Timpanaro's ongoing anxiety disorder should be kept in mind as we confront his more intellectual refutation of psychoanalysis – not to discount the substance of his thought but to contextualise it.

However, before this neurosis closed Timpanaro's world more definitively, his life was full of intellectual and political stimulation. His working life, in particular, had a huge bearing on his intellectual profile and worldview. In the early part of his career, between graduation from university in 1945 and 1959, he took after his parents in assuming teaching posts at various provincial middle schools outside Pisa (serving students aged eleven to fourteen; from 1948, Timpanaro taught at the now-defunct schools of 'professional training', aiming to equip students from less well-off backgrounds to enter the workforce).[19] Timpanaro loved the work, had deep affection for his students, and managed to hold the job down for a good fourteen years before his neurosis got the better of him and began to make public speaking – even before a class of wholesome provincial tweens and teens – beyond impossible. But this frame of his life continued to have huge consequences.[20] In particular, the requirement to teach Italian history and make the Risorgimento period especially interesting to the young pushed Timpanaro to engage in serious work on

17   See, for example, S.T. to Hugh Lloyd-Jones, 16 May 1998; S.T. to Margarethe Billerbeck, 5 March 2000.

18   S.T. to Francesco Orlando, 30 June 1974.

19   Bufarale, *Sebastiano Timpanaro*, 24. Until 1962, Italy's middle school system was divided by class: the *scuola media* allowed entry to the *licei* (academic high schools) and ultimately the university; the *avviamento professionale* led strictly to a blue-collar job at the end.

20   For Timpanaro as teacher, see the cover photo of Nuccio Ordine, *La lezione di un maestro. Omaggio a Sebastiano Timpanaro*, Naples, 2010 – with justification at xvii.

nineteenth-century Italy, which would become one of his flagship areas. He himself attributes the origins of this interest to the classroom.[21] But schoolteaching also infused his later intellectual output *in general*. As the political and intellectual historian Perry Anderson notes, one of the strange and striking features of Timpanaro's style on the page is his crystalline lucidity, bucking the trend of overwrought and byzantine sentences infusing Italian academic prose at the time.[22] While Timpanaro's philological training and Enlightenment principles were no doubt behind his anachronistic written clarity, there was also a *didactic* strand to the prose, something beaten into shape in the harsh studio of explaining history to distraction-prone students.[23] No matter what it is about, a Timpanaro book or article is always graspable, always intelligible, because he never takes anything for granted. He treats the reader as an intelligent but perhaps not quite fully knowledgeable entity, without ever being patronising.[24] We, as readers, emerge so much the better for it.

When Timpanaro made the hard decision to discontinue his teaching career, his options became more limited. The university – the institution which his philological training had naturally equipped him to traverse – was out of the question, because it would involve public speaking requirements even more terrifying than middle school. What else could the job market do with Timpanaro's cerebral skill set? He essentially needed a paid position tolerating introversion, rewarding attention to

---

21   S.T. to Giorgio Voghera, 27 December 1969. On the other impacts of Timpanaro's teaching, see Bufarale, *Sebastiano Timpanaro*, 24.

22   Perry Anderson, 'On Sebastiano Timpanaro', *London Review of Books* 23, no. 9 (May 2001).

23   On the commitment to clarity in Timpanaro's philology, see Federico Santangelo, 'Voler "capire tutto". Appunti sullo stile di Sebastiano Timpanaro', *Anabases* 20 (2014): 61–3. Piras, 'Sebastiano Timpanaro', 689, quotes Santangelo's apt description of Timpanaro's prose as a kind of 'written seminar' (57) (*seminario scritto* – thanks to Frances Muecke for alerting me to this). Such clarity also came from Timpanaro's embeddedness in militant struggle, which showed him the importance of using common, non-academic, non-jargony language (Romano Luperini, 'Testimonianza per Timpanaro: Il dibattito sul materialismo e altri ricordi degli anni sessanta e settanta', in Enrico Ghidetti and Alessandro Pagnini [eds], *Sebastiano Timpanaro e la cultura del Secondo Novecento*, Rome, 2005, 375). As Romano Luperini attests in his fond reflection on Timpanaro's person at the end of Bufarale, *Sebastiano Timpanaro*, 103, that non-academic directness extended to all his personal relationships.

24   Or as if the reader were a complete idiot, in Timpanaro's self-deflating account (S.T. to Scevola Mariotti, 30 April 1977). We can see why Timpanaro was attracted to Holbach's repetitive style in *Il buon senso* – see *BS*, lxvi; cf. the conclusion of this book.

detail, and leaving some time for him to conduct his scholarship on the side. In 1959, he ended up securing a job as a copy editor at the Florentine publisher La Nuova Italia. This four-day-a-week position left Timpanaro with a bit of time and energy to write the things he was burning to write, and to participate fully in local leftist life.[25] But it also, perhaps, gave him some on-the-ground, 'embodied' insight into a process that was already important for his intellectual orientation and would later become still more so. The technical side of classical philology known as textual criticism, tasked with the job of considering the manuscript history of a particular text across its chequered record of copying since antiquity, traffics in *error*. The common mistakes across these different manuscripts are the glitches that allow for their genealogical classification to be made (a method Timpanaro would write about in *La genesi del metodo del Lachmann* (*The Genesis of Lachmann's Method*), first published 1963) and enable informed guesswork to approximate a text closer to 'what the author wrote'. But, as an editor reading hundreds and hundreds of pages of copy every week, Timpanaro became familiar with how these errors actually occurred, and what a banal and material thing they were. His day job as a corrector of texts perhaps helped clarify to him that these kinds of human linguistic errors were just that: the stuff of a day job. They fell into certain predictable patterns, followed certain norms, and were rarely accounted for by the Byzantine Freudian analysis he would later impugn in *The Freudian Slip* (see chapter 5). In his novella *Proofs*, George Steiner makes his protagonist into a Marxist philologist-proofreader, based loosely on Timpanaro.[26] This protagonist lives a continuity between his day job and his politics around the idea of correcting an imperfect world, whether on the page or in the piazza. This metaphorical equivalence between text and world as imperfect objects to be relentlessly improved gives us the 'major corrections' of this book's title. But we should not push the neat conceptual wordplay

---

25 It also gave him genuine authority as a worker (Bufarale, *Sebastiano Timpanaro*, 29). Timpanaro stuck steadfastly to an entry-level role at La Nuova Italia and avoided all higher editorial or managerial responsibilities (cf. also Mario Bencivenni's comments, ibid., 10–11). Sociologically, the PSIUP also had much more involvement from traditional workers, and more active links to the working class via trade unions, than other New Left parties (see Daniel A. Gordon, 'A "Mediterranean New Left?": Comparing and Contrasting the French PSU and the Italian PSIUP', *Contemporary European History* 19, no. 4 [2010]: 319).

26 George Steiner, *Proofs and Three Parables*, London, 1992.

too far. Indeed, there was less connection between the real Timpanaro's day job and his Marxism (apart from, of course, experiencing the alienation of work and taking part in union activity)[27] than there was between it and his knowledge of errors later leveraged to debunk Freud. Therein lay the continuity between minor and major correction.

While Timpanaro's eccentric combination of copy editor and Marxist proved fruitful for Steiner's fiction imagination, he became almost as famous for what he was *not*. Timpanaro garnered a reputation for being an outsider partly because he never held a university position. Many other figures comparable with Timpanaro's intellectual stature on the post–World War II Italian left were incubated in ongoing posts at universities. The fact that Timpanaro worked as a rank-and-file copy editor rather than holding a lofty professorial chair certainly gave him an outsider prestige. But we should be cautious overplaying that. While he did not work in the university, his entire suite of social and political relationships were mediated by it. He was deeply, structurally hardwired into that milieu, even if he only received a pay cheque from a university as a 'professor by contract', on an outlier occasion in 1983–4 when he finally managed to pluck up the courage to teach a seminar.[28] Timpanaro was so firm a fixture of the Tuscan university scene that he was even elected, in 1989, to the Accademia dei Lincei – one of the oldest and most prestigious academies in Europe. The story of Timpanaro as outsider intellectual is partly an effect of how compelling and deep set this myth is within Western culture. We want to believe it in his case, and we desire his outstanding work to be a direct consequence of his uncompromised position outside the institution.[29] But the briefest of glances at the make-up of his lifelong correspondence puts the lie to this, showing us just how networked Timpanaro was with so many prominent university-based intellectuals of his day. Timpanaro himself would comment on how his reputation as outsider took on a life of its own: in inventing his biography, believers would make a principled virtue of a decision not to sully himself in the university, when, in fact, it was a product of neurological

---

27 Timpanaro's union activity was significant (Bufarale, *Sebastiano Timpanaro*, 41–2).

28 See Antonio Rotondò, 'Sebastiano Timpanaro e la cultura universitaria fiorentina della seconda metà del Novecento', in Enrico Ghidetti and Alessandro Pagnini (eds), *Sebastiano Timpanaro e la cultura del Secondo Novecento*, Rome, 2005, 5–6.

29 Rotondò, 'Sebastiano Timpanaro', 5, argues this line directly.

necessity and medical constraint.[30] Timpanaro's life itself thus became yet another example of the voluntarist/idealist fantasy, whereby humans would always interpret events as a direct result of human will. Timpanaro the Leopardian materialist knew otherwise: that history was often the result not of active decisions but of our bodies and minds laying down limits, and of us yielding to natural forces beyond our control.

If Timpanaro did not breathe the office air of the university, he was still, as mentioned, embedded in its networks.[31] His main institutional loyalties were twofold. Between 1942 and 1967, Timpanaro frequented the halls of the Scuola Normale in Pisa, though never in a formal capacity.[32] His other foot was firmly lodged in the Faculty of Letters and Philosophy at the University of Florence, where he did his undergraduate studies during World War II, and in whose library he would again become a regular after moving to Florence in 1967. This life split between Pisa and Florence cultured the precise overlap of callings at the heart of this book: on the one hand, formal classical philology, under the long shadow of Giorgio Pasquali (1885–1952; a professor of Greek and Latin at the University of Florence, who also taught at the Scuola Normale in Pisa); on the other, revolutionary socialism on the Italian left.[33]

Our popular concept of classical philology (if we have one) bears very little resemblance to the world of the militant left: How could a field concerned with nutting out the minutiae of classical texts share any meaningful space with a political practice devoted to change at the largest scale? What is more, there was an unseemly but concrete link, during the ventennio of Mussolini's reign, between the Latin language and Fascist nativism.[34] Going further back, many of the founding figures of

---

30   See chapter 4.

31   Rotondò, 'Sebastiano Timpanaro', 4–5, limits Timpanaro's claims to isolation. What he lacked in formal institutional power, he more than made up for in his informal position among the Florentine Faculty of Letters milieu.

32   On the intellectual and political culture of the Scuola Normale from the fall of Fascism to 1968, see Paola Carlucci, *Un'altra università: La Scuola Normale Superiore dal crollo del fascismo al Sessantotto*, Pisa, 2012.

33   See Rotondò, 'Sebastiano Timpanaro', 12–32. Timpanaro was also a student of the literary critic Giuseppe De Robertis (1888–1963), from where he developed his keen interest in Leopardi.

34   See, for instance, Han Lamers, 'Mussolini's Latin', *Symbolae Osloenses* 96, no. 1 (2022): 205–29. See also Ramsey McGlazer on Gramsci's comments on the Latin class's fascist co-optation: *Old Schools: Modernism, Education, and the Critique of Progress*, New York, 2020, 4–7.

nineteenth-century classical philology had been enmeshed with the dark side of racist ethnonationalism and the scientific scaffolding of white supremacy, a connection exposed most forcefully by the Palestinian American scholar-activist Edward Said.[35] In the red Tuscany of the 1940s, '50s, and '60s, however, the politics of philology's intellectual landscape looked quite different. There were always many philologists floating about – more than in many other European countries, thanks both to Italy's cultural heritage and its deeply classicising secondary education system. But post-war Italy also had one of the strongest lefts in Europe. Italian Communist Party (PCI) membership was extremely high, reaching a peak of 2.3 million in 1947, out of a population of around 45 million; in the '50s and '60s, the PCI newspaper *L'Unità* had a distribution of a million copies a day.[36] In the 1946 Italian elections, the socialist PSI gained 20.7 percent of the vote, and the Communists 18.9 percent. Even a relatively small party such as the Italian Socialist Party of Proletarian Unity (PSIUP) – the party in which Timpanaro later did his most intensive political work – reached a membership of 100,000 and had a peak vote of 4.5 percent in the 1968 Italian election.[37] At its summit, the PSIUP had twenty-three deputies and fourteen senators in the Italian legislature, as well as a strong share of power at the local level.[38] Frenetic activism and self-sacrificing devotion to party, for the advance of the working classes, were almost a norm.[39] With a glut of philologists and a healthy supply of Marxists, then, it was likely some would be pulling double duty.

In the red Tuscan heartlands of Pisa and Florence, in particular, philology and Marxism were starting to mingle. Timpanaro's posse included fellow Pisan philologist Vincenzo Di Benedetto (1934–2013; a professor of Greek and a founding member of the Pisan PSIUP chapter

---

35   Edward Said, *Orientalism: Western Conceptions of the Orient*, New York, 1978. There is now a significant tradition of critique targeting the complicity of philology and racism, for instance, Martin Bernal, *Black Athena: The Afroasiatic Roots of Classical Civilisation 1: The Fabrication of Ancient Greece 1785–1985*, London, 1987. See also Markus Messling, 'Philology and Racism: On Historicity in the Sciences of Language and Text', *Annales* 67, no. 1 (2012): 151–80.

36   Marco Albeltaro, 'Communism and Social Relations: The Life of a Communist Militant', in Stephen A. Smith (ed.), *The Oxford Handbook of the History of Communism*, Oxford, 2014, 446.

37   Gordon, 'A "Mediterranean New Left?" ', 310–11.

38   Ibid., 311.

39   Albeltaro, 'Communism', 449–50.

after its split from the PSI) as well as Antonio La Penna (1925–2024; a professor of Latin at the Universities of Florence and Pisa, with teaching duties also at the Scuola Normale Superiore in Pisa, member of the PCI from 1943 to 1967, and of *Manifesto* thereafter, a New Left breakaway from the PCI).[40] Tuscany may not have been crawling with Marxist philologists, but the red tinge of the universities in the area left Timpanaro with some good company in which to hone his craft.

Timpanaro's core circle in 1940s, '50s, and '60s Pisa was a discipline-transcending group which well reflected the diverse interests he would make his own. I give a fuller list of the best-known members of this sprawling intellectual network in Appendix 1. But the main point to stress here briefly is the sheer breadth of Timpanaro's interlocutors, in both the academic and political camps. On the academic side, Timpanaro maintained active friendships and intellectual exchanges with classical philologists, ancient and modern historians, critics and historians of Italian, French, and German literature, linguists, philosophers and historians of philosophy, poets, translators, and novelists. In the more political wing, Timpanaro was organically connected to many activists within his own parties (the PSI, PSIUP, and subsequently PdUP), but also beyond, sustaining a vital engagement even with many members of the party to which he often played gadfly, the PCI. At the heart of these interlocking communities were Tuscany-based print journals, the enabling and meaningful fora for intensive discussion and debate. For broad humanistic topics (political ones too), there was *Belfagor*, run between 1946 and 1961 by the then director of the Scuola Normale Superiore, the literary critic and PCI member Luigi Russo (1892–1961), and dutifully taken on by his son Carlo Ferdinando Russo (1922–2013) in subsequent years. Timpanaro published many influential cultural-historical pieces and reviews here. With a more dedicated political accent, devoted to urgent issues facing the Tuscan new left, the non-aligned journal *Quaderni Piacentini* emerged in 1962. It was edited by Marxists of a slightly younger generation, Piergiorgio Bellocchio (1931–2022) and Grazia Cherchi (1937–1995), both close friends of Timpanaro. The *Quaderni* provided a home for several of Timpanaro's classic articles of political philosophy, including those that would become the core

---

40   See Anna Maria Cimino, 'L'influenza di Gramsci su Antonio La Penna. Dalla formazione gentiliana all'empiriomaterialismo', *Lexis* 39, no. 1 (2021): 211–36.

of *On Materialism*. In general, Timpanaro was plugged into a vibrant scene of leftist intellectuals, heated conversation with whom, in print and person, served to shape and sharpen his thought in real time. Most importantly, there was a marked overlap between the more rarefied academic and more activist political circles in which Timpanaro travelled. A revolving door connected the seminar room and the socialist rally.

By far the closest thing we have to a Timpanaro in terms of a Marxist-philologist composite, however, would be Antonio La Penna. A brief comparison with the life of La Penna, born only two years after Timpanaro and living a life largely in parallel (indeed as close friends until the 1980s), might serve to throw into relief the common ground shared by this red philologist set. La Penna came from the south, a remote village called Oscata in Irpinia, an ancient mountainous region roughly coextensive with the province of Avellino in Campania. Like Timpanaro's early experiences with his father, La Penna, too, had been saturated in the idealism of Croce and Gentili, as well as the Hegelian aesthetics of Francesco De Sanctis (1817–1883) – all of which influences were rife among the teachers at La Penna's academic high school.[41] When La Penna arrived at the Scuola Normale Superiore in Pisa in 1941, he was still in thrall to such idealism. But as the scholar Anna Maria Cimino has shown in a brilliant recent piece on La Penna's intellectual formation and debt to Gramsci, La Penna soon became a fully fledged convert to materialism.[42] This was owed largely to new exposure to the historicist methods of Pasqualian philology, to a generally anti-fascist commitment among the Normale teachers (e.g., Aldo Capitini, Luigi Russo, Delio Cantimori, and Cesare Luporini), and to the radicalisation of World War II. La Penna joined the PCI in 1943 and remained an official member, with fluctuating highs and lows of political activity, till 1967. But his critiques of the PCI in the 1950s and '60s, as we shall see, were almost completely aligned with Timpanaro's: he identified as a minority anti-Stalinist in an overall Stalinist environment; he picked on the historical 'justificationism' undergirding the PCI's increasing collaboration with centrist power brokers; and he took issue with the providentialist and teleological tendencies of the PCI

---

41 Cimino, 'L'influenza', 214–5.
42 The following account of Antonio La Penna relies heavily on ibid., 214–31.

brand of Marxism in the 1960s – the idea that the collaborationist line of the PCI was all for the greater good and the eventual victory of communism, from which he took distance as a self-described resistant or 'disorganic' intellectual. In the end, La Penna's revulsion towards idealism proved stronger than his commitment to Marxism. He concluded in the '90s that Marxism was too structurally infected with Hegel to be salvaged. For him, the unresolvable problem of Marxism was that it could not liberate itself from idealism, the unforgivable philosophical cornerstone of Fascism.

As we saw above, Timpanaro would have vigorously countersigned all of this anti-Hegel sentiment. The difference from La Penna, theoretically speaking, was that Timpanaro never decided that Marxism was irretrievably lost to the Hegelian inheritance. Timpanaro's positions on Gramsci were also different from La Penna's: Timpanaro was cooler on Gramsci, thinking the latter to be bound up with the idealism from which La Penna cordoned him off.[43] There were also distinct differences in the way La Penna combined his politics with the study of antiquity: his famous works of the 1960s on the Roman authors Horace, Virgil, and Sallust were exercises in direct hegemony-critique *à la* Gramsci, studying the complex positions of their authors vis-à-vis the dominant political class of the late Republican and Augustan 'revolutions'.[44] Timpanaro, as we shall see, never allowed his politics to take such a direct seat at the table of his philological work. But the things that bound together La Penna and Timpanaro – Pasquali, the Scuola Normale, reaction against Fascism and idealism, a faith in materialism and empiricism – were much more binding than the differences. These intellectuals represented a brief, precious moment in the history of the world where the historical rigour of philology fizzed with the electricity of Marxism – and even, especially, vice versa.

The fairly unique crucible that produced Timpanaro was a vibrant intellectual culture on which it is hard not to look back longingly. From philology Timpanaro took an eagle eye for details, a tendency to scepticism and empiricism, a hatred of a priori assumptions and settled habits

---

43   As Cimino shows, La Penna's faith in Gramsci as an antidote for Marxism's idealist corruption reaches right up to 1989 (ibid., 232).

44   Ibid., 223.

of thought, and a reflex to return to first principles, to subject every piece of evidence to an intense scrutiny and independent judgement. For Timpanaro, living alongside but firmly antagonistic towards relativising theories like structuralism, scientific truth was still something out there and attainable. Philology trained him to believe in objectivity and material reality and made him dismiss as *civetteria* (intellectual 'coquetry' or 'flirtation'; see chapter 7) any pretentious attempt to problematise these workaday givens. There were many more things that philology contributed to Timpanaro's intellectual toolkit, and some of these were particular to the overlapping Florentine and Pisan circles of Giorgio Pasquali (who had a professorial chair in Florence but taught as a commissioned visiting professor at the Scuola Normale in Pisa from 1931 to 1952).[45] Among other things, Pasquali's approach emphasised examination of the tools of the field itself and its history as much as the field's objects of study – the classical texts themselves – and a democratic approach to the study of ancient texts indifferent to aesthetic value.[46] I will expand further on the concrete intellectual inheritance of Pasqualian philology in chapter 2.

Philology, for Timpanaro, was not just a worldview or a set of intellectual instruments – it was also, importantly, a professional *identity* of ongoing use to him over the course of his life.[47] But it only became especially useful to him precisely from the moment he stopped being a philologist stricto sensu and spread his wings into other disciplines. Almost excessively, Timpanaro took a single line on his intellectual activity: all told, he was a philologist at core; at a stretch, he was also a scholar of nineteenth-century Italian culture; but in everything else he went on to write about in the beating heart of his career in the '60s and '70s – materialist philosophy, linguistics, Freud – he remained, in his own self-description, a stalwart 'dilettante'.[48] And he felt professionals in

---

45   Giorgio Pasquali was even more attached to the SNS in Pisa than he was to Florence (see Carlucci, *Un'altra università*, 134; cf. 175–6. Thanks to Alessandro Schiesaro for pointing me to this).

46   Rotondò, 'Sebastiano Timpanaro', 31–2.

47   Philology brings respect for professional competence: S.T. to Antonio Perin, 30 December 1983.

48   For Timpanaro's complaints about his dispersivity, see S.T. to Giuseppe Cambiano, 26 August 1979; S.T. to Feliciano Speranza, 14 February 1980, 3 March 1980; S.T. to Ermanno Circeo, 8 March 1980; S.T. to Silvia Rizzo, 3 September 1980; S.T. to Francesca Dovetto, 8 October 1988; S.T. to Franco Giancotti, 12 May 1989. Timpanaro

those disciplines often treating him so, by dismissing his work – or worse, ignoring it. For Timpanaro, whose avowed object in writing polemical interventions was more often than not to 'raise discussion', silence was the worst fate his work could meet.[49] He resented it, but it must be said that he also drew energy from being the philological trouble-maker, creating chaos and being dismissed or ignored for his trouble.[50]

In regularly straying beyond his home field, Timpanaro was consciously traipsing in the shadow of his beloved teacher and mentor Giorgio Pasquali, who had published several collections of 'extravagant pages', that is, writings ranging beyond strictly philological subjects.[51] Not only did philology furnish the launch pad for all of Timpanaro's various Pasqualian 'extravagances'; it provided a kind of protective identity which enabled Timpanaro to make sallies into other disciplinary camps without professional grounding in them. The excuse of being a mere philologist and therefore not adequately versed in another field was certainly another modesty trope. Timpanaro often deployed it to capture an audience's goodwill before diving right into the field at hand. But the vocational identity as philologist also gave him a certain freedom and security to enter another field and ruffle feathers within it, precisely because he remained 'just a philologist' (as he remained always 'just' a 'corrector of proofs', in his own humble self-description). It was a steeling excuse of marginality that allowed him to smuggle himself into intellectual corners unused to having guest philologists rearranging the furniture. But as well as an excuse, philology was also an *anchor* to Timpanaro, a kind of recharge station for scholarly identity after moments of vertiginous disciplinary boundary crossing. His correspondence is full of declarations, at moments in which his more experimental works are nearing completion or newly complete, that he was looking forward to returning to his field of

---

also downplayed the heterogeneity of topics within individual works, such as the *AF* (S.T. to Giuseppe Valli, 10 October 1980).

49   Indeed raising debate is part of the fundamental 'restlessness' (*inquietudine*) Bufarale identifies at the heart of the Timpanaran approach to research (*Sebastiano Timpanaro*, 42–3).

50   On Timpanaro's obsession with his silent treatments, see chapter 2.

51   Original volume: Giorgio Pasquali, *Pagine stravaganti di un filologo*, Lanciano, 1933.

philology. He was due a return home.[52] Timpanaro's genuinely interdisciplinary activity is a salutary reminder that the best intellectual
roving can be predicated on this solid sense of home base. Timpanaro
was the prodigal philologist periodically ranging beyond and returning to his native field.

Philology, however, was only one home. Another, perhaps *the*
other for Timpanaro, was Marxism. I will give a fuller overview of
Timpanaro's politics in chapter 1, but for now, a brief sketch.
Timpanaro became a card-carrying member of the PSI in early 1947,
when he was twenty-three, and continued as an active member of
socialist parties until quitting formal party activity in 1976. What
did his brand of Marxism look like? Timpanaro himself gives a nice
retrospective self-definition in a letter to the German philologist
Siegmar Döpp (1941–; a professor of classical philology at the
University of Göttingen) in 1995, a passage to which we shall come
round again at the end:

> I've been a socialist of the left, Marxist and Leninist without any
> particular orthodoxy, with sympathies also for the thought of Trotsky,
> but with clear hostility to Stalinism, which I've always considered to
> be a degeneration, not a continuation, of Marxism and Leninism. [53]

As Perry Anderson has written, Timpanaro's politics were somewhat heterodox (or 'without any particular orthodoxy') for the
age.[54] A committed anti-Stalinist, he never really looked on the
Soviet Union as the great hope for socialism, even before the 1956
Soviet invasion of Hungary sparked a major crisis of confidence
in the Soviet Union for Western European socialist and communist parties.[55] He was sceptical of China and Mao in the late 1960s
and early '70s, at a moment in which the radical left was looking

---

52   For instance, S.T. to Cesare Cases, 9 January 1968.

53   S.T. to Siegmar Döpp, 25 July 1985.

54   Heterodoxy is also Timpanaro's word for his Marxism: see S.T. to Carlo
Ginzburg, 5 March 1971.

55   Timpanaro's anti-Stalinist and anti-bureaucratic leanings are some of his most
deeply held, there already as early as 1948: see Bufarale, *Sebastiano Timpanaro*, 33–4. In
this respect, he was perhaps in the minority of his party, the PSIUP: see Gordon, 'A
"Mediterranean New Left?" ', 325.

east with wilful blindness to the problems of the Chinese road. He was sympathetic to Trotsky at a moment in which Trotsky's stock was fairly low and 'Trotskyists' were considered an irritation on much of the left.[56] From where, then, did Timpanaran Marxism emerge?

It was surely based on extended, militant, and active party service. Timpanaro's political life was just as deeply felt and lived as his philological one – if not more so. By his own declaration, in his political peak from the late 1940s to the mid-1970s, he often spent more time in meetings and demonstrations than in the study:[57]

> In all these parties I didn't play the part of the basic card-carrying member, nor the 'prominent intellectual': I've served as rank-and-file militant, or else the local 'intermediate cadre' (member of the governing body of the section or federation, or of the provincial executive). I've done a bit of everything, from posting flyers to participating in meetings and river-length discussions. *As much as it may seem exaggerated to you, there have been periods of years and years in which I've dedicated many more hours to party activities than to study.* I haven't had, in the parties I've been in, what's usually known as a 'minority vocation'; I've always understood the dangers, but also the necessity of party organisation and discipline, on the sole condition that the party represent the class interests and needs.[58]

His commitment to a militant Marxism was unswerving, and this militancy took place through active service to a series of socialist parties on the fissiparous Italian left (first the PSI from 1947 to 64, followed by the PSIUP from 1964–72, and then the PdUP from 1972–76).[59] All of these were revolutionary socialist parties at the time of Timpanaro's membership, and Timpanaro's position within them was always to the left of the

---

56   See chapter 1. Timpanaro never defined himself as Trotskyist or an adherent of the Fourth International (Romano Luperini, 5 February 1975) – but sympathies he certainly had. At *AN*, 11–12, he called himself Leninist–Trotskyist at heart.

57   See the excellent discussion of a similar passage, as well as wider discussion of Timpanaro's politics of *militanza di base*, at Bufarale, *Sebastiano Timpanaro*, 29.

58   S.T. to Umberto Carpi, 10 June 1981 (italics mine). Timpanaro repeats much of this self-definition to a wider public at *AN*, 12–13.

59   For a detailed history of these parties, their political content, and Timpanaro's place within them, see Bufarale, *Sebastiano Timpanaro*, 29–51, and chapter 1.

PCI. Long and deep immersion in this culture left ingrained marks on Timpanaro's way of thinking.

If the philological environment gave Timpanaro a relentless appetite for truth and an aspiration to shun settled a priori assumptions, these leftist circles also brought a lot to Timpanaro's formation. The first thing to mention would be a kind of 'sideline' positioning that tended to reinforce the 'minor' roles on which Timpanaro drew for energy in other spheres of life – philology, copy-editing, and so on. The party in which Timpanaro was the most active – the PSIUP – was a minoritarian splinter from the mainstream PSI, formed in response to, and escape from, the currents of reformism, accommodation, and collaboration with bourgeois government creeping into the mass left parties (both PCI and PSI) in the 1960s. As the political historian Daniel A. Gordon puts it, 'in the PSIUP's case . . . the initial split [from the PSI] was not so much over specific policies as over the principle of being in a bourgeois government at all'.[60] Timpanaro was at the vanguard of this resistance: in early 1964, he was one of four initial breakaways around which the Pisan chapter of the PSIUP clustered.[61] The issues central to the early PSIUP were varied, as the Timpanaro scholar Luca Bufarale has shown: attentiveness towards the new working class comprising not just mass factory workers but also those with technical qualifications; secular state education; opposition to the North Atlantic Treaty Organization (NATO); anti-imperialist struggles in the Middle East, Latin America, and Indochina.[62] Internationalism was clearly an important part of its makeup: as Gordon notes, party documents tend to train on the political situation in several other countries before even broaching the subject of Italy.[63] Such 'other-focussed' politics were a nice complement to Timpanaro's philosophical fixation on the world beyond the self. Sociologically speaking, the PSIUP, unlike other grouplets associated with the New Left, was not a party of pure middle-class intellectuals – according to one estimate, up to 94 percent of its members were workers, peasants, or artisans.[64] And, despite having strong ties to the world of middle-class intelligentsia, Timpanaro

---

60 Gordon, 'A "Mediterranean New Left?" ', 312.
61 Bufarale, *Sebastiano Timpanaro*, 38.
62 Ibid.
63 Gordon, 'A "Mediterranean New Left?" ', 314.
64 Ibid., 320.

himself, as an entry-level copy editor at a modest-sized publisher, was also one of those workers.

The founding justification for a party like the PSIUP was to keep the goals of revolutionary socialism alive under the threat of social democratic neutralisation. Its central purpose was not to wield significant electoral power but to nip at the heels of the big parties that did, hauling them to the left, all the while tending the flame of a revolution that looked increasingly distant but still urgently necessary. (Timpanaro's correspondence after the 1950s is full of honest abandonments of aspiration to revolution 'in a brief timescale'; see chapter 7.) But, in practice and over time, the PSIUP became ever more subordinate to and reliant upon the PCI.[65] Timpanaro always maintained a position on the left flank of the PSIUP, following the current of the heterodox Marxist and anti-Soviet Lelio Basso (1903–1978; one of the founding leaders of the PSIUP and a former influential force within the left faction of the PSI).[66] From this left flank, Timpanaro engaged in remorseless critique of the 'leftist' parties to his right for cosying up to capital in the 1960s and '70s – and the PCI became his main target. This minoritarian standpoint was essentially polemical and antagonistic.[67] The PSIUP as a whole became known, condescendingly, as the 'alliance of the no's'.[68] Within the PSIUP itself, Timpanaro's opposition to any form of subservience to the PCI was total and unstinting. Indeed, the central block against which Timpanaro butted his head in political life was the spirit of consensus and accommodation with capitalism he saw infusing the PCI (and PSI) from the 1960s onwards – a spirit which would culminate in the 'historic compromise' of 1976, resulting in a collaboration between the PCI of Enrico Berlinguer and the centre-right Christian Democrats of Aldo Moro.[69] It is no coincidence that Timpanaro finally left organised party politics that very year.[70] His adversarial persona,

65   Ibid., 322.
66   On Lelio Basso, see Gordon, 'A "Mediterranean New Left?"', 316–18; 324–5.
67   Timpanaro took this position even within the party itself: he maintained that his local Florence branch was far to the left of the national PSIUP executive: see S.T. to Girolamo De Liguori, 10 April 1972.
68   Gordon, 'A "Mediterranean New Left?"', 312.
69   Bufarale, *Sebastiano Timpanaro*, 37. Timpanaro is critical of how the spirit of such compromise ends up creeping into his final party, the PdUP (S.T. to Dante Nardo, 16 March 1976).
70   See Bufarale, *Sebastiano Timpanaro*, 47.

built up from the position of revolutionary minority within the PSI and subsequently outside it, was largely formed as a means of cultivating an antagonism towards capitalism which he felt to be fast disappearing from the culture of the mainstream left. It was also about stoking the fire of free critique which, in the PCI's increasingly stale and stalling party structure, Timpanaro thought to be dying out. These spirits of antagonism and free critique are everywhere in his writing, and they were no doubt products of his formation on the minoritarian left during the period of capitalism's entrenchment and the left's recession in post–World War II Italy.

Timpanaro occupied a precarious generational position, poised between Old Left and New Left.[71] Indeed, the PSIUP, like the comparable French PSU, worked to 'form an important bridge between official politics and the new movements of 1968'.[72] While Timpanaro's main opponents were the PCI, and this partly because of the hardening of its party apparatus and lack of internal democracy,[73] he was also no big enthusiast of the groups such as Lotta Continua starting to come into prominence from the late '60s onwards as antidotes to the fossilisation of the Old Left.[74] Timpanaro was certainly on the 'New Left' side of the PSIUP in the mid-'60s, ever frustrated by the tension between the 'innovators' such as himself at the local level and the party traditionalists at the national level.[75] But he was not attuned enough to the potential revolutionary energy of the New Left to see the explosion in '68 and '69 on the horizon.[76] Timpanaro sympathised with the broad goals of that New Left, which formed partly as a means of solving the inevitable problem of inertia and sclerosis that came with party structures congealing, as

71   Timpanaro's attitude towards 1968 shifted between mildly disparaging (S.T. to Mario Untersteiner, 10 November 1968; S.T. to Alessandro Russo, 26 January 1976) and respectful of the spirit of revolutionary break (S.T. to Mario Untersteiner, 20 December 1968). Cf. Luca Baranelli, 'Sebastiano Timpanaro e i "Quaderni Piacentini" (1966–1979)', in Ghidetti and Pagnini, Sebastiano Timpanaro, 380–1. On the PSIUP's relationship with the New Left, see Gordon, 'A "Mediterranean New Left?" '.

72   Gordon, 'A "Mediterranean New Left?" ', 312.

73   This critique only intensified over the years: see Bufarale, Sebastiano Timpanaro, 48–9, and chapter 1.

74   S.T. to Luciano Della Mea, 26 March 1970, 24 May 1970, 2 July 1970.

75   Bufarale, Sebastiano Timpanaro, 39.

76   Ibid., 40.

the political historian Terry Renaud has shown.[77] But Timpanaro thought the political tactics of groups like Lotta Continua were more about making a mess than about making revolution.[78] As Luca Bufarale notes, in the late 1960s Timpanaro's relationship with groups of the New Left such as Nuovo Impegno and Potere Operaio could be characterised as 'critical sympathy'.[79] For Timpanaro, it remained important to keep the explicit ideological debate going and not to yield to the lazy temptations of ideological *menefreghismo* – 'not giving a damn'.[80] The party structure was a valuable source of discipline, without which he saw political activity as more or less meaningless. But even if he nursed a slight scepticism towards emerging leftist mess-makers such as the autonomists, the big problems they were born to tackle – the increasingly bureaucratic organisation of the big left parties, their lack of internal democracy, the deficit in direct worker participation in many of the revolutionary parties – were crucial to Timpanaro's formation.[81] He could be stubborn. But his resistance to all forms of dogma and a priori assertion came not just from the philological spirit (see chapter 2) but also from a sensitivity towards the political manifestations of such dogma and assertion within the culture of the Italian left. Timpanaro, as we shall see, was an opponent of methods overreaching themselves, of systems staking too great an explanatory claim on the world – and this too had a political genesis as resistance to the hardening pieties on the mainstream left. Free-thought and independent scrutiny had to be a feature of any party, and any left, worth the name.

As we will see reflected brightly in the detailed episodes of this book, it was at moments of threat to liberty of discussion, public access, and unrestricted scrutiny that Timpanaro pushed back most pugnaciously. His Enlightenment sensibility, insisting on openness in everything at all costs, came out in his coolness towards Maoism and outright contempt of Stalinism, both of which had, let us say, less than spotless records on

---

77 Terence Renaud, *New Lefts: The Making of a Radical Tradition*, Princeton, 2021.

78 S.T. to Luciano Della Mea, 26 March 1970; 24 May 1970; 2 July 1970; S. T to Cesare Cases, 29 September 1972 (and cf. Bufarale, *Sebastiano Timpanaro*, 42); but later, more positive appreciation of Lotta Continua's importance on the left can be found at S.T. to Luigi Pintor, 6 May 1976; S.T. to Giuseppe Pacella, 24 July 1977; S.T. to Giorgio Voghera, 15 August 1977.

79 Bufarale, *Sebastiano Timpanaro*, 41.

80 Ibid., 42.

81 Ibid., 41.

the publicisation of internal debate.[82] But this need for openness cut through every department of Timpanaro's life – political, intellectual, personal. In his scholarship, he was constantly minded to denounce mystifications and chicanery, but also conduct that compromised public access or threatened debate: the cardinal and philologist Angelo Mai (1782–1854), Timpanaro's nineteenth-century antitype, got a dressing down for his unthinkable practice in restricting access to manuscripts while librarian of the Biblioteca Ambrosiana in Milan.[83] Freud himself, another enemy of Timpanaro's, was rendered unsavoury partly because of his possessive looming over the field he created, his tendency to shut down debate like a disciplinary paterfamilias.[84] Even in his personal life, Timpanaro hated any form of secrecy or protectionism: when some young literary historians got in touch to excavate more of his mother's poetic past, Timpanaro maintained that her wish to conceal that past should *not* be respected.[85] Mother, like everything, had to be in the public domain. Truth should not be stopped at the front door when it comes a-knocking.

Timpanaro, like everyone, was cut from his time, and my brief attempt to contextualise him within his intellectual and political universe assumes as much. But the last important thing to mention here is that Timpanaro was also *not of his time at all*. His Enlightenment principles were unfashionable among a 1960s and '70s cultural left taken with Freud, Althusser, and the Frankfurt school. His faith in science landed badly among those for whom science was no more than pure bourgeois ideology (a critique emerging from many on the radical Italian left, who were, thanks to the strict humanities/science apartheid legacy of idealism, already predisposed towards spurning it).[86] Timpanaro was an eighteenth-century fish out of water, and this characteristic – what he would call *inattualità*, the state of being uncontemporary, productively out of relevance – kept him going. He was so drawn to Leopardi partly because he saw him as a kind of Enlightenment, materialist, pessimist

---

82 See chapter 1. Timpanaro exalts the early Bolsheviks and Lenin also because they maintained freedom of discussion: *VR*, 121.

83 *AF*, 238–9.

84 S.T. to Luigi Blasucci, 10 August 1974.

85 S.T. to Carlo De Matteis, 10 July 1983.

86 On the particularly strong 'two cultures' divide in twentieth-century Italy, see Pierpaolo Antonello, *Contro il materialismo*, Turin, 2012.

outlier in an overall romantic and mystifying age.[87] When the main-stream media and ruling class tried to claim Leopardi's 'relevance' with an outpouring of banality on the 150th anniversary of his death, Timpanaro reacted with outright disgust.[88] He saw himself as playing a parallel anti-relevant role within his own culture and time, though he would never be caught claiming outright that he was Leopardi *redivivus*. His letters creak with admissions of being a dinosaur, a relic, prema-turely old and out of date (see chapter 7). But in the Timpanaran system, where truth and value are often stored in apparently antiquated vessels such as Leopardi, hailing from another age was not necessarily a bad thing. Given the non-linearity of intellectual history, truth and progress come and go.[89] Knowledge proceeds more in step with the rhythms of philology, in which old contributions can never quite be discounted; so it is that in the future, Pavlov might prove to be more useful for under-standing our minds than Freud.[90] Steps back could also be steps forward: a theme of Timpanaro's *Classicismo e illuminismo nell'Ottocento italiano* (Classicism and enlightenment in the Italian nineteenth century) and the message apothegmatically contained in one of Timpanaro's favourite Verdi quotes, 'Let's return to the past and it will be progress' (*Torniamo all'antico e sarà un progresso*).[91] Timpanaro made it one of his most solemnly sworn duties to be resolutely at odds, and out of joint with, his age. But to be out of fashion is not the same thing as being out of ideas. This is why I think he can be dusted off, why we need him now, and why he will be relevant again – for in every fossil, in every relic, there is some hard truth.

Timpanaro's reception across the varied disciplines in which he worked has been inconsistent. His contributions to so many scattered fields also render this reception difficult to summarise. If his name still resonates at all, it means distinct things to distinct communities. The differences between his respective receptions in the contexts I know best – Italy and the anglophone world – are instructive. In Italy, the memory of his sheer

---

87   Timpanaro was also dismissive of any attempts to *attualizzare* Leopardi, that is, to bring him 'up to date': see Bufarale, *Sebastiano Timpanaro*, 69, and chapter 1.

88   *VR*, 153–4.

89   *OM*, 54, 217.

90   *OM*, 54.

91   Giuseppe Verdi, letter to Francesco Florimo, 5 January 1871.

range of contributions is still very alive (even if the celebration can tend to cultic levels of respect at times): Timpanaro remains one of the great Latin philologists of his day, an eminent intellectual historian of the nineteenth century who helped transform our understanding of Leopardi, a fascinating materialist, and a committed (if slightly single-minded and eccentric) opponent of Freud in an environment otherwise very responsive to him. Although comparatively little has been written on Timpanaro in Italy in the last twenty years (with the happy exception, now, of Luca Bufarale's 2022 *Sebastiano Timpanaro: L'inquietudine della ricerca*), the spate of (hagiographic, but useful) edited volumes that emerged in the wake of his death in 2000 are remarkable for giving such a comprehensive coverage of all the various Timpanaros. Most of these contributions were written and edited by friends and comrades. The proximity helps to excavate Timpanaro's thought. Sometimes, however, the network effect can be a hindrance. The important social function of mourning and memorial that this kind of scholarship provides does not necessarily make for the sharpest critical lens. What is more, these contributions tend to be short, thematic, and divided by discipline, with each expert author giving their two cents on a particular segment of Timpanaro's output. With the exception of a synthetic 1985 article by literary critic and classical philologist Emanuele Narducci and now Luca Bufarale's excellent 2022 book, there have been few attempts to give a fulsome and attentive account of Timpanaro as a whole, drawing contrasts and connections across his corpus, using both published and unpublished material.[92] Bufarale's *Sebastiano Timpanaro*, to which I refer throughout, in particular should be singled out as an outstanding account of Timpanaro's formation and contribution as an 'anti-moderate' socialist, as well as a fascinating attempt to truly co-ordinate his lived politics with his philosophy. In this book, generally, I lean on this comprehensive spirit of Timpanaro scholarship in Italian, for it has proved vital to appreciating him as a thinker. There is, however, still an urgent need for something even more ambitious. Narducci's contribution, at only article length, is too short to treat topics in depth; and Bufarale sticks mainly to Timpanaro's politics and philosophy, without much excavation of his philological and linguistic work. Instead of siloing Timpanaro's sides off from one another, or assigning his bit parts to

---

92   Emanuele Narducci, 'Sebastiano Timpanaro', *Belfagor* 40, no. 3 (1985): 283–314.

various experts within larger edited volumes, I am attempting to bring them all together and see what comes out.

The pattern in the anglophone reception of Timpanaro is very different, and quite remarkable in its own right. As Perry Anderson has noted, there is a strange paradox in operation when we look at Timpanaro's work travelling to the English context.[93] Timpanaro's frame of cultural reference was almost exclusively continental – Italian, German, and French were his strongest modern languages, and his coverage of those national literatures and intellectual histories (particularly on topics that interested him, such as the French Enlightenment) was immense. English, not so much: Timpanaro, like many of his generation of Italian intellectuals, could neither speak nor write it. He read it, but laboriously, and his linguistic struggle is reflected in the relative poverty of his references to anything coming out of the Anglosphere (apart from in his home field philology; and outside of that, Timpanaro only had knowledge of English works long translated into Italian). Moreover, when it came to philology, Timpanaro was outright dismissive of the English tradition, which, as we shall see, he associated with outrageous entitlement to indulge in 'conjecture', the freewheeling and arrogant textual interventionism of famous English philologists such as Richard Bentley (1662–1742) or A. E. Housman (1859–1936). It was not just a cultural *gap* for Timpanaro; sometimes it was also a snub.[94]

The paradox is that this relative disdain towards anglophone cultural production was by no means reciprocated. Timpanaro became a well-known figure in England in the '70s and '80s, with his thought gaining wide currency via two major transmission routes. The first was philological. His esteem as a philologist and historian of philology among English classical scholars remained high for most of his scholarly life, especially after his *Genesis of Lachmann's Method* was taken up by prominent professors like E. J. (Ted) Kenney (1924–2019; Kennedy Professor of Latin at Cambridge), who hailed it as a masterpiece and paid it a lot

93 Perry Anderson, 'Timpanaro among the Anglo-Saxons', in Riccardo Di Donato (ed.), *Il filologo materialista. Studi per Sebastiano Timpanaro*, Pisa, 2003, 178; a revised version of the article was republished under the same name in 2021 in *New Left Review* 129.

94 Alessandro Schiesaro points out that this hostility towards anglophone scholarly production was common to Timpanaro's coevals, such as Antonio La Penna and Alfonso Traina.

of tribute in his own work. The lines of communication between Italy and England were opening up in the discipline of classical scholarship from the '70s and '80s onwards (especially between Pisa and Oxford), and two of Timpanaro's close England-based correspondents also had very strong ties to Tuscan philology: Eduard Fraenkel (1888–1970; a professor of Latin at Oxford) and Arnaldo Momigliano (1908–1987; a professor of ancient history at University College London). The politics of language in European academia were fast changing at this time (with English overtaking French as the dominant continental lingua franca), but disciplinary expectations around linguistic competence meant that the footnotes of classics tomes had to be littered with references to all the big European languages or risk being written off as sloppy work. This guaranteed a basic degree of engagement with Italian philology on the part of the English.

But there was something about Timpanaro's work which gave him particular added traction in English classics. So much of an outlier in this respect was Timpanaro that he was even elected a corresponding fellow of the British Academy as early as 1975 – with no other Italian philologist winning election for another thirty years. This burgeoning reputation in England was helped by the motors of correspondence, which Timpanaro maintained vigorously. He had active letter exchanges ongoing with some of the biggest names working in England in the second half of the twentieth century – Fraenkel and Kenney, as well as Harry Jocelyn (1933–2000; a professor of Latin at Manchester), Michael Reeve (1943–; Kenney's successor as Kennedy Professor of Latin at Cambridge), and Otto Skutsch (1906–1990; a professor of Latin at University College London). But it was more than an effect of Timpanaro's prolific typewriter. His Enlightenment principles, commitment to empiricism, and lucid style brought him oddly in tune with some of the most treasured points of self-definition in English classical scholarship.[95] This virtual shared culture of reason, clarity, and empiricism meant that Timpanaro could have as easy a time keeping up a cordial and functional scholarly relationship with an incorrigible reactionary like Hugh Lloyd-Jones (1922–2009; a professor of Greek at Oxford), as he could with the more liberal-centrist Jocelyn. If you want a strange

---

95 Timpanaro thought English philologists admired him precisely because of his *noterelle*, details-based philology (S.T. to Nino Scivoletto, 6 April 1983).

mix of mutual admiration over good philology combined with intense clashing over the relative merits of the working classes, Timpanaro's correspondence with Lloyd-Jones, the conservative Oxford don, cannot be beaten.[96] Responding to Timpanaro's *On Materialism* with lordly understatement, Lloyd-Jones says, 'Considering how much I detest socialism, it is surprising how much of your argument I can accept.'[97] High praise.

The other line of reception has been through Timpanaro's broader political and philosophical writings, particularly via Perry Anderson and the *New Left Review* throughout the '70s and '80s. The *NLR* translated and published segments of both Timpanaro's most provocative and interesting works, later publishing them whole through the imprint New Left Books: *On Materialism* and *The Freudian Slip*. Both of these texts, still in print with Verso, found a good home in and wide diffusion through the intellectual circles of the British New Left.[98] Timpanaro was grateful for (as well as a little bamboozled by) the vigorous take-up of this work in the Anglosphere. Even if *The Freudian Slip* did not win many fans in psychoanalytic circles, its arguments were at least engaged at a serious intellectual level by psychoanalytic literary critic Jacqueline Rose and British psychoanalyst Charles Rycroft in the pages of *NLR*.[99] It was taken up even more earnestly by the German American philosopher of science Adolf Grünbaum in his lengthy critique of the methods and evidential base of Freudian psychoanalysis.[100] The pattern was similar with *On Materialism*. Timpanaro's strange brand of Marxism–Leopardism stirred the pen of no lesser leftist luminary than Raymond Williams.[101] Timpanaro's memory is still alive and well enough in those circles and their descendants for Perry Anderson to publish 'Timpanaro among the Anglo Saxons' in a 2021 issue of the *NLR*[102] and, now, for

---

96   See, for instance, S.T. to Hugh Lloyd-Jones, 20 June 1973, 30 June 1973.

97   S.T. to Hugh Lloyd-Jones, 20 June 1973.

98   Timpanaro himself acknowledged that *On Materialism* had a better reception in England than Italy (S.T. to Girolamo De Liguori, 14 April 1984).

99   Jacqueline Rose et al., 'Four Comments on *The Freudian Slip*', *New Left Review* 94 (1975): 74–84.

100   Charles Rycroft, 'Timpanaro and The Freudian Slip', *New Left Review* 118 (1979): 84.

101   Raymond Williams, 'Problems of Materialism', *New Left Review* 109 (1978): 3–17; cf. Anderson, 'Timpanaro among the Anglo-Saxons', 189.

102   See n. 93 above.

Verso to publish a whole monograph on him. Such was the warmth of Timpanaro's reception into the *NLR* fold that sociologist Michele Barrett flatteringly relayed to him an anonymous but revealing comment: that if Timpanaro 'didn't exist, NLB would have had to have invented him'. She goes on: 'There certainly is a feeling in some Marxist quarters that your position on materialism has introduced a note of sanity into the absurd debates that have developed here.'[103]

What accounts for Timpanaro's enduring popularity on the anglophone New Left? There was perhaps an over-representation of high humanities background among the *NLR* set in the 1970s, a common endowment of Oxford equipment, which made Timpanaro's particular profile of cultural knowledge – a combination of hard-nosed historical and philological scholarship, with serious doses of European literature and Marxist classics – not only palatable but *legible*. The *NLR* took learned intellectual history seriously. Products of high literary culture and canonical Marxist theory were part of that, and these were exactly Timpanaro's strong suits. But there was also a profoundly English tradition of Marxism behind the *NLR* which made Timpanaro's push for a restoration of science among the New Left a particularly resonant goal. Part of Timpanaro's mission was to challenge the excessive abstraction and cerebral theorising of leftist politics under the sign of 'Western Marxism': to Timpanaro, *en vogue* obscurantist theory emerging from France – especially Lévi-Strauss and Althusser – but also from germanophone Europe – Freud, the philosophers of the Frankfurt school – was all allied to his major philosophical enemy, idealism. It was, in his estimation, corroding the true materialist essence of Marxism. And it was partly the reason why the left was losing ground. Timpanaro's critique of Western Marxism, then, was not too far removed from Perry Anderson's[104] – except Anderson's scepticism perhaps built on a long English tradition of pragmatic reservation about continental theory which would culminate in *NLR* founder E. P. Thompson's 1978 *The Poverty of Theory* (though Anderson himself was no simple exponent of Thompson's views, and his even-handed response to Thompson shows the diversity within the *NLR* scene).[105] While the English New Left was,

---

103   Michele Barrett to S.T. (numbered 1 in Timpanaro archive).
104   Perry Anderson, *Considerations on Western Marxism*, London, 1976.
105   Perry Anderson, *Arguments within English Marxism*, London, 1980.

of course, very alive to new directions coming out of the continent, it also featured strains of suspicion towards some theory emerging from it.[106] Timpanaro could have written much of *The Poverty of Theory* – Thompson's extended critique of Althusserian Marxism – himself. Perhaps the thing that endeared Timpanaro to Hugh Lloyd-Jones was not so different from what endeared him to Perry Anderson. At the very least, Timpanaro was attuned to the urgent debates being waged within the English New Left at the time he found his reception channel via Anderson.

This double-headed reception history in the Anglosphere – philology on the one hand, Marxism on the other – generates a few problems, for which this book is designed as a partial correction. The first is that it amplifies only two aspects of Timpanaro's intellectual life, to the detriment of those aspects less familiar or interesting to anglophones unversed in Italian history and culture – for example, Timpanaro the nineteenth-century cultural historian, Timpanaro the sharp reader of Leopardi, and Timpanaro the genealogist of linguistics never became very well known simply because a misalignment of cultural literacy made these things hard to apprehend from the outside. The project of this book is thus, partly, to give English-speaking readers a fuller picture of this fascinating figure. The second problem is the mutual indifference, verging on mild disdain, between circles of philology and circles of the left. Philology and the left, it would be an understatement to say, are not exactly natural bedfellows. But such mutual indifference is a missed opportunity because it perpetuates the notion that philology has nothing much to do with, nor much to offer, politics. This is perhaps the working assumption of most active philologists. Glenn Most's introduction to Timpanaro's *Genesis of Lachmann's Method* embodies some of that bias, taking Timpanaro's more politically inflected output as something occasion based, ephemeral, and by now superannuated – as opposed to the philology which *lasts*.[107] As we shall see, this separation is partly something which Timpanaro – ever the divided soul – was invested in maintaining (see also the conclusion of this volume). But the

---

106   On the anglophone reception backdrop – English traditions of empiricism, as well as the weakness of the tradition of theoretical Marxism in England – see Anderson, 'Timpanaro among the Anglo-Saxons', 178.

107   See Most, introduction, 6–7.

rationale of this book is that, when it comes to Timpanaro, we cannot, and should not, discuss his philology without his Marxism, nor vice versa. Indeed, the thing that makes Timpanaro such an acute thinker is precisely this combination of philological punctiliousness and Marxist commitment. In Timpanaro, we have a rare meeting: a thinker trained in a field whose point was to interpret small bits of the world, with a militant working in a tradition whose objective was to change the whole thing. That strange contradiction is the essence of Timpanaro. And it is the basis of all the corrections we will mark in the following chapters, starting with the most major: Timpanaro's politics.

1

Red to the End

'I've always been a modest rank-and-file comrade, and I've written things on Marxism that are (I hope) clear, but not original. But between my past and my present there's no contradiction.'[1]

As we saw in the introduction, Timpanaro's politics were one of the great organising principles of his life. After his entrance into the Italian Socialist Party (PSI) in 1947, he remained a staunch and committed Marxist for over fifty years, till the very end. There were, of course, compressions and rarefactions, fluctuations and flattenings, along the way; stints of greater or lesser activity both inside and outside the official parties of the Italian left, and evolutions of stance in step with the rapid shifts in international politics that rattled the second half of the twentieth century. As new problems such as the ecological crisis emerged, Timpanaro took note and rethought. But less remarkable than the occasional nuancing and inflection of his politics in this period is the fact of pure continuity. From the late 1970s onwards, a moment in which former radical Marxist comrades were abandoning the socialist and communist ship in droves, Timpanaro's basic politics barely changed at all.[2] He held firm to his

---

1   S.T. to Edo Cecconi, 29 August 1979.
2   For this firmness in the wake of collective abandonment of former comrades, see the postscript to *OM*, 255. Timpanaro affirms that his politics had not changed much even in one of his final political writings, published in 2000 (*VR*, 233).

brand of Leopardian Marxism: Leninist, Trotsky sympathetic, non-dialectical, libertarian, and, ultimately, red with a late tinge of *green*. Timpanaro's deeply felt Marxism was his North Star. A short history of this commitment is the best way to approach his thought, because it is the closest thing (apart from philology, for which see chapter 2) to the glue unifying this thinker resistant to synthesis. We will return to this issue in the conclusion.

While politics will feature as prominent theme throughout the book, this chapter will provide a compressed chronological overview of Timpanaro's political history, folding into its contexts brief mentions of his major intellectual contributions, in various fields, that form the base matter of the following chapters. This chapter, then, pulls double duty as overview of both Timpanaro's politics and his intellectual output. I have drawn on Timpanaro's main published political writings, *Il verde e il rosso. Scritti militanti, 1966–2000* (The green and the red: Militant writings, 1966–2000), conveniently collected by Luigi Cortesi, as well as some choice letters in the correspondence. But, for the overall narrative of Timpanaro's political life below, I am deeply indebted to Luca Bufarale's brilliant 2022 book, the first of its kind to treat Timpanaro's politics sensitively and comprehensively.[3] As we see in the epigraph above and shall see throughout the following chapters, Timpanaro took special pleasure in claiming unoriginality. I am thankful to Bufarale for allowing me the same.

Timpanaro was not born into a socialist family; his family *became* socialist at the same time he did. By 1947, mother, father, and son in the Timpanaro family were enrolled in the Italian Socialist Party. Even before this, the pre-war period and the war itself had allowed Timpanaro the opportunity to develop a fairly firm, even precocious, academic and philosophical identity. Learning his classical philology trade under Giorgio Pasquali and Nicola Terzaghi between the University of Florence and the Scuola Normale Superiore in Pisa, Timpanaro was already, by the mid-1940s, producing undergraduate work of an uncannily high standard on the thorny and fragmentary early Roman poet Ennius. As we saw in the introduction, he was also gaining a clear sense of identity

---

3   Luca Bufarale, *Sebastiano Timpanaro: L'inquietudine della ricerca*, Pistoia, 2022. I am especially reliant on the chapter 'Il socialista antimoderato' (27–56).

as a hardened scientific materialist, in conscious counterpose to his father's woolly idealism. But, at a moment rich with opportunities for political action for a young Tuscan man hovering around twenty years of age – as Timpanaro was towards the end of World War II – Timpanaro was not quite in the thick of it. He did not participate in any forms of organised resistance under Fascism and Nazi occupation. He was not politically 'born', as it were, under the sign of the heroic age of red anti-fascism, part of whose glory accounted for the subsequently gargantuan strength of the left in post-war Italy. Timpanaro was missing in action.

At least this is how Timpanaro himself, ridden by a crippling guilt over this inaction that would haunt him for the rest of his life, would come to see it.[4] But, apart from this self-imposed sense of inadequacy, a lack that Timpanaro felt as a compromising question mark marring his authority as a 'front-line' socialist, non-participation in the resistance seems to have had some more positive shaping effects on Timpanaro's political bearing. Firstly, the guilt made his subsequent commitment strong and enduring. It helped to power his Marxism through challenging times. Secondly, not being actively involved in this 'heroic' generation meant he was less susceptible to the voluntarist currents of the post-war left, which tended to valorise action and praxis, the human power to effect concrete historical change, to the detriment of the equally important brakes in the Marxist account of the world: material conditions as *conditioning* forces limiting such action. Timpanaro would become deeply sceptical of the praxis-worship he saw in Western Marxist thinkers such as Gramsci, Lukács, and Korsch, all of whom he would come to criticise in his work on materialism (see chapter 4). Such hostility was as much about philosophical temperament as political consequence. But Timpanaro's sympathy for the constraints and limits of scientific materialism also emerged from the fact that he did not fully live a political moment in which humans were truly making their own history – and so never laboured under any illusions that this was an easy thing to do.

When Timpanaro entered the PSI after World War II, it was not in quite the rude health it had been in its heyday (it attained almost a third of the vote at the 1919 general election). But it was still the major leftist

---

4 See Timpanaro's autobiographical reflections on his political conversion at *VR*, 179–80.

party in Italy, narrowly outperforming the Italian Communist Party (PCI, which had been formed from the rib of its seceding left wing in 1921) in the 1946 elections by 20.7 to 18.9 percent. It was also a very different party in terms of political content and conduct compared to what it would be in 1964, when Timpanaro finally left for the newly minted Italian Socialist Party of Proletarian Unity (PSIUP). Compared to the PCI, there was markedly greater party democracy and freedom of discussion – two things that would become obsessions in Timpanaro's political imaginary in the years to come. There was less degree of compromise with centrist and right parties, and less subservience to the Soviet Union; a bold accent on internationalism; and a principled resistance to imperialism and colonialism, a direct inheritance from the PSI's stand against the 'bourgeois' World War I. But, just as important as this political content were the political demographics of the party. There was still a strong worker presence in the PSI when Timpanaro joined. This would change in the subsequent years and decades as the PCI monopolised working-class representation ever more. But the party Timpanaro joined was not a party of intellectuals; it was a party with active and solid roots in the workers' movement.[5]

In the late 1940s, the PSI stood at an existential crossroads as it strove internally to work out its relationship with the PCI – which was either a natural ally or rival, depending on whom in the party you asked. Two major currents formed: autonomists, who pushed for greater independence from the communists, and unitarians, who wanted to maintain unity of action with them. The schism was deep enough to drive Timpanaro to write a tragedy, ancient-Greek style, satirising the rift in the PSI polis. In the 1948 general election, unity of action remained the official PSI policy under then leader Pietro Nenni (1891–1980), who presided over the party in its strategic alliance with the PCI: the Popular Democratic Front (FDP). But this alliance gave the autonomist wing of the PSI under Giuseppe Saragat (1898–1988) an excuse to break off into the Socialist Party of Italian Workers (PSLI). If Timpanaro was no blind fan of Nenni, he was even further from the PSI's right flank as led by the reformist Saragat. But what enabled Timpanaro and his fellow revolutionaries to practise their politics energetically within the PSI for that crucial late '40s period was the leading role given to Lelio Basso, in

5   *VR*, 180–1.

whose leftist faction Timpanaro saw himself as a rank-and-file member until Basso led the split of the PSIUP in January 1964. Saragat's departure in 1947 opened up a crucial space for Basso in the party leadership; he served as party secretary for two years, till the Genoa congress of 1949. Timpanaro's faction was thus represented at the highest levels of party leadership for these two golden years; but from 1950 onwards, the road started to get bumpier. Basso was a firm opponent of the Stalinism he saw creeping into the PSI, which put him in patchy (at best) favour with the upper echelons of the party over the course of the 1950s. It was under these formative conditions that Timpanaro developed his deep aversion to Stalinism and bureaucratisation – pillars of his thought that were already visible in letters to his friend and comrade Antonio La Penna, probably dating from 1948.[6]

In the early 1950s, Timpanaro was settling into his life teaching at provincial schools around Pisa. His intellectual activity was taken up with bits and pieces on classical philology, but he was also working on what would become his first major work in the world of academic scholarship: *La filologia di Giacomo Leopardi* (The philology of Giacomo Leopardi, 1955). The book uncovered genuinely new evidence to make the irrefutable case that this treasured national poet – to whom Timpanaro periodically returned his whole life, and who will feature prominently in the chapters ahead – was a technical philologist as much as an inspired poet. In Timpanaro's reading, Leopardi had fallen victim to idealist attempts to cordon him off as a 'pure poet', padded in his velvety creative realm. Timpanaro considered it his task to bring him back to the world as (at least in the earlier part of his career) a jobbing classical philologist, a practitioner of the most up-to-date techniques of German philology, and a thinker who believed in the Enlightenment values of science and reason over the randomness of romanticism. The defence of Leopardi as Enlightenment thinker from what Timpanaro saw as the distortions of scholarship would be a lifelong task, which would come back in two further Leopardi-heavy contributions: *Classicismo e illuminismo nell'Ottocento Italiano* (Classicism and Enlightenment in the Italian nineteenth century, 1965) and *Antileopardiani e neomoderati nella sinistra italiana* (Antileopardians and neomoderates on the Italian left, 1982). While it was not quite fully

---

6   See Bufarale, *Sebastiano Timpanaro*, 33.

evident in the 1955 book, this twisting of Leopardi was a politicisation deeply embroiled with Italian cultural politics at the time. When Timpanaro talks of Leopardi, he is often talking of himself. But he is also handling a loaded symbol that tended to bear the weight of contemporary politics and projection.[7]

A year after *La filologia di Giacomo Leopardi* came out, the monumental events of the Soviet invasion of Hungary drove a wedge in the core alliance of the old Italian left. The PSI may have picked the right side of history in opposing Soviet actions in 1956 (while the PCI defended them), but this left the PSI open to even more distasteful collaborations to its right. The party's direction in the late 1950s and early 1960s leaned increasingly towards a cosiness with the centrist Catholic party, the Christian Democrats (DC), from 1946 till 1994 the largest party in Italy's successive governing coalitions, and certainly its most powerful political force throughout the 1950s. Timpanaro's articles and letters in the late 1950s and early 1960s are full of complaints about this PSI strategy of DC-courting.[8] He was particularly piqued by the suggestions of diluting Marxism in the party to accommodate Catholicism (and we should not underestimate the strength of Timpanaro's aforementioned repulsion towards the church, inherited from his mother).[9] But there were also other concerns building: the dual threats of encroaching currents, Stalinist on the one hand, social democratic on the other;[10] the party leadership only representing one faction, the Nennians, and the party newspaper, *Avanti*, only voicing that single perspective;[11] the evacuation of a politics of opposition in favour of a politics of inserting themselves into the mainstream led by the DC;[12] and, finally, the PSI merely

---

7   Timpanaro's defence of Leopardi from ideologically dubious reclaimings continued till very late in his life: see his response to Adriano Sofri's attempt to 'green' Leopardi at *VR*, chapter 13.

8   See for instance, Sebastiano Timpanaro, 'Dibattiti ideologici e politica concreta', *Problemi del socialismo*, August–September 1960: 780–4; S.T. to Lelio Basso, 5 November 1960.

9   S.T. to Lucian Paolicchi, 19 September 1959.

10   S.T. to Pier Carlo Masini, 20 December 1958 (numbered 8 under 'PSI' in Timpanaro archive).

11   S.T. to Giovannini, 13 June 1959 (numbered 15 under 'PSI' in Timpanaro archive).

12   S.T. to Grimaldi, 7 March 1961 (numbered 22 under 'PSI' in Timpanaro archive).

supporting the improved living standards of boom-time economic growth.[13] For Timpanaro's left faction of the PSI, an internal way forward through the party now seemed blocked.

The solution was the tried and tested way of the Italian left: a split. In early 1964, Timpanaro joined a relatively modest exodus of some of the PSI left faction into the new PSIUP, led by Lelio Basso. So began Timpanaro's most intense decade of militant activity, pivoting around the local maxima of Italian leftist politics that were the years 1968 and 1969. Timpanaro was part of the first small cluster of breakaways in the Pisan chapter of the PSIUP, which included his mother, another philologist called Vincenzo Di Benedetto, and the historian Giovanni Miccoli. Timpanaro was instrumental in the secession and is listed as the contact for communication in the newspaper announcement of January 1964.[14] Initially, few people showed up to the party, and Timpanaro was quite gloomy about the PSIUP's prospects at the start. Even by March 1964, however, the situation had begun to improve, with an influx of union heavyweights entering the party.[15] The initial motion of the party was about minimising distance between leadership and base, and keeping all meetings open to all comrades, not just the executive. These issues of party governance – direct democracy, openness, transparency – were the most pressing pieces of housekeeping after the frustrating experience of the PSI. But there were also a host of other political issues coming through the party agenda in this period: the matter of the new working class and how it should be represented; the struggle for secular state education; opposition to NATO and active support for anti-imperialist struggles across the Middle East, Latin America, and South East Asia. It was, in fact, the anti-imperialist work that got Timpanaro and other comrades arrested for a demonstration in 1965 against US involvement in Vietnam, as well as the closer-to-home presence of US military bases on the coast between Pisa and Livorno. It should be remembered that, for red Tuscans in the post-war period, the US military machine was a very local as well as a global pest.

The early to mid-1960s were not only politically intense for Timpanaro; they also hosted some of his most brilliant works of

---

13   S.T. to Alceste Angelini, 18 April 1963.
14   In *Cronaca di Pisa*, 21 January 1964 (numbered item 7 under 'PSIUP' in the Timpanaro archive); see also Bufarale, *Sebastiano Timpanaro*, 38.
15   S.T. to Giorgio Voghera, 27 March 1964.

scholarship and intellectual history. The 'history of classical philology' follow-up to 1955's *La filologia* was an even more ambitious book called *La genesi del metodo del Lachmann* (*The Genesis of Lachmann's Method*, 1963; based on articles first published in 1959 and 1960; see chapter 2).[16] While *La filologia* had been interested in restoring credit to Leopardi for his original philological contributions, this work carried out the opposite task on one of the feted 'fathers' of modern classical philology: Karl Lachmann (1793–1851). In the historiography of the development of scientific philology in the early nineteenth century, Lachmann had come to occupy a prime position as the 'inventor' of a rigorous system of manuscript classification into 'family trees', or *stemmata*, which allowed for better reconstruction of a given text's tradition, and a supposedly closer approximation to an 'archetype' (in principle the closest thing possible to 'what the author wrote'). Timpanaro reconstructed a deep and intricate prehistory of the stemmatic method before Lachmann, which showed its evolution to be modest and gradual – removing from Lachmann many of the things that the subsequent compressions of intellectual history had unthinkingly rendered unto Lachmann. At the same time, Timpanaro was hard at work on another work of the intellectual and cultural history of the nineteenth century: *Classicismo e illuminismo* (1965; see chapter 3). Through painstaking profiling, and again, fine-grained intellectual historiography of some of the great (yet, in Timpanaro's political moment, marginalised) thinkers of nineteenth-century Italy – figures like Leopardi, Pietro Giordani (1774–1848), and Giosuè Carducci (1835–1907) – Timpanaro quested to show that this period of Italian history was not just one for the romantics. It was a moment that also featured countercultural figures who chose classicising over romanticising aesthetics and harked back to the Enlightenment principles of the eighteenth century rather than getting bogged down in the mystifications of the day. For Timpanaro, Leopardi and his ilk could not be dragged to the idealist dark side of romanticism; this was his defence of an eighteenth-century materialist tradition that had new life breathed into it in the nineteenth.

---

16   Sebastiano Timpanaro, 'La genesi del metodo del Lachmann I', *Studi italiani di filologia classica* 31 (1959): 182–228; 'La genesi del metodo del Lachmann II', *Studi italiani di filologia classica* 32 (1960): 38–63.

The PSIUP started strong and consumed much of Timpanaro's time. Of course, it was not all homogeneous; intra-PSIUP conflicts were quick to appear. The main structural schism was between the traditionalists and innovators within the party, mapped roughly onto a division between the national leadership and the provincial sections. The national leadership maintained very active political links to the two main traditional left parties, the PCI and PSI. Timpanaro's regular complaint here, just as with the PSI, was that this created subservience to, and fear of criticising, the USSR.[17] Timpanaro roundly identified with the local and provincial chapters of the PSIUP because the politics of the party at that level were much more independent and openly critical of the Soviet Union.[18] In a sense, the 'provincial innovator' faction of the PSIUP had natural sympathies with the brewing forces that would come to be known as the New Left.

As Luca Bufarale nicely formulates it, Timpanaro's approach to the emerging forces of 1968 and the New Left – organisations such as Lotta Continua – was one of 'sympathetic criticism'. He emphatically disapproved of the voluntarist and idealist strands informing their political discourse, which resulted, for Timpanaro, in a worldview more philosophical than economic-social. This, in turn, spawned an excessive intellectualism and pretentious language that was unintelligible to the average worker. As we have seen, and will see again, this was a red flag to Timpanaro's didactic mind that prized Enlightenment clarity. At the same time, Timpanaro identified a paucity of intellectual discipline in the up-and-coming generation of the New Left: confusing 'making a mess' with 'making revolution', as we saw, but also their ideological *menefreghismo* – their purposeful 'not giving a damn' about live issues in Marxism, and their lack of awareness about their own ideological positioning within the Marxist tradition. It was in this context – of needing to talk to a new generation threatening to practise a voluntarist/idealist Marxism, to prize action at all costs, to lose Marxism's true materialist essence – that Timpanaro took on his brilliant interventions that would become his most famous work on Marxism: *Sul materialismo* (*On Materialism*, 1970, the first three chapters of which were

---

17 S.T. to Claudio Bolelli, 10 December 1968.
18 S.T. to Grazia Cherchi, 14 October 1972.

published in 1966, 1967, and 1969; see chapter 4).[19] Timpanaro's work on materialism sought to counter what he saw to be a general distaste for 'vulgar materialism' as a coded dismissal of scientific materialism per se, across the spectrum of Old Left *and* New Left; but, in publishing the initial interventions in one of the key publications of the burgeoning Tuscan New Left, the *Quaderni Piacentini* (see below), he certainly had the younger generation in mind as prime audience.

While Timpanaro had his reservations about the rising mess-makers of organisations like Potere Operaio and Lotta Continua, he also shared a lot of their political convictions.[20] Timpanaro was, by temperament, wholly opposed to any kind of authoritarianism, whether in the organs of the bourgeois state like the bureaucracy, the legal system, the army, the school, even the patriarchal family, or in his own backyard, the party itself. He was also totally opposed to the capitalist leveraging of unequal wages to exploit and divide the workers – another talking point of the New Left in the late 1960s. In fact, the differences, such that there were, between the PSIUP-supporting Timpanaro and the New Left were not so much in political content but in method of struggle and worldview. Timpanaro still saw the party itself as the central vehicle of politics, despite its flaws, and anything beyond it had the tinge of undisciplined chaos about it.

In terms of everyday political action in the late '60s, however, Timpanaro lived a harmonious existence with the primarily workplace-oriented struggles of the New Left. Timpanaro lived the politics of 1968, and the 'hot autumn' of 1969, in his workplace – by then, as we saw in the intro-duction, the Florentine publisher La Nuova Italia. Timpanaro's status as an average worker gave him true credentials as the 'militante di base' (rank-and-file militant) he would later claim as so critical to his political self-definition.[21] Florence was a centre of the Italian publishing industry in this period, and so there were many opportunities for sector-wide organising. In the early 1970s, Timpanaro teamed up with fellow copy editors such as Vittorio Rossi and Franco Belgrado (see below, on Trotsky),

19   Sebastiano Timpanaro, 'Considerazioni sul materialismo', *Quaderni Piacentini* 5, no. 28 (1966): 76–97; 'Prassi e materialismo', *Quaderni Piacentini* 6, no. 32 (1967): 115–26; 'Engels, materialism, "libero arbitrio" ', *Quaderni Piacentini* 8, no. 39 (1969): 86–122.

20   Timpanaro's estimation of the 1968 movement also improved over time: see Cortesi, introduction to *VR*, ix.

21   See, for instance, *VR*, 215.

taking an active role in organising strikes and pickets with other workers in Florentine publishing houses. Timpanaro's workplace provided the real-world context for him to put his PSIUP principles into practice.

While Timpanaro was more or less aligned with the New Left–driven agitation of the late 1960s and early '70s at a practical level, serious theoretical differences were starting to percolate. Apart from the abandonment of materialism, there were two other problems starting to nag him: firstly, the younger generation's seemingly uncritical adulation of China and Mao, pouring all their libidinal energy into this new hope for socialism, and identifying it with everything the essentially Stalinist Soviet Union could not be: egalitarian, anti-bureaucratic, a haven of synergy between party and masses. Timpanaro did not share such cheeriness. As we shall see, the signs of non-publicised debates, hardening bureaucracy, the Mao cult of personality, and the repetition of empty slogans meant the writing was already on the wall that China was no utopia.[22] The second issue was the sidelining, across the left, of the thought of Leon Trotsky, which Timpanaro took as a signal of an even more worrying congealment of anti-Leninism among his comrades. He felt so strongly about the unfair treatment of Trotsky as pariah that he teamed up with Franco Belgrado to write a spirited defence intended for publication in the *Quaderni Piacentini*, just as he had done with his articles on materialism. But the second time around, things did not go as planned. Let us dwell for a moment on this episode, which crystallises some crucial aspects of Timpanaro's politics at their height.

Towards the end of 1971, Timpanaro and his PSIUP comrade Franco Belgrado pitched an article on Trotsky to their favourite journal of the extraparliamentary left, the *Quaderni Piacentini*.[23] This journal had furnished the forum for Timpanaro's materialist interventions, which stirred (as intended) a flurry of debate.[24] As a cat-among-the-pigeons

---

22 See *VR*, 32–6. Timpanaro is even clearer in his condemnation of China after the death of Mao in the 1980 edition of *OM*, 260–1.

23 Eventually published as 'Quel "cane morto di Lev Davidovic" ' [That 'dead dog Lev Davidovich'], *Giovane critica* 30 (1972): 56–9; reprinted in *VR* as chapter 3.

24 See, for instance, Jervis's response in QP, 29; and QP, 30, ballooned even more due to the discussion on materialism (S.T. to Grazia Cherchi, 7 April 1967). For a list of responses, particularly to the first materialism article, see Michele Feo, 'L'opera di Sebastiano Timpanaro', in Ricardo Di Donato (ed.), *Il filologo materialista*, Pisa, 2003, 213.

event fomenting robust discussion and ideological challenge, these interventions had been a resounding success.[25] Timpanaro perhaps had a similar vision in mind when he started workshopping the proposal for the Trotsky piece with Piergiorgio Bellocchio, founder and co-editor (along with Grazia Cherchi) of *QP*.[26] The countercultural Timpanaro was no doubt rubbing his hands together: such periodic acts of provocation were necessary to the health and diversity of leftist culture, and Timpanaro loved being behind them. If there was space to discuss maligned materialism, surely there was space to reconsider the hot potato that was Leon Trotsky.

Why was Trotsky so untouchable on much of the Italian left in this period? Timpanaro's view was that he had become an unfortunate victim of a category conflation in the same way as with 'romanticism' (see chapter 3). 'Trotskyists' had become a tainted crew: they were a byword on the non-Trotskyist left for being particularly divisive, tribal, and prone to underhand tactics like entryism – the deliberate infiltration of one political group by another in order to thwart the first group's political objectives. But the Trotskyists, in Timpanaro's view, had simply given Trotsky a bad name. What Timpanaro and Belgrado wanted to do with their article was start the process of Trotsky recuperation, precisely for the non-Trotskyist left.[27] Their point was that there was still a huge amount of contemporary value in the thought of Trotsky – particularly on the matters of internationalism, on permanent revolution, and on the relationship between party and masses – and that this value was getting lost in the blanket condemnations doing the rounds in Timpanaro's political circles.[28] What is more, rampant anti-Trotskyism was often a cover for anti-Leninism.[29] So there was much at stake in salvaging something of Trotsky. As usual for Timpanaro, the consummate anti-cancellation thinker, the legacies of political theorists were complex and mixed, a grab-bag of errors and pearls. Timpanaro and Belgrado thought that the invocation of the Trotskyist nuisance was usually a way of

---

25   S.T. to Attilio Chitarin, 25 June 1972.

26   On this episode, see also Bufarale, *Sebastiano Timpanaro*, 44–5.

27   Internationalism: S.T. to Stefano Merli, 5 March 1976; permanent revolution: *VR*, 43; party democracy: *VR*, 45–6.

28   *VR*, 45.

29   S.T. to Siegmund Ginzberg, 19 June 1972; see also Bufarale, *Sebastiano Timpanaro*, 45.

defanging Trotsky himself – of shearing his thought of its contemporary edge (*attualità*) by complaining of its current debased incarnation.[30] But Trotsky, like Leopardi or, for that matter, any member of Timpanaro's living graveyard of written-off thinkers, was not to be dispensed with so easily.

The correspondence with Bellocchio over this proposal, as well as the ambient letters with other correspondents around it, give a fascinating glimpse both into Timpanaro's most deeply held political convictions and ethics, and into the touchy spots of the Tuscan left in the early 1970s. Bellocchio tried to steer Timpanaro and Belgrado towards a more neutral and desiccated historical piece on Trotsky, pitched explicitly *not* as an invitation to debate.[31] He expressed some concern that if this went wrong, *QP* would be clogged with endless factional warfare; he would rather not upset the apple cart.[32] Once it became clear Timpanaro and Belgrado had no intention of mincing words, Bellocchio proposed certain moderating strategies, such as giving space to a reply piece immediately after the Trotsky article, to balance things out. Timpanaro pushed back to suggest the reply should come in the next issue, as was the case for the materialism debate. An immediate reply would suggest the whole point of this exercise was to refute a misplaced airing of Trotsky's thought.[33] Eventually, Timpanaro withdrew the proposal altogether, when it became clear (at least to him) that Bellocchio was trying to take the wind out by subtly changing the accent of the article, from Trotsky himself to the more abstract question of party democracy. The two Trotsky sympathisers ended up taking their business elsewhere to *Giovane Critica*, another key journal of the 1968 radical left. But the piece certainly did not generate as much heat there as it would have done in *QP*.[34] As a cultural intervention, the Trotsky piece's impact was tiny compared to Timpanaro's materialism articles. But the engine room dynamics of its frustrated publication journey do show something interesting about Timpanaro's ethics and politics.

---

30   *VR*, 47.
31   Piergiorgio Bellocchio to S.T., 29 December 1971.
32   Piergiorgio Bellocchio to S.T., 12 January 1972.
33   S.T. to Piergiorgio Bellocchio (n.d., numbered 7 in Timpanaro archive).
34   Among Timpanaro's correspondence, I could only find a strong dissenting reaction to the article in Siegmund Ginzberg to S.T., 15 June 1972.

Timpanaro was an expert at not just tolerating but actively building open disagreement into the fabric of his friendships. This kind of tension is typical, seemingly to the point of the unremarkable. But the friendly dissolution of the conflict – *No problem, we will take it elsewhere* – belies the fact that this was, for Timpanaro, an important litmus test for an issue that went far beyond Trotsky. Timpanaro suspected that the editorial principles of *QP* were becoming more and more closed over time. He was fond of telling Grazia Cherchi (the other founding editor, along with Bellocchio) that their original benevolent dictatorship of a two-person editorial team was actually much better for a democratic and diverse ventilation of opinions than it was after getting several other members of the radical left on the editorial committee.[35] Timpanaro caught a whiff of various political biases forming, with the added effect of crystallising certain politically untouchable topics. Luxemburg and Mao were in;[36] Trotsky and China-scepticism were out.[37] A once broad-church leftist publication like the *QP* was bunkering down – and for Timpanaro, this was a deeply worrying sign.

Why did this touch a particular nerve for Timpanaro? He was, as we have seen and will see again and again, genuinely committed to the open, anti-aprioristic evaluation of intellectual contributions; and it was perhaps true that Trotsky was getting excessively short shrift, or was even being totally ignored, at that historical moment (although Timpanaro did have a tendency to overstate silence and neglect for effect).[38] But it was more the meta-issue of 'free debate' that Timpanaro

---

35   S.T. to Grazia Cherchi (n.d.; 18 in Timpanaro archive).

36   Timpanaro thought that the Trotsky piece would have been accepted had it been advocating Luxemburgism or Maoism (S.T. to Luca Baranelli, 24 February 1972). On the related recurring themes of criticism of Mao, revival of Trotsky, and defence of authentic Leninism, see Bufarale, *Sebastiano Timpanaro*, 43.

37   S.T. to Attilio Chitarin, 17 September 1975.

38   Conspiracy of silence around Trotsky: S.T. to Stefano Merli, 5 March 1976. The silence met by the *LF*: S.T. to Antonio Perin, 30 December 1983; Pagnini introduction to *RF* (14), *RF*, 39. As Fabio Stok says, Timpanaro hyped up the universal silence with which the *LF* was supposedly greeted in Italy (Fabio Stok, 'Dal Lapsus alla Fobia Romana', in Nuccio Ordine [ed.], *La lezione di un maestro: Omaggio a Sebastiano Timpanaro*, Naples, 2010, 81). The complaint about various critical silences threads throughout Timpanaro's pessimistic assessment of his work's impact. On the fourth chapter of *SM*: S.T. to Piergiorgio Bellocchio, 7 September 1979; on the *Antileopardiani* pieces: S.T. to Ersilia Alessandra Perona, 18 September 1976. On the silent treatment Timpanaro claimed for his wider works of nineteenth-century cultural history: S.T. to Nino

found so agitating – and this, I think, is crucial to understanding his politics. Like many figures in the vast coalition of forces that would come to be known as the New Left, Timpanaro was fiercely anti-Stalinist, but particularly in relation to the ossification of public debate and censorship. Any sign of sclerotisation or bureaucratisation was anathema to him; thus, any attempt to stifle debate or deoxygenate certain lines of inquiry became a cardinal sin. Dialoguing with Nino Scivoletto, a philologist at the more centrist/liberal end of the spectrum, Timpanaro found that the two had common ground on the question of liberalism, understood not as economic liberalism but as freedom of thought:

> I should have already understood by myself, without needing your clarification, that for you liberalism isn't the political expression of capitalism, and not even of economic 'liberalism' pure and simple, but it's the constant need for free thought and free discussion, the constant struggle against every tendency to the scleroticisation and bureaucratisation of any political or ideological system. In this sense, I have no difficulty considering myself also 'liberal' or 'libertarian'. I'd add one thing: perhaps it's not even about 'betting' more on the need for social justice or on that of individual freedom, because in reality I think that the two needs are closely interconnected, and the one can't stand without the other.[39]

This strand of liberalism – of thought and inquiry – ran right through Timpanaro's entire intellectual output. And it was perhaps the central part of the Venn diagram that helped him maintain meaningful conversations with people of radically different political persuasions, from the most conservative Oxford philologist to the most provocative autonomist.[40] Any time this Enlightenment thinker caught a hint of a stifled debate, he perceived it as a genuine existential threat to the ongoing life

---

Scivoletto, 28 November 1981. By the time of the *AN* (1982), it is almost as if he courts the expected response of readerly silence for effect (*AN*, 9). Timpanaro was also keen to point out these silences wherever they may obtain in the intellectual history of his favourite precursors, for instance, 'il lungo silenzio sul Meringer': *RF*, 169.

39   S.T. to Nino Scivoletto, 28 November 1981.

40   Timpanaro maintained long exchanges with several correspondents with whom he fundamentally disagreed on political matters, for instance, Hugh Lloyd-Jones and Giorgio Voghera.

of the left. The promise of socialism, for Timpanaro, was also a promise about liberty of thought and discussion. To Scivoletto, again, he cited the famous snippet from Marx and Engels's *Manifesto* that a future socialist society will be 'an association in which the free development of each person will be the condition for the free development of everyone'.[41] Cancelling Trotsky was no way to prefigure that libertarian vision.

With this deeply held commitment in mind, it is no surprise that Timpanaro and Belgrado gravitated to the specific *content* of Trotsky's thought most aligned with that commitment: the question of improving party democracy.[42] The encroaching logic of Stalinism was always trying to stamp out debate and reduce direct involvement of party rank-and-file. For Timpanaro and Belgrado, Trotsky still proved most useful for keeping the party accountable to and representative of the masses it claimed to be agitating for. The meta-issue of this whole Trotsky affair was really about freedom of debate, just as the content of Trotsky's thought that Timpanaro sought to highlight was about that very same democratic principle. Trotsky should be the intellectual property of the *whole left*, not just the Trotskyists[43] – even as his thought could make it a more robustly democratic place. If *QP* did not end up taking the bait, no matter; Timpanaro would fight it wherever he could write it.

While the Trotsky affair was symbolically important for what Timpanaro saw as an increasing closure and theoretical waywardness of the left, the left was now facing bigger problems. The year 1972 was particularly brutal for the PSIUP. In the general election of 1968, the PSIUP had garnered considerable electoral support, with around 1.5 million votes. In 1972, they attracted half that. The drastic collapse of support prompted a flight of much of the leadership back into the PCI and PSI – and, according to Timpanaro, the pro-PCI positions of that leadership were partly what accounted for the crisis in the first place.[44] Timpanaro

---

41 S.T. to Nino Scivoletto, 28 November 1981.

42 Timpanaro and Belgrado are also attracted to other parts of Trotsky's thought of particular contemporary relevance (Bufarale, *Sebastiano Timpanaro*, 44): genuine internationalist organisation and opposition to socialism in one country, and a transitional programme for advanced capitalist countries. But it was the anti-bureaucrat Trotsky that resonated with Timpanaro most deeply.

43 Bufarale, *Sebastiano Timpanaro*, 44.

44 S.T. to Giuseppe Anceschi 9, 28 June 72.

decided to stay in the PSIUP, but some kind of renewal had to happen. In December 1972, the new PSIUP ran together with the Workers' Political Movement (MPL) to form the Proletarian Unity Party (PdUP). Timpanaro had a mildly optimistic sense that this new political entity, purged of the strong links to the PCI and PSI that left the PSIUP hamstrung and subordinate, could start properly acting as the anti-PCI gadfly Timpanaro wanted his party to be. Alas, not much changed.

Subservience to the PCI would not necessarily have been such a problem, had the PCI's politics remotely continued to honour their communist origins. They were, however, drifting ever rightward. Though the PCI, under its new leader Enrico Berlinguer (1922–1984), was abandoning links with the Soviet Union in favour of 'Eurocommunism', this foreign policy realignment was not correlated at all with a left turn at the domestic level. This was the era of the great 'historic compromise', a naked cooperation between the PCI and DC first proposed by Berlinguer in 1973.[45] Its full political fruit was harvested only in 1976, when the first government of national solidarity was formed – a coalition of the DC (headed by Giulio Andreotti [1919–2013]) and its junior partner, the PCI. Here truly began the heaviest of the Italian 'Years of Lead' (*anni di piombo*), a period marked by economic crisis, crippling levels of unemployment, and acts of violent resistance on the extreme left (e.g., the kidnapping and assassination of the politician and former prime minister Aldo Moro [1916–1978]), with yet worse terrorist atrocities from the neo-fascist right (e.g., the Bologna railway station bombing of 1980, which killed eighty-five people). In 1976, the worst was still to come – but Timpanaro had had enough. The historic compromise was a stain on the Italian left, and there was no meaningful opposition to it left in the PdUP.[46] Timpanaro chose to leave the PdUP that year, and with it, the organised party politics of a left he had served dutifully for almost thirty years, never to return again. He was now a Marxist unmoored.

These declining years of Timpanaro's involvement in party politics were also some of his most intellectually fruitful. His work on nineteenth-century culture now took a turn towards the history of linguistics in earnest, with a profile of the Italian linguist Graziadio Ascoli

---

45   See *VR*, chapter 8, for Timpanaro's analysis of the emergence of Eurocommunism under Berlinguer.

46   S.T. to Alceste Angelini, 30 Dec 1976.

(1972), an article on the German linguist Friedrich Schlegel and the early phase of Indo-European linguistics (1972), and an intricate untangling of the distinct approaches to the structure and genesis of Indo-European languages in three influential early scholars of the field: the aforementioned Friedrich Schlegel, August Wilhelm Schlegel, and Franz Bopp (1973).[47] These articles would form the substance of the collection in *Sulla linguistica dell'Ottocento* (On nineteenth-century linguistics; 2005), the subject of chapter 6. They bear the imprint of a time in which Timpanaro was deeply engaged in the debate over materialism – and they prosecute the case for the value of that materialism by showing its beneficial role in linguistics (particularly in the thought of Ascoli).

Timpanaro continued this defence of scientific materialism through other means in what is nowadays perhaps his most famous book, *Il lapsus freudiano* (*The Freudian Slip*), first published in 1974 (see chapter 5). This book took on what Timpanaro saw as a compromised new darling of the Marxist left – Freudian psychoanalysis – and tried to show how a particular treasured principle of the Freudian system, the parapraxis (or slip), is in most cases not as revealing of the dark workings of the unconscious as the Freudians would have it. If Freudian analysis of particular slips in *The Psychopathology of Everyday Life* revealed anything, it was the intellectual dishonesty of Freud's methods. To prove their anti-scientific qualities, Timpanaro would lean on nothing less than his skills as a classical philologist used to explaining everyday errors of a similar kind in the manuscript transmission of classical texts. In 1975 and 1976 – the last years of Timpanaro's party-active life – he published four trenchant interventions in the Tuscan cultural journal *Belfagor* around the new alignments on the Italian left which were serving to rehabilitate nineteenth-century Tuscan 'moderates' as well as malign his beloved Leopardi; these articles would constitute the nucleus of the 1982 book published under the same name (see below), *Antileopardiani e neomoderati*. After Timpanaro properly withdrew from the PdUP in 1976, political disenchantment served to re-energise his home fields of philology and nineteenth-century cultural history, no

---

47   Sebastiano Timpanaro, 'Graziadio Ascoli', *Belfagor* 27 (1972): 149–76; 'Friedrich Schlegel e gli inizi della linguistica indeuropea in Germania', *Critica storica* 9 (1972): 72–105; 'Il contrasto tra i fratelli Schlegel e Franz Bopp sulla struttura e la genesi delle lingue indeuropee', *Critica storica* 10 (1973): 553–90.

doubt partly as a coping mechanism.[48] The year 1978 brought the long-awaited publication of a gigantic collection of his philological and linguistic contributions, many of them reprintings of articles published years earlier, but several of them new and bracing works; 1980 brought the follow-up to *Classicismo e illuminismo* (1965) in *Aspetti e figure della cultura ottocentesca* (Aspects and figures of nineteenth-century culture), with a whole new suite of pieces on nineteenth-century culture, and further intellectual profiles of both prominent figures such as the librarian Angelo Mai (1782–1854) and the poet Ugo Foscolo (1778–1827), as well as lesser-known figures such as the writer Ludovico Di Breme (1780–1820). Timpanaro was finding a powerful scholarly momentum that would carry him through an incredibly productive 1980s, well into the '90s. Scholarship stepped into the breach of politics.

The late 1970s and early '80s were also the moment Timpanaro decided to revisit the defence of Leopardi with *Antileopardiani e neomoderati* (1982; but based on four articles published in 1975 and 1976), a long and impassioned intervention against the strange effects of the Italian left's political realignment on certain interpretations of the nineteenth century.[49] To better understand Timpanaro's movement back to the Leopardi question in these years, we should spend a moment clarifying Timpanaro's political co-ordinates at this time. Despite his step back from party life, his socialist commitments were as strong as ever – and this manifested primarily in an intensification of hostility to the PCI. Timpanaro's resentment of the PCI was deep set, going back to Togliatti's politics of national unity in 1944, perhaps even to the popular fronts of 1936.[50] But in this period, Timpanaro truly raised the intensity.[51] The PCI had by this point lost most of its communist and anti-imperialist identity: it accepted Italy's presence in NATO and fell into line with standard capitalist recommendations for coping with the economic crisis; and the 'Eurocommunism' that was meant to mark a break from Stalinism in the party was essentially hollow because the party structure still suppressed dissenting currents against Enrico

---

48   S.T. to Alceste Angelini, 30 Dec 1976.

49   Original articles: Sebastiano Timpanaro, 'Antileopardiani e neomoderati nella sinistra italiana', parts 1–2, *Belfagor* 30 (1975): 129–56, 395–428; 'Antileopardiani e neomoderati nella sinistra italiana' parts 3–4, *Belfagor* 31 (1976): 1–32, 179–200.

50   *VR*, 100.

51   See particularly chapters 7, 8, and 9 of *VR*.

Berlinguer, with the single notable exception of Umberto Terracini (1895–1983; one of the founding members of the PCI, part of the original Gramsci–Togliatti generation, and a lone PCI voice against the historic compromise in the 1970s). By 1979, Timpanaro was issuing particularly blistering and bitter attacks on the PCI, claiming they no longer even merited the faint-hearted epithets 'social democratic' or 'reformist'. They were, in his estimation, an unreconstructed Stalinist party now committed to serving capitalism.[52] These were strong words, and Timpanaro meant every single one of them. Behind them, we see the rage launched against a political entity that had, in Timpanaro's view, torpedoed the revolutionary left and any hope of real socialism.

This political resentment towards the PCI was also firing Timpanaro's work on the cultural plane. Nor was this cultural work considered secondary in a period whose purpose Timpanaro came to see as cultivating an antagonistic popular spirit that might one day come in handy, should the revolution re-emerge as a prospect.[53] As early as 1976, he noted the distorting impact of the new politics of 'historic compromise' on the historiography of the nineteenth century:[54] certain scholars, most of them (such as Umberto Carpi) with a strong PCI identity, were starting to rehabilitate historical figures such as the Tuscan moderates around Gian Pietro Vieusseux (1779–1863) and Gino Capponi (1792–1876) merely because they exerted cultural and political power in their time. As intellectuals, they were habituated and integrated into the dominant class, 'organic' to that class, and hence had an impact on history. Timpanaro sensed a strong whiff of 'justificationism' here – the idea that these nineteenth-century figures were being used to validate the PCI's current direction of greater integration with the mainstream. This historiographic tendency was also having a negative effect on Leopardi's reputation. This was plummeting precisely because Leopardi was considered an isolated refusenik who chose to stand at an antagonistic angle to society rather than accommodate it and participate in it. Timpanaro would not accept this slight to his favourite poet's honour. And, in the absence of a party into which he might pour his energy for

---

52   S.T. to Edo Cecconi, 29 August 1979; reprinted as chapter 9 in *VR*. See also *OM*, 255–6.
53   *VR*, 165, reiterated at 190; cf. 196.
54   S.T. to Vanna Gazzola Stacchini, 11 February 1976.

more concrete struggle against the PCI and against capitalism, the issue provided an important version of that struggle, transplanted to the plane of cultural memory.

Timpanaro's political work in the '80s and '90s – his phase of being, as Luca Bufarale calls it, a 'socialist and ecologist without a party' – largely took place on this cultural level. He continued to write about politics even if this did not, at first appearance, seem the core subject. In 1984, he wrote a stunning book ostensibly about a very obscure piece of late nineteenth-century literature: the recently discovered unpublished novel of the late nineteenth-century socialist Edmondo De Amicis (1846–1908), entitled *Primo Maggio* (May first; see chapter 7). The book is a wonderfully lucid act of Timpanaran 'setting the record straight', getting us to see the serious political content in a book that had instantly been written off as a piece of failed sentimental claptrap from an annoying nationalist and bland school-curriculum-style author. But Timpanaro's reaching for this topic at such a political moment was no accident. In its evocation and restatement of the fundamentals of Second International–era socialism, this was Timpanaro's way of reconnecting and refreshing his commitment to his roots. A beautiful passage of the book, quoted by Bufarale, reflects on the current fate of the left through thinking about parallel figures, the roads travelled and not travelled by certain comrades like Lucio Colletti (1924–2001). Colletti, a direct contemporary of Timpanaro, had once been as staunch a Marxist as he, even if they disagreed on certain things. But once Colletti had diagnosed an irredeemable component of Hegel as poisoning Marxism forever, he converted to bourgeois democracy.[55] For Timpanaro, the philosophical and economic rights and wrongs of Marx – too much Hegel, or the fact that the rate of profit was not falling as predicted – did nothing essential to invalidate Marxism. The essence of Marxism was a deeply *felt* opposition to an unjust system of profit and exploitation. As long as that system existed, Marxism was the only principled way of responding to its brutality. *Il socialismo* is a beautiful book because it sees Timpanaro remaking the case for scientific socialism but also, in the process, allowing emotion to keep the flame of Marxism flickering as the light became ever dimmer.

---

55   On Colletti's 'conversion', see *VR*, 107. Timpanaro responds to Colletti's abandonment of Marxism in a postscript to the 1980 edition of *OM*, reprinted as chapter 10 of *VR*.

In addition to this excavation of a socialist predecessor in the form of De Amicis, Timpanaro's mid- to late 1980s were characterised by a turn of his philology towards the end of curating predecessors even further back in time. In 1985, he published a translation with notes on a classic Enlightenment text, *Il buon senso* (*Good Sense*) by Paul-Henri Thiry d'Holbach (1723–1789). This was a very direct, no-nonsense statement of a radical materialism and atheism penned by one of Timpanaro's favourite Enlightenment thinkers, who embodied for him, more than Diderot or Voltaire, the best of that tradition. There was also the very closely related edition in the same series, of another 'Enlightenment' thinker in the broad sense, Cicero's *Della divinazione* (*On Divination*, 1988). Timpanaro saw this text, in its second book a refutation of Roman practices of interpreting signs, omens, dreams, and portents, as one of Cicero's great contributions to the war against religious superstition. Timpanaro may not have had many active comrades left to struggle alongside in organised form, but, in his own way, he was still recruiting to the ranks of Enlightenment materialism and atheism. He was also writing comrades into existence in the history of philology (see chapter 2) with the publication of *Per la storia della filologia virgiliana antica* (Towards the history of ancient Virgilian philology, 1986) which sought to revalue the late antique commentators on Virgil (e.g., Valerius Probus) as honest guardians of Virgil's text, rather than fraudulent meddlers in it. In other words, these original scholars were appointed as rigorous precursors of Timpanaro's own tradition. Even on the topic of psychoanalysis, Timpanaro busied himself with philologically caring for his predecessors in producing a translation of Rudolf Meringer, a prominent Austrian linguist (1859–1931) who had anticipated Timpanaro's criticisms of Freud in *The Freudian Slip*. In short, this was a time of political and intellectual consolidation among a community drawn from the past. Timpanaro was restating the case for the causes dearest to his heart by revisiting the authors who had best made it before him. As we shall see in the conclusion of this book, Timpanaro held 'originality' and 'innovation' cheap – especially because these intellectual vacuities had led his one-time comrades, as he put it in a postscript to the 1979 edition of *On Materialism*, to invent under the guise of the new 'something very old:

capitalism'.[56] Better to keep shoring up the best of the Enlightenment left's tradition than destroy it by reinvention.

But Timpanaro's explicitly political writings continued alongside such indirectly political ones, right through the '80s and '90s. And while this was a period of consolidation and return towards the end of his life, it was also a period of growth and change. The contributions collected in *Il verde e il rosso. Scritti militanti, 1966–2000* (The green and the red: Militant writings, 1966–2000) show an increasing focus, from the 1980s onwards, on the ecological crisis – the 'green' in the volume's title. In *On Materialism*, Timpanaro had gravitated towards Engels's image of the cooling of the Earth after the Sun's explosion to show that Engels was aware of the physical limits that would ultimately impose themselves on the cosmos and the humans within it (see chapter 4).[57] Timpanaro and Engels rejected the anthropocentric in favour of the long historical view. Timpanaro admitted later in life that this image of the end of the world had plagued him and vexed his neurosis long before he encountered it in Engels; even as a child, it kept him up at night.[58] This limit was a material property of the universe, and that was scary enough. But what dawned on Timpanaro in the 1970s and '80s, particularly after reading Dario Paccino's 1972 *L'imbroglio ecologico* (The ecological swindle) and Jean Fallot's 1976 *Sfruttamento, inquinamento, guerra* (Exploitation, pollution, war), was that the end of the world was also a property and a logical conclusion of *capitalism* – and this end of the world would arrive far sooner than the Sun's death.[59] Nuclear war was one threat; but the more serious one, that which Timpanaro judged more likely to materialise in the not-so-distant future, was the slower self-elimination of the human species through capital's inherent processes of environmental degradation and resource depletion.[60] The revelation was energising for an ageing Timpanaro because it provided fresh reasoning to overturn capitalism. Socialists were not just fighting for humankind's liberation but for its very survival on earth. The end of the world was stripped of its abstract qualities as a consequence of the universe's finite nature.

---

56   *OM*, 261.
57   *OM*, 98–9.
58   *VR*, 185.
59   See *VR*, 191, and *VR*, chapter 15; see also Cortesi's introduction to *VR*, xxxiii–iv.
60   *VR*, 188.

Instead, it was given the face of a clear and present enemy, a blameworthy political agent, the same one Timpanaro had been combatting his whole life: capital.[61]

Was this, then, a political change? It was closer to a new way of framing the problem, not a shift in substance. The story of 'the green and the red' is not one of red to green, a change of colour from socialism to a liberal environmentalism that many of Timpanaro's former comrades, such as Lotta Continua's Adriano Sofri, would undergo. It is really a story of *acquiring green-coloured reasoning for the red*.[62] Timpanaro was scathing about vague liberal formulations of the environmental problem, which failed to put that problem squarely at the door of the large polluting corporations and the capitalist system itself. For Timpanaro, there could be no green without the red.[63] The red was the core principle which could not be abandoned. And the environmental crisis had merely underscored another, even more existentially urgent, reason for why that was the case. In other words, the green became, late in Timpanaro's life, another way of recommitting to the red.

This new green hue did not mean that Timpanaro would consent to the past being distorted through it. In one of his best later essays, Timpanaro responded to Sofri's 1987 attempt to co-opt both Leopardi and Timpanaro to the cause of fuzzy green humanism.[64] According to Sofri, Leopardi's broad-based call for widespread solidarity in the face of nature's merciless hostility could help in banding together as one in a newfound struggle *for* nature. This was just the kind of ahistorical sophistry that always made Timpanaro's blood boil. How could a poet who explicitly advocated the principle of 'nature as stepmother' (*natura matrigna*; see chapter 3), and took the natural world to be an uncompromising enemy of humanity, be twisted into acting as a rallying post for *protecting* that nature?! Timpanaro rejected these ideological attempts to bring Leopardi 'up to date', to make him speak to facile contemporary concerns (*attualizzare*) as he was made to in the dreaded recent 150th anniversary of his death, which launched a series of vapid attempts to ventriloquise Leopardi with contemporary concerns. Just as Timpanaro

61   *VR*, 189.
62   Cortesi, introduction to *VR*, xxxv.
63   *VR*, 162–3.
64   Sebastiano Timpanaro, 'Il "Leopardi Verde" ', *Belfagor* 42, no. 6 (1987): 613–37; reprinted as *VR*, chapter 13.

resisted any attempts to make Leopardi a Marxist avant la lettre, as well as the attempts to sideline him from cultural relevance merely for not being a slippery 'organic intellectual', so he made one final intervention against Leopardi's co-option to green centrism. The green could be a new way of shading the red, but not a way of colouring over the anti-nature Leopardi. And it could not neuter or domesticate the radical materialist pessimism we will discuss in chapter 4.

Timpanaro's active political life spanned the entire second half of the twentieth century. It reached from the high watermark of the post–World War II Italian push for socialism and communism, right up to the post-Soviet world and new neoliberal order of the 1990s. There was, of course, evolution in his positions on various issues in this time. But the base of his political thought and practice – anti-Stalinism, uncompromising Leninism and sympathy for Trotsky, a constitutional hatred towards all forms of authoritarianism in party or society, belief in free debate, a concomitant scorn for the PCI, certitude of the need for a proper scientific materialism in an age of Marxism's dilution under the influence of other ideological distractions – remained hardy and unshakeable throughout. If Timpanaro's politics stayed remarkably stable, the development in the breadth and depth of his intellectual work was, by contrast, staggering. In the chapters that follow, we will focus on the particulars of this work to show this development, but also to tease out the overriding concerns that powered him to produce genuinely original contributions in so many fields. We will start with the only activity that can boast a longer claim on Timpanaro's attention than politics: classical philology.

2
Philology and Its Histories

Among those civilians with any knowledge of classical philology, the field has various connotations – few of them good. Abstruse, pedantic, trivial, minor, the preserve of Oxbridge or Ivy League elites, a cloistered study of disconnected points of textual detail in the already-hermetic classical tradition: this is perhaps the impression given off by its perceived dusty and fusty practitioners (assuming people care enough to notice them at all). To the vast majority of people, however, philology would mean little more than an unpronounceable word.

Philology is the art and/or science of working through linguistic, literary, and historical problems in Latin and Greek texts. The job of the philologist is manifold but could be split into two purposes. The first and historically most prestigious, textual criticism, has as its goal the establishment of the form of classical texts as close as possible to what the ancient author wrote. The second, something like 'comment' or 'exegesis', is about interpreting the meaning of these difficult and crux-strewn texts. Timpanaro was more at home in the latter (see below), though he was constantly engaging with problems germane to the former. Latin and Greek works are cultural objects battling against thousands of years of natural entropy, human error, and the loss of cultural and historical literacy needed to understand them. Their interpretation requires a special kind of vigilance: a huge amount of attention to detail, with a thousand micro-decisions finessed into final calls often involving extremely marginal degrees of probability. Classical philology, in short, is the discipline of the nitpicker, a field of microbial humanities seemingly standing infinite levels of magnification beneath the huge concatenation of material forces we call politics.

Timpanaro, one of the twentieth century's greatest practitioners of this art, oddly tended to agree.[1] He was trained in one of the most (if not *the* most) eminent hubs of the discipline at a moment when its centre of gravity, after a long nineteenth century tarrying in Germany, had swung towards Italy; in fact, his particular school, the University of Florence under the monumental and all-shadowing professorship of Giorgio Pasquali, laid claim to the inheritance of the best German philological tradition of the previous generations.[2] While Timpanaro – unlike other students of Pasquali who diffused across the peninsula to spread the gospel to its other corners of higher education – never worked in a university, due to his crippling neurosis around public speaking, he always considered philology his central métier: the thing he was actually trained in, as opposed to the bouts of intellectual 'dilettantism' he would engage in over the rest of his wide-ranging writing career.[3] But despite these dual signs positively centralising philology in Timpanaro's life – intellectual maturation in a context where philology was taken deadly seriously, and then his ongoing identification as a card-carrying *filologo* for the rest of his working days – Timpanaro's prose is full of self-deprecating apologies for his field. It takes away precious time from political struggle; it languishes as a kind of 'micrology', a study of microscopic minutiae far below the care or concern of humans gravitating to graver matters.[4] Such

---

1   For philology as antithetical to politics: S.T. to Grazia Cherchi (n.d., probably 1971; numbered 20 in Timpanaro archive); as distraction and drain: S.T. to Attilio Chitarin, 16 March 1973, 25 March 1973, 16 September 1977; as apolitical: S.T. to Luciano Della Mea, 10 May 1976. For Timpanaro's claim that philology does not serve the task of understanding the contemporary world or combatting capitalism at all: S.T. to Luciano Della Mea, 28 November 1970. Timpanaro comes across as almost ashamed of his *CF* for their concealment of his politics (S.T. to Ambrogio Donini, 25 May 1979). Cf. also S.T. to Dario Paccino, 28 May 1976; S.T. to Mario Geymonat, 24 April 1981.

2   The Pasqualian group identity and pride was tight: see S.T. to Nino Scivoletto, 28 November 1981.

3   Timpanaro's self-description as dilettante outside philology: S.T. to Giorgio Voghera, 21 February 1967; S.T. to Arnaldo Momigliano, 30 August 1970; S.T. to Dario Paccino, 12 March 1971; S.T. to Alceste Angelini, 25 April 1971; S.T. to Giuseppe Cambiano, 26 August 1979; S.T. to Nino Scivoletto, 28 November 1981.

4   S.T. to Attilio Chitarin, 16 March 1973, 25 March 1973, 16 September 1977. On philology as micrology: S.T. to Silvia Rizzo, 4 June 1975; S.T. to Arnaldo Momigliano, 8

self-deprecation, of course, was part and parcel of Timpanaro's evergreen rhetorical positioning as minimal or marginal, which he maintained even within the allegedly narrow scope of philology itself: he described his main collection of philological work 'the minor writings of a philologist with no major writings to his credit'.[5] The rendering of slim pickings in a programmatically thin discipline, such minimising self-presentation, as we have seen and shall see, was not just pathological or lordly modesty; the reduction of the ego to vanishing unimportance was, rather, a crucial lodestone of Timpanaran materialism, which played down individual subjectivity for the truth 'out there'. Even so, Timpanaro's multiple protestations of philology's triviality serve to quarantine it from his more ambitious forays into politics, culture, history, psychology, and philosophy. It is as if the minimal detail and the broader sweep were two warring factions in a conflict within a 'non-integrated personality', a conflict that Timpanaro was always invested in keeping unresolved because of a deeply held belief in the principle of unresolvability (over and against the vague abuses of the 'dialectic' rife in Timpanaro's intellectual culture).[6] The small and the big, philology and politics: never the twain should meet.

While respecting Timpanaro's modus operandi of conflict and contestation, in this chapter I want to show that he was not entirely right about the missing overlap between these different spheres. Not only did philology equip him with an intellectual toolkit on which he would draw again and again for all his subsequent activities, but its history, methodologies, obsessions, filters – its worldview – supplied him with a distinctive means

---

Jan 1979; S.T. to Nino Scivoletto, 6 April 1983; *SLO* 289–90. This restriction to the 'minor', the nitty gritty, is almost Timpanaro's most important constituent for philology: Foscolo cannot be classed as a philologist because he never made such micrological contributions (*AF*, 106, 110).

5   *CF*, 7.

6   See, for instance, S.T. to Carlo Ginzburg, 5 March 1971, where Timpanaro denied any fusion of his philological pedantry and broader, more cultural-political voice. As Cases noted (Cesare Cases to S.T., 24 December 1990; cf. 3 January 1986), Timpanaro always combined his philology and politics by keeping them distinct; he observed a conjugation rather than a synthesis, unlike, for example, the communist classical scholar George Thomson (1903–1987), famous for spearheading explicitly Marxist interpretations of Greek drama. Cf. Timpanaro on the non-unity of his philological technique in the *LF* with the political-ideological content (S.T. to Emilio Bigi, 13 July 1975). Timpanaro retained the principle of unresolvability right up to one of his very last works, on the antinomies of Aeschylus' *Agamemnon*. Sebastiano Timpanaro, 'Antinomie nell'*Agamennone* di Eschilo', *Giornale Italiano di Filologia*, 1998: 169; cf. S.T. to Hugh Lloyd-Jones, 16 May 1998.

of sense-making that would express itself, in different ways, in all his subsequent work. What big things, then, can this small field teach?

Before tackling that question, we might first ask a more basic one: What *is* this small field? I will offer here a very short potted history, focussing particularly on some of the key themes and characters that shaped Timpanaro's sense of his home turf. I focus particularly on classical philology, as opposed to the other related European traditions of philology – Biblical, Romance, Medieval, comparative, and so on – solely because this was Timpanaro's intellectual grounding.[7] Classical philology boasts a vast history stretching back to the Hellenistic period of antiquity, when scholars in the early third century BCE first started codifying and correcting the flawed texts they had inherited.[8] But classical philology as the disciplinary practice we recognise today was formulated largely, like many academic disciplines, in the nineteenth-century German university. Two rough areas of pursuit were defined and refined in that period: firstly, *recensio* (recension), a review process of collating and analysing the available manuscripts of a given text such as Virgil's *Aeneid* or Plato's *Republic* in order to constitute a kind of genealogy leading back to a hypothetical 'original' text, ideally as close as possible to what the author wrote. Secondly, *emendatio* (emendation), the process of locating and ironing out various errors and 'corruptions' which had become evident in the process of *recensio*. The complicated history of both of these areas runs much deeper than the nineteenth century. Below, I engage in the butchery of a simplification. But these initial categories go some way towards rooting Timpanaro's understanding of what philology was.

Two important historical influences, embodying two different phases of modern philology, underlay Timpanaro's work – but in a negative sense. These figures also map nicely on to the division between *recensio* and *emendatio*. The first figure was the English philologist Richard

---

7 For a recent synthesis of various traditions of world philology, see Sheldon Pollock, Benjamin A. Elman, and Ku-ming Kevin Chang (eds), *World Philology*, Cambridge, MA, 2015.

8 For an up-to-date account of the major currents in European classical philology from the eighteenth century to the late twentieth, see Gherardo Ugolini and Diego Lanza (eds), *History of Classical Philology: From Bentley to the 20th Century*, transl. Antonella Lettieri, Berlin, 2022.

Bentley (1662–1742).[9] Bentley was renowned, in particular, for his work as an inspired critic who leveraged supposed sympathy with the original author and a vast command of Latin and Greek to make a host of active *changes* to the inherited text – as we will see below, the practice known as conjecture. Bentley thought of this process very much as an art involving a degree of innate genius – and though he is still held up as a scholar of peerless vision and insight in the English philological tradition, Italian philologists such as Timpanaro tended to be more sceptical. Bentley was the first to make extensive revisions to texts – indeed, his (in)famous edition of the Roman poet Horace made an unprecedented number of such changes. Such 'heroic interventionism' was based partly on a practice of heavy 'analogism' – the belief that classical authors wrote in a regular and predictable way, and so, if a mountain of parallel expressions found in other texts of that author could be found to justify a change to a manuscript reading, the change should be made. Bentley was a great believer in applying this rule of an author's habitual practice (known as *usus scribendi* in philology, the 'usual practice of writing') to regularise a text, and to eliminate exceptions. The changes always needed to be reasoned and justified. But Bentley became the patron figure for a philological tradition which Timpanaro largely positioned himself against, as we shall see below.

The history of philology cycles through various forms of disagreement over whether it is an art or a science – and if Bentley was one of its great artists, the next antagonist for Timpanaro was one of its most eminent scientists: Karl Lachmann (1793–1851).[10] Nineteenth-century German philology did what German scholarship was doing in many disciplines at that time: it attempted to put the field on a more rigorous and scientific footing, with predictable, trustworthy, and generally applicable methodologies. Lachmann and others' contribution was in generating a particular method for manuscript classification: a 'set of criteria used to establish the relationships between the manuscripts that transmit a text to us'.[11] In other words, Lachmann became known for

---

9   For information on Bentley, I draw on Francesco Lupi, 'Richard Bentley and Philology as the Art of Conjecture' (2002), in Ugolini and Lanza, *History of Classical Philology*, 9–33.

10   For information on Lachmann, I draw on Sotera Fornaro, 'Karl Lachmann: Method and Science', in Ugolini and Lanza, *History of Classical Philology*, 117–31.

11   Ibid., 117.

inventing a simplifying system of rules for the process of recensio, and endowing the method with uniformity. The system came to be known as the 'stemmatic method', after *stemma* (family tree), because the way the manuscript relationships were visualised resembled a genealogical tree – a technique that would, in fact, emerge in several branches of science during the nineteenth century, from the biological to the linguistic. While Lachmann can be thought of as a kind of 'purifier' and stream-liner of this system, arguably it was not fully refined into a 'geometric', mathematical version of itself till Paul Maas's *Textkritik* (*Textual Criticism*) of 1927 – to which Timpanaro's teacher Giorgio Pasquali responded very vocally (see below).[12] So, even though Lachmann may feel remote to us, he had been given a new lease on life, as it were, in the philological epoch immediately preceding Timpanaro. This contempo-rary relevance was partly why Timpanaro felt it timely to tackle the history of the method.

Another legacy of the German philological nineteenth century was a very formative debate about what philology was, and was not. This period did not just generate or codify new methods but also debated the identity of the discipline fiercely. In the early nineteenth century, two competing 'branches' of classical philology emerged, clustering around the conflict between two leading philologists, Gottfried Hermann (1772–1848; a professor at the University of Leipzig), and August Boeckh (1785–1867; a professor at the University of Berlin).[13] Hermann, the elder of the two, had already established himself as perhaps *the* eminent philologist in Germany, becoming representative of a very technical and formal approach. Boeckh proved the young maverick, challenging what he saw as Hermann's constrained approach to move the goalposts of philology to consider the broader social and cultural history of antiquity (not just its words). The Hermannian branch would come to be known as *Wortphilologie* (philology of the word), so called because it trained on language, on the finicky minutiae of words, gram-mar, and metre, aiming to reconstruct the texts themselves and stick strictly to the linguistic and stylistic analysis thereof. The Boeckhian

---

12   Paul Maas, *Textkritik*, Leipzig, 1927.
13   For the Hermann-Boeckh conflict, I rely on Gherardo Ugolini, 'Hermann contra Boeckh: Formal Philology and Historical Philology', in Ugolini and Lanza, *History of Classical Philology*, 133–62.

branch, on the other hand, was known as *Sachphilologie* (philology of the object). This approach was oriented more towards the concrete objects that made up the overall world of ancient societies and aimed at the more holistic reconstruction of these societies in all their totality – not just the language as left behind in their patchy textual artefacts. Interestingly, Timpanaro would always define his own philological practice as more Hermannian than Boeckhian: rigidly formal and technical, interested much more in the nitty-gritty of the textual and linguistic problems thrown up by ancient texts, rather than the grander, more zoomed-out ambitions of the Boeckhian tradition. This was perhaps also because Hermannian philology was also about recognising one's own cognitive limits and cultivating what Hermann called an 'art of not knowing' (*ars nesciendi*) – and Timpanaro's temperament, as we shall see, also leaned towards inscribing such limits on the human ability to make the world with one's mind (see chapter 4).

But the most emphatic reason for Timpanaro's feeling of connection to this tradition of nineteenth-century German philology was his undergraduate teacher and mentor Giorgio Pasquali.[14] Pasquali had spent his crucial formative years in Germany learning the philological trade from titanic descendants of the Lachmann–Hermann–Boeckh generation. Pasquali cut his teeth with a broad selection of professors skilled in various branches of philology: Jacob Wackernagel (1853–1938) on historical linguistics, Friedrich Leo (1851–1914) on the relationship between Latin and Greek literature, Eduard Schwartz (1858–1940) on the historical reconstruction of classical texts and manuscript traditions, and Ulrich von Wilamowitz-Moellendorff (1848–1931), perhaps the most forbiddingly impressive of the Boeckhian line of German philologists, who worked to treat the ancient world as a totality and philology as inherently interdisciplinary.[15] When Pasquali returned to Italy in 1924 and took up the chair of philology at the University of Florence, there was still some resistance to the scientific tradition of German philology among the older generation of Italian philologists such as Giuseppe Fraccaroli (1849–1918) and Ettore Romagnoli (1871–1938; see chapter 6). But Pasquali managed

---

14   For information on Pasquali, I here draw on Luciano Bossina, 'Giorgio Pasquali and Philology as a Historical Science', in Ugolini and Lanza, *History of Classical Philology*, 239–75.

15   See Gherardo Ugolini, 'Wilamowitz: Philology as "Totality"', in Ugolini and Lanza, *History of Classical Philology*, 189–210.

to prevail in installing a school of philology that was less modelled on analogy with the natural sciences (à la Lachmann), and more based on the form of historical analysis. Pasquali's legacy in Italian philology, and world philology in general, became monumental. A devoted teacher at both the University of Florence (1924–52) and the Scuola Normale Superiore in Pisa (1931–52), he trained a host of golden age Italian Latinists who would go on to make a huge impact on the field, including Antonio La Penna (1925–), Scevola Mariotti (1920–2000), and Timpanaro himself.

Pasquali's major principles were largely in service of a well-rounded philological practice that tried not to neglect any helpful strand of the tradition: he made no attempt at *recensio* of manuscripts without the ability to comprehensively interpret what was in them; he also argued that certain more recent manuscripts could not necessarily be ruled out of contention when constituting a text (*recentiores non deteriores* – 'more recent does not mean worse' – see below). But Pasquali's most important line of research, for our purposes, was the one embodied in his magnum opus, *Storia della tradizione e critica del testo* (History of tradition and textual criticism, 1934). This book was a direct challenge, through extensive nuancing, to the recently codified system of manuscript classification in Paul Maas's above-mentioned *Textkritik* – a kind of hyper-mechanical, mathematical version of the so-called method of Lachmann. Pasquali's problem was that Maas tended to banish anything from his system that did not make sense within it – that is, any manuscript traditions that could not be reduced to a clear family tree. He tended not to consider messy issues of 'horizontal' contamination – cases where a scribe producing a manuscript refers to more than one manuscript, thus mixing up branches of the tree. Maas's drastic system prematurely eliminated many manuscripts from consideration – manuscripts which, according to Pasquali, might still have value for reconstructing a text. Maas's response to all this was to legislate it out of interest. Maas thought Pasquali put too great an accent on the *exception* over the *rule*, giving too much importance to 'singular, atypical cases', and merely refused to do the harder thing: describe the rule. This was also the general response to the Pasquali–Maas debate within the philological community: one went to Maas for the rule, to Pasquali for the anomalies; to Maas for general anatomy, to Pasquali for specific physiology.[16] This emphasis on

---

16   Bossina, 'Giorgio Pasquali', 261–2.

both anomaly/exception and specificity, as well as a resistance to all forms of blindly applied law, would become pivotal for Timpanaro's own philological practice. And it would inform all his other work too.

Pasquali's other major torch handed to Timpanaro was a firm imperviousness to Italian idealism. As we shall see in chapter 6, one wing of Florentine philology among Pasquali's predecessors (the above-mentioned Fraccaroli and Romagnoli) was heavily informed by the idealism of Benedetto Croce, which treated poetry not as a material phenomenon with a prehistory but as a kind of sacred creative act of a poet, spontaneous and without precedent. The Pasqualian method, whether in 'Arte allusiva' ('Allusive art') or *Preistoria della poesia romana* (Prehistory of Roman poetry), was, rather, about tracing the long back-story to every slice of language surviving from antiquity.[17] There were no miraculous creative conceptions in the world of Pasqualian philology. Nothing happened in a vacuum. Every classical artefact had long roots to disentangle. In virtually all of Timpanaro's future work, this ability to unravel long and complex intellectual histories with painstaking patience was something he would make his own.

Timpanaro's philological output falls into a few different brands. First, there is the 'practice' of philology pure and proper, as embodied in two collected volumes which were both published relatively late in his career but act as retrospective repositories of material first released much earlier: the *Contributi* (1978) and the *Nuovi contributi* (1994). These are collections of articles on very specific, targeted problems in classical philology, for instance, the interpretation of a strange phrase in Virgil (*ut vidi, ut perii*); or nutting out the history of the Latin word *ilicet*.[18] Timpanaro referred to these as *ricerca puntuale* or *esegesi puntuale*, or *adversaria*, or the self-deprecating *noterelle*.[19] 'Ricerca puntuale' means

---

17   Giorgio Pasquali, 'Arte allusiva', *Italia che scrive* 25 (1942): 185–7; *Preistoria della poesia romana*, Florence, 1936.

18   *CF*, 219–87.

19   *Ricerca puntuale*: S.T. to Cesare Cases, 11 January 1974; S.T. Alfonso Traina, 11 January 2000; *CF*, 219; cf. Emanuele Narducci, 'Sebastiano Timpanaro', *Belfagor* 40, no. 3 (1985): 286. *Esegesi puntuale*: *CF*, 219. *Noterelle*: S.T. to Nino Scivoletto, 28 November 1981, 6 April 1983; S.T. to Alessandro Russo, 21 September 1996; S.T. to Mario Untersteiner, 8 January 1979. Cf. *adversaria*, also used of Leopardian philology: Piergiorgio Parroni, 'Timpanaro e la filologia', in Nuccio Ordine (ed.), *La lezione di un maestro: Omaggio a Sebastiano Timpanaro*, Naples, 2010, 60–1; *FGL*, 177.

something like 'precision pieces', research focussed on the resolution or thinking-through of a very circumscribed snag in making sense of an ancient text – and it was the need for comprehensive comprehension, the need to understand *in full* (*capire tutto*) that Timpanaro took as central to the philologist's task.[20]

Next, there are two more discursive and extended works on the history of philology, both texts forming a complementary meta-disciplinary study on the evolution of the discipline in the nineteenth century (as well as its deeper historical roots). The first of these – Timpanaro's debut major work, launched to great acclaim in 1955 – is a focussed account of the philology of Giacomo Leopardi. Timpanaro's main thesis in *La filologia di Giacomo Leopardi* was to show that the famous poet was not *purely* a poet but, particularly in the early part of his career, a philologist of the highest, most up-to-date order at a historical moment in which Italy had very few specimens worthy of the name. The second of these is Timpanaro's path-breaking *La genesi del metodo del Lachmann* (*The Genesis of Lachmann's Method*, 1963), which, for the first time, prised apart the myth of a revolutionary break in the practice of editing classical texts with a genealogical method of manuscript classification supposedly cooked up by Karl Lachmann himself.[21] Timpanaro showed here, with the most granular and subtle historical analysis, that the so-called method of Lachmann was really a cumulative result of many different individual philological contributions between the renaissance and the early nineteenth century – a testament to Timpanaro's conviction on the longue durée 'progress' of philology, a field of human endeavour subject to the laws of gradualist reformism rather than the kangaroo-leaps of revolution. We might be

---

20 *DD*, xcix; Federico Santangelo, 'Voler "capire tutto". Appunti sullo stile di Sebastiano Timpanaro', *Anabases* 20 (2014): 62–3; S.T. to Garzanti Editore Milano, 14 January 1986. Timpanaro's defence to Antonio Perin that philology is more than mere pedantry is interesting for the way it talks of philology as serving the ancients, who themselves have a right to be understood ever better (S.T. to Antonio Perin, 30 December 1983). Timpanaro also attributed this philological act of understanding to Marx and Engels (S.T. to Arnaldo Momigliano, 4 August 1967). For interpretation as fundamental to the philologist's task, not just pure memory or conservation: S.T. to Giorgio Voghera, 27 Dec 1969. Timpanaro expanded on this crucial point of detailed philological understanding, and counterposed it to the chicanery of postmodernism, in 'La filologia e il postmoderno: Intervista a Sebastiano Timpanaro', *Allegoria* 3, no. 8 (1991): 95–108; see Luca Bufarale, *Sebastiano Timpanaro: L'inquietudine della ricerca*, Pistoia, 2022, 24–5.
21 *La genesi del metodo del Lachmann*, 1st ed., 1963; nucleus originally published in 1959 as articles in *Studi italiani di filologia classica* 31: 182–228 and 32: 38–63.

tempted to sequester these two works in an altogether different category from the workaday *minimalia* of Timpanaro's *esegesi puntuali* – which, however model in their clarity and often novel in their results, flashed nowhere near the same originality, nor bore the same cultural impact, as their more 'historical' cousins. But in practice, the school of philology from which Timpanaro came – that of Pasquali's Florence – never really distinguished between the two kinds of enterprise.[22] As Pasquali's influential masterpiece, *Storia della tradizione,* had already established in writing – and as Pasquali apparently affirmed in his teaching over and over again – the practice of philology was inseparable from a self-conscious study of the history of its methods.[23] Philology was also its histories.

The last major strand of Timpanaro's proper philological activity was another diptych of monographs on the Virgilian tradition of antiquity, both, again, relatively late works: *Per la storia della filologia virgiliana antica* (Towards the history of ancient Virgilian philology, 1986) and the posthumously published *Virgilianisti antichi e tradizione indiretta* (Ancient Virgilians and indirect tradition, 2001).[24] In some ways, Timpanaran philology functioned as a kind of ring-fence of security around a career whose central block was characterised by breathtaking interdisciplinary expansion and violation. The Virgilian tradition, in Timpanaro's purview, was the late-antique practice of commentary and editing on the authoritative texts of Virgil, and for Timpanaro, it was a treasure trove of textual variants sometimes pickled better than in the manuscripts of Virgil's actual poetry. Timpanaro had an abiding interest in these somewhat marginal grammarians his whole career, but he only treated them in earnest relatively late – in a period where he too was concerned with the curation and divulgation of the texts of his own 'materialist' predecessors, his own tradition (including d'Holbach and Cicero).[25] What these works allowed him to express, as we shall see below, was a full working out of philology's

---

22   See this book's introduction.

23   See Antonio Rotondò, 'Sebastiano Timpanaro e la cultura universitaria fiorentina della seconda metà del Novecento', in Enrico Ghidetti and Alessandro Pagnini (eds), *Sebastiano Timpanaro e la cultura del Secondo Novecento*, Rome, 2005, 31–2; Giuseppe Cambiano in the same volume, 98.

24   *PLS* and *VA*.

25   Salvatore Settis interestingly groups the *FGL* together with *Il buon senso* and *DD* as Timpanaro's *scelta dei propri antenati* (the script of a speech given by Settis at the Accademia Lincei in Rome; numbered 8 under 'Settis' in the Timpanaro archive).

case-by-case judgement, its inability to write anything off or treat anything as valueless. This radical democratism of evaluation, the absolute (or at least attempted) suspension of all a priori prejudice, cashes out in much Timpanaran work. It was philology that trained him to rehabilitate these neglected corners of intellectual history, and to never take anything for granted.

It is worth noting here something that may be opaque to the non-initiate: the philology that Timpanaro did not do, or did not quite do. Unquestionably, the summit goal of a philological career in Timpanaro's mid-twentieth-century heyday was one thing: the production of an edition of, often with an explanatory commentary on, a given classical text. Such an enterprise was thought to require all the philologist's Herculean strength in many areas of labour: collating and organising manuscripts (recensio), deciding between textual variants, making informed conjectures about the form of the original text when such variants did not yield ready sense (emendatio), and finally, often, synthesising the history of scholarship on that particular text to then offer one's own detailed interpretation of its form and content, its linguistic and metrical (if poetry) oddities and typicalities. Timpanaro never produced an exemplar of such gold standard philology, even if his undergraduate work placed him well to produce an authoritative edition of Rome's first major poet, Ennius, and even if older titans in the field such as Eduard Fraenkel (1888–1970, a professor of Latin at Oxford, 1935–53) thought he should apply his preternatural gifts to no lesser flagship than the editing of Virgil (in classical philology, a sort of holy grail).[26] In the former case, Timpanaro's awareness that the leading London-based German scholar Otto Skutsch had a more advanced Ennius edition already in the works discouraged him from the prospect of doubling up.[27] In the

---

26   Santangelo, 'Voler "capire tutto"', 55–6. See also Mario De Nonno, 'Timpanaro tra filologia e storia della lingua latina', in Enrico Ghidetti and Alessandro Pagnini (eds), *Sebastiano Timpanaro e la cultura del Secondo Novecento*, Rome, 2005, 120, on the continuing fallout of Timpanaro's refusal to produce an Ennius edition; and Vincenzo Di Benedetto, 'La filologia di Sebastiano Timpanaro', in Riccardo Di Donato (ed.), *Il filologo materialista*, Pisa, 2003, 83–4, on Timpanaro's keener feeling for the missing Virgil.

27   See Sebastiano Timpanaro, 'Otto Skutsch's Ennius', *Bulletin of the Institute of Classical Studies Supplement* 51 (1988): 2 – although Timpanaro did suggest to Mariotti (S.T. to Scevola Mariotti, 15 October 1986) the possibility of doing a small edition of Ennius's fragments.

latter, Fraenkel's appeals fell on deaf ears, fobbed off by Timpanaro's pathological pleading of incapacity and lack of patience.[28] The closest Timpanaro came to producing an edition was outside the strict remit of academic philology: his much-admired volume of Leopardi's *Scritti filologici* (Philological writings, 1969), a kind of follow-up to *La Filologia*, co-edited with Giuseppe Pacella (whose presence Timpanaro admitted was absolutely crucial to force him to bring such painstaking work to term); and his popular translations of two critical 'Enlightenment' (in the broad sense) texts, Cicero's *On Divination* and d'Holbach's *Bon Sens*.[29] Both of these latter, especially the Cicero, had the hallmarks of a kind of 'public-facing', accessible philological edition – more than half their battle was in offering detailed explanatory notes (i.e., commentary) to the lay reader. This was by design of the series in which they appeared – the Italian publisher Garzanti specialised in textbooks and school reference works. But there was a reason Timpanaro took on these jobs. They were, in a sense, the natural philological outgrowth of Timpanaro's didactic impulse. So Timpanaro did indeed channel the iron gravity of his discipline's expectations into producing serious editions – only that the business was transacted off site, as it were, away from the intense glare of professional classical scholarship.[30] But for the rest of his life he remained deeply self-conscious, indeed abashed, that he had never generated a 'proper' scholarly edition – a state of affairs giving added context to his 'minor writings of a philologist with no major works' comment cited above.[31] What did this blatant philological lacuna – the missing edition – obstruct, and what did it enable?

It was, perhaps, a very mild drag on Timpanaro's reputation as a philologist; or, more to the point, it became a gatekeeping slight his critics could throw at him to qualify the validity of some of his findings, particularly in his more synthetic 'history of classical scholarship' works.[32] In *La genesi del metodo del Lachmann*, for example, Timpanaro

---

28   And lack of inspiration – S.T. to Eduard Fraenkel, 27 December 1955. See also Narducci, 'Sebastiano Timpanaro', 283. Cf. also S.T. to Ferruccio Bertini, 7 March 1979.

29   *SF*; S.T. to Giuseppe Pacella, 2 August 1963.

30   Cf. Di Benedetto, 'La filologia di Sebastiano Timpanaro', 74.

31   *CF*, 7. On Timpanaro's worry about only writing *noterelle* but no edition or commentary: S.T. to Nino Scivoletto, 28 November 1981.

32   Cf. James Zetzel, 'Review of Sebastiano Timpanaro and Giuseppe Ramires,

made certain claims about the process of recension – the construction of textual genealogies – without ever having actually *done* this for any text. Such 'lack of experience' left Timpanaro open to accusations of overestimating the limitations of Lachmann's method, particularly in its most recent and mathematically systematic incarnation in the work of Paul Maas.[33] Timpanaro could give as good as he got here, later slinging the same accusation of improper preparation – a favourite among hard-core philologists – at the young scholar who would turn into one of classical scholarship's most eminent historians, Anthony Grafton.[34] But if such a lack of edition could be an Achilles heel among the arrow glances of spiky professional philologists, it was also, from a wider perspective, an unmitigated boon. Instead of spending ten, twenty, even thirty years painstakingly plumbing the depths of a particular text and its tradition, Timpanaro was free to read widely and peruse the history of philology synoptically.[35] And because he could see clearly the best of its methods, he could put them to best practice – even beyond the confines of a field not so used to having its perimeter breached.

So much for the forms of Timpanaran philology. Now we must discuss some of Timpanaro's specific obsessions within it. At the top of the list is something that Timpanaro could never leave alone: conjecture. Conjecture is the practice of suggesting a change to a classical text – usually at the level of an individual word, more rarely at a more substantial scale – which is unattested in extant manuscripts of that text. Because of the rough and ragged state of most classical texts, whose modern editions are products of centuries of copying in variable conditions, with perishable materials, involving huge degrees of scribal error (both innovated and carried), conjecture is often the only way to restore sense to an unintelligibly corrupt text. For example, say we found the sentence 'Laura had to go to the ticket' in a group of related manuscript copies of an ancient text. Such

---

Carteggio su Servio (1993–2000)', *Bryn Mawr Classical Review*, 14 April 2014. Timpanaro himself points out his practical inadequacies here at *GLM*, 211.

33   On the importance of Pasquali's critique of Maas in the genesis of the *GLM*, see Glenn Most, introduction to *The Genesis of Lachmann's Method*, Chicago, 2006, 16. On Timpanaro's opposition to Maas's abstraction: S.T. to Arnaldo Momigliano, 20 December 1968.

34   S.T. to Anthony Grafton, 12 June 1981.

35   Cf. Santangelo, 'Voler "capire tutto" ', 49.

a phrase would ring strangely in our ears, given our knowledge of the English language. If another group of manuscripts featured the version 'Laura had to go to the title', we would continue to be suspicious but would have little help from this alternative as to the state of the original text. Ideally, then, we would use our formidable sleuthing abilities as textual critics to make a suggestion based on principles such as likely linguistic usage and stylistic habit of that particular author (usus scribendi).[36] In this case, we would probably offer an educated guess like 'Laura had to go to the toilet'. That guess would be called a conjecture, and if we managed to convince others sufficiently of its likelihood, we might hope to see it migrate into the next official edition of said text. Or we might convince ourselves and put it in the edition we ourselves were editing.

This may not sound like much; and perhaps it is not. Philology is, after all, the art of subtle tugs and tweaks. But conjecture as a practice is actually one of the most contentious topics in the history of classical philology: its range and bounds are in almost-constant dispute across time, and its triumph or, conversely, constraint come to define both philological nations and epochs. On the philological axis, 'radicals' are those who readily make their own interventions (however aggressive) into a classical text, and those interventions are often in the form of conjecture; 'conservatives' are those who respect the forms furnished by the manuscript tradition at all costs and invest in manuscript authority as the only empirical guarantor, or at least approximator, of editorial truth. Since philology is a 'human science', its technical toolkit straddles both art and science, poetic creativity, and sober rationalism – and the radicals often channel the spirit of the former, the conservatives that of the latter. The window of acceptable conjecture is constantly shifting over time and between national traditions. For example, the 'arrogant English', to Timpanaro, embodied the absolute extreme of conjecture-happy behaviour, with their leading lights such as Richard Bentley and A. E. Housman winning fame for bold and inspired conjectures that sometimes risk outdoing or improving the poets they claimed to be merely fixing.[37] Or, again, late nineteenth-century Germany became a

---

36   On the history of usus scribendi: *GLM*, 68.

37   The complaint is everywhere in Timpanaro: *GLM*, 56, on Bentley; S.T. to Giancarlo Giardina, 16 January 1983; conjecture as the 'morbus Anglicus' (English disease), S.T. to Vincenzo Tandoi, 14 August 1984. Timpanaro claims that this Bentley–Housman style conjecture is still in the majority today, particularly in the work of David

hotbed of conjectural fever.[38] The fundamental question at issue, here, is who has the right to fiddle with the historical given of a classical text and its imperfect tradition – and under what terms, what limits? Philology and philologists tend to pick corners on this question and fight trenchantly in their nooks of choice. Few things fire them up more.

Timpanaro's politics may be radical by many definitions – but on this seemingly minor philological question, he certainly skewed towards conservative.[39] His earliest, most formative philological experience with the text of Ennius made him extremely cautious treading the speculative ground of conjecture, because Ennius was a poet subject to particularly abject abuses of scholarly licence.[40] No manuscripts containing complete sections of Ennius's poetry survive. Rather, only fragments of his verse – often no longer than a single line – have come down to us via quotation in other, later texts. This was a classic example of the value of the 'indirect tradition' Timpanaro would come to respect so deeply in the case of Virgil – perhaps partly because, in Ennius's case, such sources were not just a handy help or supplement to the textual tradition but literally its lifeline, sustaining the only surviving parts of Ennius's shattered corpus. But since Ennius, on account of his extreme fragmentation, lacked the quantity to furnish resolutions of textual problems by the standard principle of usus scribendi (i.e., what the author wrote elsewhere), and since his verse also appeared embedded in less luminous texts, more subject to scholarly entitlement to intervene, the sport of conjecture on this poet was rife.[41] Timpanaro did not like it. He praised Johannes Vahlen, late nineteenth-century editor of Ennius, partly because he was anachronistically sober in his conjectures.[42]

Roy Shackleton-Bailey: S.T. to Josef Doltz, 15 August 1989, cf. *NC*, 460; and Hugh Lloyd-Jones does it too (Vincenzo Di Benedetto, 15 May 1998). The gripe is already there in Giorgio Pasquali, *Filologia e storia*, Florence, 1971 [1920], 81. See also Di Benedetto 'La filologia di Sebastiano Timpanaro', 30.

38   S.T. to Eduard Fraenkel, 27 December 1955.

39   Timpanaro identifies as a 'conservative' on these matters – or at least thinks that's what Housman would have called him ('Otto Skutsch's Ennius', 4). On Timpanaro's 'moderate' or 'enlightened' conservative position on these matters, see Di Benedetto, 'La filologia di Sebastiano Timpanaro', 26; cf. Narducci, 'Sebastiano Timpanaro', 287.

40   This early experience with Ennius also made Timpanaro more interested in problems of *emendatio* rather than *recensio* (Di Benedetto, 'La filologia di Sebastiano Timpanaro', 21)

41   On the dangers of analogism applied to the fragmentary Ennius, see S.T. to Armando Golzio, 20 February 1986.

42   S.T. to Paul Maas, 2 December 1955; S.T. to Aldo Lunelli, 30 July 1979.

So it was here, deep in the weeds of philological work on a poet stuck in a right textual state, that Timpanaro developed his aversion to what he vilified as arbitrary 'rewriting' (*rifacimento*) – the point at which the sometimes-necessary art of conjecture passes over into the all-out renovation of a text.[43] For someone whose lifeblood was largely creative – concerned with generating new ideas and studying the intellectual innovations of others – Timpanaro developed a deep suspicion of originality and ingeniousness via his early engagement with conjecture.[44] What is more, the antipathy towards conjecture, if not a causal determinant or seed of Timpanaro's later thought on subjectivity and materialism, was, at least, an early manifestation of the same fundamental principles governing such thought: that the individual human subject was not entitled to generate its own reality; and that such external reality, like the extant manuscripts and knowledge of parallel passages limiting the philologist's budding conjectures, formed an insurmountable brake on any transcendent power of human creativity to bend or make the world its way.

Timpanaro explicitly confronted the problem of conjecture very early in his career. His 1953 'Delle congetture' (On conjectures) clearly draws on some of his crystallising work on the philological activity of the young Leopardi, which bears fruit in the above-mentioned full monograph of 1955.[45] Already in the 1953 piece, Timpanaro is characteristically suspicious of the 'humanist' tendency of scholars such as Emil Baehrens (1848–1888) and the early Girolamo Vitelli (1849–1935) to

---

Timpanaro is also critical of Vahlen's over-conservatism: 'Otto Skutsch's Ennius', 4; but he respects his defence of manuscript readings for being grounded in solid philological argument (see Vincenzo Di Benedetto, 'Discutendo di Timpanaro e di congetture', *Rivista di cultura classica e medioevale* 47, no. 1 [2005]: 166).

43 See *CF*, 663; Otto Skutsch to S.T., 30 June 1969.

44 Conjecture was judiciously subjected to critique in Timpanaro's early work on Ennius, the published parts of his undergraduate thesis: 'Per una nuova edizione critica di Ennio, I', *Studi italiani di filologia classica* 21 (1946): 41–81; 'Per una nuova edizione critica di Ennio, II e III', *Studi italiani di filologia classica* 22 (1947): 33–77 and 179–207; 'Per una nuova edizione critica di Ennio, IV', *Studi italiani di filologia classica* 23 (1948): 5–58. As Timpanaro says ('Otto Skutsch's Ennius', 2), his fundamental disagreement with the Skutschian approach to Ennius of hardcore analogism and corrective conjecture was already set in the late '40s.

45 Sebastiano Timpanaro, 'Delle congetture', *Atene e Roma*, 1953: 95–9; reprinted in *CF*, 673–81. For in-depth historical tracing of Timpanaro's thoughts on conjecture, see Giuseppe Ramires, 'Timpanaro e la questione del congetturare', *Il Ponte* 60 (2004): 242–50; and Di Benedetto's ('Discutendo') supplementation and extension.

embellish passages of ancient text through conjecture, defacing even 'healthy' text liberally via the principle of *mallem scripsisset* – 'I'd prefer the author had written . . .' Hostile to such 'artistic' and arbitrary injections of the critic's ego into the text – a hostility that would intensify in Timpanaro's subsequent hatred of structuralist interpretations of literature – Timpanaro was rather attracted to the ideal practice of a more scientific 'historical philologist', who subjects the intuitive element of making conjectures to *limiting* factors: wide knowledge of the language of a given historical period, of the style of a given author, of the history of the transmission of ancient texts both generally and in particular.[46] These limiting factors become a kind of structure of accountability to keep the philologist honest: to rein in an impulsive genius threatening to cross the boundary from scientific research *on* into artistic collaboration *with* vulnerable, long-dead authors. If conjecture is pure intuition, it is no more than an 'elegant game'; it needs hard knowledge to lift it into the serious realm of the probable, if not the certain.[47] Best philological practice keeps human subjectivity in check and balance.

This conviction in the *right* kind of conjecture is affirmed throughout Timpanaro's works on philology and the history of philology. His work on Leopardi's philology is largely tasked with separating out Leopardi's 'poetic' subjectivity from his activity as a hard-nosed philologist; he is more conjecturer-scientist than conjecturer-artist, in Timpanaro's book.[48] We can also read Timpanaro's objection to Nietzsche's naive unification of Leopardi philologist with Leopardi poet – the denial of which works for Timpanaro as a justification for the very possibility of one's philology having nothing to do with the rest of one's life.[49] But such a binary at the level of conjecturer – the scientist versus the artist – also comes to inform one of Timpanaro's most defining philological conflicts in the 1980s. His work on the tradition of Virgilian commentators in late

---

46   *CF*, 675.

47   *CF*, 676; see also S.T. to Luciano Canfora, 9 February 1973. Leopardi comes in for praise for not playing such a dainty humanist game: *FGL*, 145–6.

48   See *FGL*, 147; Salvatore Settis, speech given at Accademia Lincei, 23 April 2004 (numbered 8 in the Timpanaro archive), citing Luigi Blasucci. Di Benedetto, 'La filologia di Sebastiano Timpanaro', 28, points out that Timpanaro was correcting Pasquali's emphasis on the subjective/artistic qualities of the conjecturer.

49   S.T. to Cesare Cases, 28 February 1970; see also S.T. to Sergio Solmi, 22 November 1972, Luigi Blasucci, 'Sugli studi Leopardiani di Timpanaro', in Di Donato, *Il filologo materialista*, 111.

antiquity – while a long-standing interest – was partly aroused by the local spark of James Zetzel's *Latin Textual Criticism in Antiquity*, which argued that these ancient grammarians were, at base, unscrupulous philologists fudging and faking their way into guardianship of the canon: they may have claimed to be preserving Virgilian text, but often they were just making it up, inserting their own conjectures without marking them as such.[50] For Timpanaro, this was baseless slander of the poor dutiful incubators of the Virgilian tradition. They were not, in his estimation, smuggling in conjectures; they were merely deciding between textual variants in circulation. These ancient scholars did make *some* conjectures, but they were also, according to Timpanaro, very conservative.[51] The core of this spat was about whether these ancients were licensed (or *felt* licensed) to make stuff up as they liked. Zetzel thought yes, Timpanaro no. Perhaps this was not just a dual act of imagining ancient scholars in their respective own images, as Zetzel noted, but a testament to the very different national traditions and contexts of conjecture in which the two found themselves doing the imagining.[52] Crudely put, the Anglo-American right to meddle and invent squared up against the Italian injunction to collate and preserve.

Timpanaro's philology could not abide that particularly anglophone appetite for innovation. In fact, the kind of conjecture that Timpanaro gravitated towards – apart from that backed up by the solid arguments of historical philology – was the conjecture that was *least* original, in the sense that it had been suggested before, somewhere in the long and deep history of scholarship; or in the sense that it was confirmed by a subsequent manuscript discovery, that is, that in the fullness of time a human individual's guesswork was confirmed as already *there* in the textual past. Timpanaro seized on many cases of both kinds of conjecture in the career of his Leopardi.[53] And he experienced the first kind – finding his conjecture already proposed by a philologist predecessor – first hand. This experience made him think of conjecture as the derivation of an unoriginal result, something multiple people could arrive

---

50   James Zetzel, *Latin Textual Criticism in Antiquity*, New York, 1981.

51   *VA*, 7–8.

52   James Zetzel, 'Review of Sebastiano Timpanaro, *Virgilianisti antichi e tradizione indiretta*', *Bryn Mawr Classical Review*, 2002.

53   *FGL*, 124, 126; S.T. to Luigi Blasucci, 23 October 1967; S.T. to Giuseppe Pacella, 22 July 1967, 18 August 1967.

at given certain constraining data (a little like the ideal replicability of the scientific method itself).[54] If August Boeckh coined the ideal of philology as *die Erkenntnis des Erkannten*, the 'knowledge of what has been known before', Timpanaro took this to heart in valuing a kind of intellectual practice whose objectivity was all the greater for its unoriginality; if a conjecture passed from an individual stab to an intersubjective approximation converged on by two or more people over time, well, all the better to admit it into the text.[55] This almost-sublime experience of losing priority in intellectual history, of not being the first to suggest something – an experience very typical of (good) conjecturers – became a reference point for Timpanaro across his career, even when it came to broader ideas rather than mere single words. He pointed out moments of lost intellectual priority for himself (e.g., in giving due credit to Rudolf Meringer for many of the points Timpanaro made in *The Freudian Slip*; see chapter 5) as well as others (e.g., the genesis of Lachmann's method having a long gestation of precursors, or Adam Smith anticipating the Danish linguist Otto Jespersen [1860–1943] by 150 years on the notion in linguistics that rules in language were recent and systematising, but exceptions were more ancient).[56] For Timpanaro, good conjecture revealed not the boundless virtuosity of the human mind but the limits of our intellect, constantly reinventing the wheel to arrive at the truth over and over again. Nothing created from nothing: the history of conjectural philology a perfect Petri dish for a materialist in the making.

If conjecture proved a charged discursive point for Timpanaro to work through some of his early ideas on the balance between human subjectivity and the limiting world 'out there', a closely related debate in contemporary philology also did its formative bit: the linguistic

---

54   S.T. to Margarethe Billerbeck, 20 July 1999.

55   August Boeckh, *Encyklopädie und Methodologie der Philologischen Wissenschaften*, ed. E. Bratuschek, Leipzig, 1877, 10; see Constanze Güthenke, *Feeling and Classical Philology: Knowing Antiquity in German Scholarship, 1770–1920*, Cambridge, 2020, 115.

56   On the common experience of finding conjectures already proposed in the past: S.T. to Giorgio Voghera, 20 November 1965; on Timpanaro's experience of it: *NC*, 338, S.T. to Margarethe Billerbeck, 20 July 1999, S.T. to Guglielmo Cavallo (n.d.; numbered 1 in the Timpanaro archive); on Timpanaro's anticipation of it happening again: *CF*, 551, cf. *NC*, ix. On Smith and Jespersen: *SLO*, 98.

controversy between 'analogy' and 'anomaly'.[57] For Timpanaro's particular standards of Pasqualian historical philology, any emendation to, or for that matter 'defence' of, the transmitted text required a vast working knowledge both of the shape of the Greek or Latin language at a given historical moment, as well as of the individual practice of the particular author under consideration.[58] 'Analogists' tend to change or preserve certain texts on the principle of authorial homogeneity: if an author deploys a word like so in this context, well, it is likely they will use it similarly elsewhere. 'Anomalists' allow more space for non-systematicity and variation in language use; for them, the 'usus scribendi' is never a straightforward case for choosing another variant or offering a conjecture, because it does not account for the huge range of variation in linguistic usage at any given historical moment, nor for the reserved right of every author to opt for something stranger, spicier, more eccentric.[59] Often it does not square with the principle of *lectio difficilior*, 'the more difficult reading', which sees manuscript errors smoothing out the unruly bumps of the original literary text by a process of unintentional standardisation or 'banalisation'. The limits of language are often much wider than the capacity for variation we ascribe to particular authors – but, given we already see such linguistic variation in them, why should we not allow for this when we make textual decisions?

If Timpanaro skewed towards the 'unimaginative' on the question of conjecture, we might be forgiven for our surprise that his taste on this question bent towards hardcore *anomalist*.[60] But the two issues were closely bound. In fact, Timpanaro distinguished between two kinds of conjecture: the imaginative/genius/Housmanesque style on one hand, and the unimaginative, rule-abiding style on the other, which was

---

57   The debate goes back to antiquity: see the entry 'Analogy and Anomaly' in the *Oxford Classical Dictionary*.

58   An active ability to defend the transmitted text through philological reasoning was crucial for Timpanaro; it was one of the reasons he thought Ugo Foscolo did not qualify as a proper philologist (*AF*, 119–20).

59   Timpanaro defends his anomalism and his antipathy to slavish observation of usus scribendi at *NC*, viii.

60   Timpanaro's anti-analogism was already important in his 1963 article on *ilicet* (*CF*, 17–38); it will become more characteristic of his philology later on (De Nonno, 'Timpanaro tra filologia', 111).

powered by a mechanical observation of analogism.[61] The scholar who embodied the latter, and did the most to radicalise Timpanaro's anti-analogism, was Otto Skutsch, the eminent (and famously obstinate) editor of Ennius, whose hyper-analogism caused him to make corrective conjectures to the Ennian text to make them conform to particular prosodic 'laws'.[62] Timpanaro took a dim view of this, partly for its over-extension of rigid scientific certainty into a context unfit for it – indeed he would always moderate Skutsch's language of 'law' to a more flexible and non-committal 'tendency'. Timpanaro's mentor Pasquali also thought of philological laws – insofar as they were laws – as very different from physical laws, a mass of exceptions more akin to grammar than gravity.[63] Applying those laws too stringently à la Skutsch made for no model exercise in scholarly caution, but for a too-audacious meddling in the text.[64] Analogism, particularly the Skutschian form applied to Ennius, was about disciplining poetry according to a preconceived theory of how early Latin language and metre worked; Timpanaran anomalism, avowedly, was about stripping away that theory and allowing the text some breathing space to vary in tune with language and literature as human products. Timpanaro took it upon himself to single out such anti-analogism for praise whenever he saw it upheld in the history of philology, for instance on Theodor Gomperz (on whom see chapter 3), whose restrained, non-virtuosic conjectures formed the antitype of the unfortunate analogist and freewheeling conjecturalist Carel Gabriel Cobet.[65]

At stake here, I think, were two intellectual questions dear to Timpanaro's heart. The first we might call something like the problem of

61   Timpanaro, 'Otto Skutsch's Ennius', 4; see also Di Benedetto, 'La filologia di Sebastiano Timpanaro', 31.

62   Such complaints about Skutsch's observation of mythical laws are rife in Timpanaro: see S.T. to Mariotti, 25 July 1962, 26 July 1963, 6 May 1968, 2 July 1969, 3 September 1970, 22 January 1973; S.T. to Vincenzo Tandoi, 22 November 1969. On the general risk of conjecture becoming hyper-analogistic, see CF, 679.

63   Pasquali himself stresses the difference between philological laws, full of exceptions and similar to grammatical rules, and physical laws of gravity and the like (Filologia e storia, 54). See also Timpanaro's remarks on the empiricism of philology rendering it only able to talk of tendencies rather than laws (OM, 189).

64   Timpanaro's philology becomes even more reserved towards hyper-analogist conjecturalism from the late '70s on (De Nonno, 'Timpanaro tra filologia', 114, 119–21).

65   See AF, 393.

'methodological overreach'. Human thinkers tend to overcook their systems and methods to the point of producing totalising frameworks which iron out the creases of reality. Just as analogists tend to work with a certain constrained concept of an author's language and defend repetitions or metrical strictures based on analogy, so, in Timpanaro's view, do Freud and the Freudians make reductive interpretations based on a narrow set of bluntly applied first principles (see chapter 5).[66] Timpanaro thought that for Skutsch, the text of Ennius was not an object to be viewed empirically but a kind of diagnostic laboratory to prove the laws he had already decided were in operation, but which he had to conjure into empirical existence via conjecture. In this, Skutsch maintained a culpable *amor di tesi* – literally a 'love of thesis', which makes the object of study simply an excuse to 'just make a point', a crutch on which to build a tendentious reading and bend the evidence in service to a particular predetermined idea[67] – that Timpanaro would go on to skewer in all the examples of structuralist and Freudian chicanery he so despised. These cases were, of course, distinct in their complexions – on the one hand, the overly rationalistic, and on the other, the overly mystificatory – but in Timpanaro's view, they were equally culpable of violating scientific principles. Not even Leopardi escaped these rigorous standards. Timpanaro points out that the great poet-philologist was often guilty of overly rationalistic interventions into classical texts to make them conform to system, despite also showing a Timpanaran abstinence in going easy on conjecture and defending transmitted manuscript readings in many cases.[68] And Leopardi himself had suffered the same thing in his scholarly reception: Timpanaro criticises the classical philologist Claudio Moreschini's habit of overcorrecting and regularising Leopardi's written Latin.[69] As with excessive conjecture, so with excessive analogism: the enemy here was the human

---

66   As Alessandro Schiesaro rightly points out, Timpanaro will abandon his anti-analogism when dealing with Freud and Meringer, opting there to emphasise the strict rules of phonetics rather than contextually varying lapsus. Schiesaro *per litteras*: 'Timpanaro is fond of the "specificità causale" in philology, but when applied to psychoanalysis he thinks it becomes "specificità magica"' (cf. Francesco Orlando to S.T., 22 June 1974).

67   S.T. to Otto Skutsch, 26 November 1983; cf. S.T. to Vincenzo Tandoi, 22 November 1969.

68   *FGL*, 103–4, 147–8.

69   S.T. to Emilio Bigi, 9 September 1984.

tendency to remodel the world the way it wished, to make it *conform* to theory rather than *make* the theory.

This hostility to a priori thinking, as we have already sketched, is one of Timpanaro's most treasured philological convictions. We could also reformulate it another way (and we will return to this issue in chapter 7): Timpanaro believed in the sanctity of *content*, the stuff – whether in the world or in the text – that remained intact independent of the human thinker's attempts at ideological reconstitution of it. Timpanaro's ethics on this were ironclad. It was not just overzealous conjecture, or the excessive rationalism of the analogists, that piqued him. In the philological sphere, he also had strong opinions on translation. He expressed hearty approval to poet and translator Alceste Angelini over his conservative thoughts about translation and affirmed his distaste for translator-artists (like conjecture-artists) who 'embellished' the original text.[70] Fidelity to the 'given' at all costs. Pasqualian philology was not about improving or superimposing upon a text but, in a sense, working out the limits which bracket it into existence. Timpanaro's close fellow Pasqualian Antonio La Penna puts it nicely when he says he learned from Pasquali the art of philology: to 'extract from the text everything that conditions it: preceding texts, historical context, life of the author.'[71] This notion of a 'conditioning' limit will become important in Timpanaro's work on materialism, where the philological notion of limiting forces such as historical context becomes the conditioning, constraining force of biological reality over human life.

But the issue of superimposing on content can also have bigger political stakes. In *On Materialism*, Timpanaro gripes at the way structuralist Marxists present their modifications of (and additions to) Marx's thought as mere readings or interpretations of his text.[72] He deems such symptomatic readings of Marx 'falsificatory', and calls these interpreters out for deceptively anchoring new theory as a type of 'discovery' of the 'Real Marx'.[73] For Timpanaro, the content-man, all of these activities – creative conjecture, rationalising analogy, unfaithful translation, and

---

70   See S.T. to Alceste Angelini, 10 March 1961.

71   See Anna Maria Cimino, 'L'influenza di Gramsci su Antonio La Penna. Dalla formazione gentiliana all'empiriomaterialismo', *Lexis* 39, no. 1 (2021): 218.

72   *OM*, 194. Timpanaro also uses his philological skills to tease out particular elements of Marx and Engels's thought at *OM*, 94, 104.

73   *OM*, 212–13.

tendentious interpretations of Marx – were on the same continuum and manifestations of the same infuriating intellectual behaviour: an idealist flouting of the sanctity of content, and an idealist conviction that the human mind had the right to override the world. For Timpanaro, such wilfulness was art, not science. Philology would have to come to the rescue of what was *there* at the expense of what was *desired*.

The analogist–anomalist controversy also shows another crucial separation in Timpanaro's thought between *reason* and *system*. While Timpanaro remained committed to a rationalist science, for him that meant not the blind and inflexible imposition of methodological system but the empirical commitment to analyse each phenomenon in its particularity, on a case-by-case basis. The analogy–anomaly conflict helped him earn and hone his stripes as an agile fox in a hedgehog's world. Anomaly thus became, for Timpanaro, the linguistic manifesta-tion of the primacy of exception, of individual eccentricity, heterodoxy, and weirdness, of things that stand aloof from any attempt to domesti-cate them into this or that regularising framework. Such a feel for eccen-tricity blooms at the historical level with Timpanaro's major studies on nineteenth-century Italy, the common denominator of which is often an enthusiasm for thinkers pitched 'against the grain' vis-à-vis their domi-nant contemporary ideological contexts (see chapter 3): Leopardi and Giordani, as 'classicists' resisting the pull of mainstream romanticism, become the spirit of anomaly breathed into culture. As with language, so with history, so with the individual: a mess of exceptions and conflicts to be attended to in the most granular specifics. Each exception becomes as important as the rules they show to be not as unbendable or inevita-ble as first thought.

Timpanaro's fondness for anomaly thus bleeds into a second meth-odological priority dear to his heart: the feel for *particularity*, which is, I think, a fundamental part of his conception of philology.[74] Timpanaro embodies this in the type of philology he praises in *theory*: the

---

74   See *CF*, 11; Giuseppina Magnaldi, 'Questioni di metodo: Plauto e Lucrezio', in Enrico Ghidetti and Alessandro Pagnini (eds), *Sebastiano Timpanaro e la cultura del Secondo Novecento*, Rome, 2005, 235; Narducci, 'Sebastiano Timpanaro', 286. It was also, of course, a feature of Pasqualian philology: cf. Sebastiano Timpanaro, 'Giorgio Pasquali', *Belfagor* 28, no. 2 (1973): 196. This taste for the particular was part of Gramscian philol-ogy too: see Joseph Buttigieg's introduction to his edition of Gramsci's *Prison Notebooks*, New York, 2011, 58–64.

'Hermannian' branch, detail-heavy formal philology which eschews the more Olympian vistas of the Boeckhian. This was a programmatically 'bitty' philology for which Timpanaro's model Leopardi had also been underrated. But Timpanaro also pursued this kind of small-scale philology in practice.[75] He described his *Contributi* as 'little jottings, very arid and disorganic' (*scrittarelli molto aridi e disorganici*), and apologises for his history of producing mere 'little notes' (*noterelle*) rather than an organic volume.[76] He devalued his own philological accomplishments in comparison with the more sweeping work of Antonio La Penna, Alfonso Traina (1925–2019; a professor of Latin literature at the University of Bologna), Scevola Mariotti (1920–2000; a professor of classical philology at Sapienza University of Rome), and Franco Munari (1920–1995; a professor of classical philology at the Free University Berlin), who in Timpanaro's view managed to produce more synthetic or organic work.[77]

The minor status is not the whole story. Timpanaro defended his formal philology as not necessarily lacking through the size of individual contributions, in the same way that no one would say a lyric poem is worth less than a long novel.[78] And Timpanaran philology is characterised by a see-sawing between the micro-details of the text and the broader issues of language and history.[79] But the important polarity here is not so much the small versus the big, but the bitty versus the whole, the 'disorganic' versus the organic. This became not only a habitual way in which Timpanaro self-deprecatingly positioned his work next to his contemporaries, but also a way of pitching an ideal of the relation of the individual to its historical context, to itself, and even, perhaps, to one's own political party. As we shall see, Timpanaro resisted the grip of the Gramscian fetish for the 'organic intellectual' and expended a lot of intellectual energy showing the often-progressive function of 'inorganic intellectuals', such as Leopardi, standing at a raspingly oblique angle to their

75   On the details-focus of Hermannian philology and its art of slow reading: *CF*, 10. On Leopardi's bitty philology: *FGL*, 177.

76   *CF*, 7; S.T. to Mario Untersteiner, 8 January 1979.

77   S.T. to Alfonso Traina, 23 October 1993, 11 January 2000.

78   *CF*, 680–1; cf. *AF*, 380. Cf. Timpanaro's defence of micrological philology (S.T. to Silvia, Rizzo, 4 June 1979).

79   Narducci, 'Sebastiano Timpanaro': 286–7; cf. Pietro Cataldi, 'Il metodo di Timpanaro', *Allegoria* 2, no. 4 (1990): 143–68; Alfonso Traina to S.T., 18 March 1995.

societies.[80] The 'inorganic' or 'non-integrated' self became a means for Timpanaro to process his interdisciplinary 'extravagance', permitting of self-internal warring factions with no need for dialectical resolution.[81] Of course, the self-flagellating Timpanaro retrospectively judged his lack of intellectual coherence as a failure.[82] But it was also one of his most salient and powerful philological techniques. For Timpanaro, *splitting* is always preferable to lumping – and philology's special mode of splitting, down to the individual follicle and whatever might lie inside it, is the model for how it should be done.

Timpanaro's commitment to a case-by-case methodology, the ideal of weighing every problem and person without aprioristic prescriptions stacking the decks, comes out clearest in his later work on the textual reception of the Roman poet Virgil (70–19 BCE) in later antiquity, known as the Virgilian 'indirect tradition.' Here, a heavy scholarly bias against late-antique commentators and compilers meant many genuine textual readings in Virgil had been unjustifiably discounted. Timpanaro revels in examining each possibility on its individual merits and recuperates many particular variants, as well as cumulatively salvaging the general reputability of the indirect tradition containing them.[83] But, although the full efflorescence of this anti-apriorism arrives relatively late in the piece, its basic stance was seeded much earlier. One of the biggest markers of Pasqualian philology was the principle of 'recentiores non deteriores': in summary, when it comes to the constitution of an edition of a text, more recent manuscripts should not be considered *necessarily* inferior to older manuscripts, because, through the possibility of horizontal cross-contamination, more recent manuscripts can preserve better readings than their more ancient cousins.[84] Such a

---

80   On Leopardi as inorganic intellectual, see chapter 3; cf. Timpanaro's sympathy for Pietro Giordani, who became one of the nineteenth-century greats without ever writing an organic work (S.T. to Giorgio Voghera, 18 February 1966). We might note that Timpanaro's coeval and longtime friend Antonio La Penna understood his own position in similar terms: see Antonio La Penna, *Memorie e discorsi irpini di un intellettuale disorganico*, 2012; Cimino, 'L'influenza', 229.

81   On Timpanaro's resistance to dialectical 'resolution', see chapter 4.

82   S.T. to Giorgio Voghera, 27 December 1969.

83   *PLS*.

84   Giorgio Pasquali, *Storia della tradizione e critica del testo*, Florence, 1934, chapter 4. Timpanaro perhaps also absorbed an appreciation for indirect tradition from Pasquali's treatment of figures like Charisius (ibid., 64–5).

principle may sound insignificant, but it was quietly radical in the context of responding to the strict, mathematising philology of Paul Maas, hell bent on eliminating as many 'derivative' manuscripts as possible from the process of constituting a text. Pasquali and others' contribution was to step in and say, *Hold it, not so fast*: the messiness of the textual tradition means that almost no manuscript (not even relatively recent ones) can be automatically written off from consideration. That general guideline was a rejoinder, again, to the methodological overreach embodied by the followers and purifiers of Lachmann, particularly Maas, whose mode of reasoning was (according to Pasquali and Timpanaro) far too rigid and mathematical for the mess of the material world that housed transmission of manuscripts. But the guideline also had a kind of politics to it.[85] As a statement of philological egalitarianism – no manuscript is valueless, no manuscript left behind – recentiores non deteriores was crucial in sealing Timpanaro's method of anti-apriorism, of taking nothing for granted. It also passed into Timpanaro's incredibly high standards for comprehensive preparation before making a case – the 'not so fast' pause to weigh *every last bit* of evidence prior to constructing the line of best fit through it. The classic example of this was Timpanaro's obsessively extensive preparation to writing *The Freudian Slip*, involving a reading, among other things, of every single thing Freud had ever written.[86] It was perhaps this need for comprehensiveness that disabled Timpanaro before the task of producing a major philological edition – which, in the case of a poet like Virgil, would have required an impossibly arduous sifting through 2,000 years of thick scholarship. Pasqualian philology taught Timpanaro to treat all elements in a set as potentially relevant. Timpanaro obliged, to the highest standards. But only, perhaps, when that set had some natural limits.

In a sense, however, pinning this feel for open-minded and comprehensive consultation of a range of evidence onto recentiores non deteriores is perhaps too narrow. The tradition of Italian philology in which Timpanaro was trained was, and still is, a tradition priding itself on a particularly indifferent, inclusive, non-evaluative consideration of all of its objects of study.[87]

---

85 Parroni, 'Timpanaro e la filologia', 63; S.T. to Luciano Canfora, 30 October 1964.

86 *FR*, 43; On comprehensiveness as a marker of Timpanaro's philology, see Salvatore Settis, speech given at the Accademia Lincei, 23 April 2004 (numbered 8 in the Timpanaro collection), citing Vincenzo Di Benedetto.

87 As Timpanaro says in *FGL*, 17–18, true philology is indifferent on the question of a text's worth.

From the mid- to late nineteenth century onwards, Italian philology saw its work as giving focussed care to every single text of the classical tradition without regard for a given text's 'value' or 'quality', its status as famous or obscure, the enjoyment gained from studying it, or the ongoing 'relevance' of it – the continuing legacy of which has been pointed out by the classical philologist Marco Formisano.[88] It was Leopardi's equitable attention across the board, perhaps even a skewing towards the minor or unappreciated classical texts over the canonical heavy-hitters, that made him into a philologist for Timpanaro to imitate. But Timpanaro took the principle even further, not only paying attention to the minor as much as the major, but in launching a project of 'retrospective justice' to make sure that minor players in the history of philology itself got the credit they deserved.[89] Again, this ethic of revisionist intellectual history played out in Timpanaro's work recuperating the value of the late antique Virgilian tradition. But its earliest and most powerful expression would have to be *La genesi del metodo del Lachmann.*

La genesi is Timpanaro's great fulfilment of the best version of Enlightenment philology: apportioning credit where credit is due and, in the process, lifting the neglected minors behind a major intellectual revolution into the limelight.[90] The project is partly motivated by a kind of resentment at a historical injustice. Karl Lachmann ended up getting all the praise for a method – genealogical classification of manuscripts – that should not be assigned solely to him. In Timpanaro's words, the fame of Lachmann has obscured other contributors to the method – and so it is high time for Timpanaro's bright Enlightenment floodlight to lift these others out of obscurity.[91] Timpanaro had already prepared the ground for this kind of redemptive, redistributive project with *La filologia*: the hero of that book was Leopardi, whose philological contributions were still yet to be tabulated and celebrated.[92] The villain was Angelo Mai, Leopardi's nemesis and Timpanaro's philological opposite,

---

88   Marco Formisano, introduction to Marco Formisano and Christina Shuttleworth Kraus (eds), *Marginality, Canonicity, Passion*, Oxford, 2017, 6–11.

89   See *PLS*.

90   This principle of retrospective justice informs both Timpanaro's politics and his intellectual history: see Rudolf Führer to S.T., 27 May 1981; Perry Anderson, 'On Sebastiano Timpanaro', *London Review of Books* 23, no. 9 (May 2001).

91   *GLM*, 116.

92   Most of Leopardi's emendations and interpretations had up to that point been ignored (*FGL*, ix).

an unscrupulous appropriator who stole from Leopardi (and many more distant philologist predecessors) without a hint of acknowledgement.[93] But what *La filologia* does to restore the balance of credit between certain individual actors in nineteenth-century philology, *La genesi* does for our intellectual history of an entire philological method. We emerge from this book completely wrong footed as to the very nature of intellectual progress, so deeply rooted is our sense of the history of scholarship as one of big individual contributions from big names, changing the landscape forever. Timpanaro's book pours cold water over the genius model. It cuts the big names down to size. In its devastating 'rescaling' of individual contributions to the history of scholarship, *La genesi* scales back the power of originality, just as Timpanaro had done for conjecture.[94] In a field like philology, there were no shuddering revolutions in method but merely a series of inchings forward, whose granularity was quickly lost to the simplifications of retrospective intellectual history.[95]

If these studies in the history of philology honed Timpanaro's ethics of redistributive justice, they were also attempts at 'correcting' the past.[96] Both Timpanaro's day jobs – philology and copy-editing – trafficked heavily in the concept of 'error'. In philology, patterns of error were the things that enabled manuscript collation, as well as the

---

93   *FGL*, 29, 32, 40; cf. *AF*, 237, 241. As Blasucci notes, Timpanaro was often talking about himself when pitting Leopardi's or Niebuhr's good practice against Mai's unscrupulous ways (Blasucci, 'Sugli studi', 98). Failure to credit someone else's contributions is one of the cardinal sins of Timpanaran philology – for instance, Franco Ferrucci (S.T. to Franco Ferrucci (n.d.; numbered 2 in the Timpanaro archive), or Willis's Macrobius (*CF*, 352, S.T. to Scevola Mariotti, 13 March 1963). Antonio La Penna notes this sin may even be partially behind Timpanaro's will to cut Lachmann down to size: Rotondò, 'Sebastiano Timpanaro', 46.

94   *Ridimensionare* ('to rescale, resize') was one of Timpanaro's favourite words for re-evaluating an intellectual contribution for better or worse: for instance, Angelo Mai, *AF*, 226.

95   See also G. F. Gianotti, 'Prima e dopo Lachmann', in Ghidetti and Pagnini, *Sebastiano Timpanaro*, 145–6.

96   Timpanaro often uses the language of correction to identify progress in intellectual history; for instance, his original *OM* was designed to 'correct extremes of voluntarism and pragmatism which can hardly serve as a basis for refounding a communism at once "scientific" and revolutionary'. *OM*, 22. Other scholars respond to this language: see, for instance, Narducci, 'Sebastiano Timpanaro', 298, on Timpanaro applying 'significant corrections' to the work of Cesare Luporini and Walter Binni on Leopardi.

wrinkles to spot and smooth out; in editing and proofing, errors were, of course, the things to weed out. But for Timpanaro, errors are not just verbal slips to sort through; they are deep misdirections in intellectual history, wrong turns needing the full address of constant correction. Timpanaro got this impulse from philology – especially, I would say, the manic drive to *self*-correction. In Timpanaro's book, no case is ever closed. One of his most distinctive features as a thinker is the depth of the revisions he plied over the course of his career to almost all of *his own* major contributions.[97] Timpanaro despised stubbornness and inflexibility in other scholars (e.g., Maas), though he could be guilty of those sins himself.[98] But in general, over the course of his career, he remained ever encouraging of challenges to his arguments – this another Pasqualian trait, namely the courting of obsolescence via robust debate – and many times, those challenges led to full recantations when Timpanaro saw that he was clearly *wrong*.[99] The last edition of *La genesi* happily capitulates to the eminent Cambridge philologist Michael Reeve on the subject of bipartite stemmata in textual transmission (the question of why most manuscript 'family trees' tend to split into two main branches, rather than, say, three or more),[100] to the point where Timpanaro actively resisted the classical philologist Glenn Most's proposal to do an English edition because he thought the book was

---

97   *FGL, GLM, OM, CI* all had at least two editions. Edward Kenney ('To Search out a Matter', *Classical Review* 57, no. 1 [2007]: 241) remarks on the vast number of modifications Timpanaro made across his editions of Lachmann, and rightly says the changes 'deserve study in their own right as the index of a mind that never rested in its unflagging quest after the truth'. Timpanaro's arm was twisted to collect his philological contributions into a volume (the *CF*) partly because it would allow him the opportunity to correct, add, and update: *CF*, 10, S.T. to Scevola Mariotti, 4 November 1972, 5 December 1976; S.T. to Arnaldo Momigliano, 8 January 1979; S.T. to Piero Treves, 6 March 1979. The *Antileopardiani* book contained previous articles redone and massively expanded, with three new long appendices (*AN*, 7, S.T. to Antonio Piromalli, 16 August 1982). For Timpanaro's obsession with self-correction: Blasucci, 'Sugli studi', 99, S.T. to Christopher Collard (letter only dated to 1999; numbered 1 in the Timpanaro archive), Ordine, introduction to *La lezione*, xiii, xv; as Parroni (introduction to *VA*, vi) says, he was never scared of 'palinodes'. Cf. Gianotti, 'Prima e dopo', 142. On constant corrections as part of the scientific process, see S.T. to Silvia Rizzo, 4 June 1979.

98   S.T. to Arnaldo Momigliano, 20 December 1968.

99   Pasquali, *Storia*, xii; S.T. to Guglielmo Cavallo (n.d.; numbered 1 in the Timpanaro archive).

100   *GLM*, 207–8, 214–15; S.T. to Michael Reeve, 16 September 1987.

definitively superannuated and ready to be put to bed;[101] and the *Contributi* are full of significant revisions to early philological pieces, even containing a full section ('ripensamenti Enniani') devoted to the rethinking of Timpanaro's earliest work on Ennius.[102] Timpanaro's publications, like many of his correspondence chains, are works that never end; countless of his letters sign off with *ma ne riparleremo*, or similar – 'but we'll talk about it again' – and such an implicit signature could be added sensibly to any given piece of published Timpanaran text too.[103] While many other scholars would simply write the books or articles and be done with them, Timpanaro felt a constant obligation to remodel his former conclusions by taking new evidence and arguments into account. It as is if, in the throes of several rounds of rigorous self-scrutiny, he sought to model the distinctive shape of philology as a science of slow, halting progress.

For, ultimately, not only did philology furnish Timpanaro with an intellectual tool belt or a disciplined way of seeing the world; it also gave him a particular reference for how history works beyond the standard drivers of class struggle and revolution which form the corner-stones of Marxist discourse. The introduction to the *Contributi* contains an ode to the basic unoriginality and incrementalism of philology: it is a field spurred not by giant methodological leaps forward but by gradual chipping away at certain particulars.[104] When Timpanaro apologised for his traditional form of philology here, he advanced two reasons for the constraints of his practice: firstly, it was his personal shortcomings;[105] secondly, it was the nature

101   S.T. to Michael Reeve, 24 July 1990; cf. S.T. to Lindsay Waters, 1 December 1982. Timpanaro's belief in the absolute obsolescence of *GLM* perhaps had something to do with his obsessive proclamations of ageing (Giovanni Fiesoli, 'A colloquio con Timpanaro: Note a margine di storia della tecnica filologica', in Ghidetti and Pagnini, *Sebastiano Timpanaro*, 208). Timpanaro claims *SM* as old even as the book comes out (S.T. to Giulio Lepschy, 27 July 1975).

102   See Timpanaro's reconsiderations on Ennius fr. 9 for a typical example: defending what he thinks is still right, yielding when he's wrong (*CF*, 629–30). On these Timpanaran shifts regarding Ennius, see Narducci, 'Sebastiano Timpanaro', 285.

103   See, for instance, S.T. to Cesare Cases, 6 August 1958.

104   On Timpanaro's philological gradualism, see Parroni, 'Timpanaro e la filologia', 60.

105   Cf. S.T. to Arnaldo Momigliano, 8 January 1979; S.T. to Nicholas Horsfall, 12 December 1982.

of the field.[106] And its distinctive nature is precisely an unfolding in non-revolutionary time:

> That depends, in the first place, obviously, on the limits of the author's talent; in second place, on a characteristic inherent to philology itself, which in the course of its history has certainly not ignored methodological innovations, but overall (even one who isn't particularly happy with it has to note it) has proceeded more 'gradualistically', more by successive refinements than by noisy re-foundations or 'epistemological ruptures'. Enough to think that, while in many natural and human sciences almost everything that doesn't belong to the last decades preserves a historical value but is by now without contemporary interest, in philology (especially in philology understood in the strict sense, as restoration and interpretation of the text) contributions at this point generations-old are still valid now, and often they have to be re-exhumed against more recent and less persuasive proposals.

Often it is required to dust off old interpretations and defend them with new arguments.[107] Sometimes, philology can be ahead of its time in offering an interpretation that will eventually be dusted off.[108] 'Gradualistically' is a charged term here: Italian leftist politics of the post-war era was rent by the conflict between *gradualismo* – the politics of social democratic reform and incremental change – and *massimalismo* – the politics of big revolutionary change.[109] This gradualism forms a backbone of Timpanaro's unorthodox attunement to all the models of history which are *not* dialectical progress: the longue durée, reformist

---

106   Cf. Timpanaro also defending Leopardian philology from Antonio La Penna's critique of lack of methodological innovation (Blasucci, 'Sugli studi', 100). Timpanaro makes similar remarks on philology's slowness and non-innovation at S.T. to Scevola Mariotti, 26 June 1976.

107   CF, 219; S.T. to Scevola Mariotti, 27 February 1976. This is exactly what Timpanaro claims to be doing in his *quam* for *magis/potius quam* and *ut vidi ut perii* pieces in the CF: S.T. to Scevola Mariotti, 14 January 1970, 4 November 1972; it's also his point in the *ilicet* article, which shows how ancient interpreters had got the meaning right: CF, 28. See similar moves at CF, 290, 337, 636. Timpanaro theorises this form of non-original philology further at NC, ix.

108   Timpanaro's *ut vidi ut perii* article is a masterclass in finding new scaffolding to defend an old argument (see, for instance, CF, 277).

109   Thanks to Alessandro Schiesaro for this point.

(rather than revolutionary) advances in the treatment of biological illness, always buying us a little time but never making a dent in the hard limit of human mortality; the slow and bumpy evolution of thought within an individual over time, for instance, Leopardi's move to cosmic pessimism; or language as an entity developing out of step with socio-economic time.[110] Philology, in its *history*, is the paradigm for a logic of snail-paced, modest human progress worked out beyond the bolts and jolts of revolution – a progress often contingent precisely on a timely salvage of the old and neglected from the storehouse of time. And, as the prospect of actual revolution within a brief term retreated from political life, and Timpanaro decided to retrieve the antiquated Leopardi to revive a Marxism flagging beneath that frustrating reality, it is not hard to see where the principle of eternal relevance came from: none other than the finicky art of Pasqualian philology – where nothing, ever, is declared dead and buried.[111] Indeed, just as old Latin words that seem to be archaic are often indistinguishable from vulgar and up-to-date forms, age should be no barrier to currency.[112] Philology offered a framework to guarantee that Marxism would never go out of date.

Philology, in the end, gave this unusual twentieth-century thinker a way of thinking through various problems that would become crucial to his broader non-philological work: the abuses of conjecture alerted Timpanaro to the limits of human subjectivity and the dangers of excessive 'ingenuity'; the analogy-versus-anomaly debate allowed him a crucible in which to forge his deep aversion to oppressively (and obsessively) applied systems; and philology in general furnished Timpanaro a feel for the case-by-case and an allergy to the a priori, an egalitarianism of treating evidence, a feel for the minors of intellectual history and a will to give the neglected their dues, a practice of restless self-revision that never considered the case closed, a sense that no ideas and no past could ever fully be discarded. But philology also gave this heterodox Marxist a way of apprehending that history itself, particularly the history

---

110   Illness: *OM*, 62; S.T. to Cesare Cases, 18 December 1964. Leopardi's evolution: *CI*, 153–5; cf. the gradual evolution of Leopardi's hostility to nature: *CI*, 394. Language: Umberto Carpi, 'Timpanaro e il problema del romanticismo', in Di Donato, *Il filologo materialista*, 153.

111   Timpanaro also believes in the persistence of old forms from a linguistic standpoint, for instance, the conscious archaising of the *carmen Priami* (*CF*, 112).

112   *CF*, 366.

of ideas, sometimes plays out very slowly. Sometimes, a return to old ideas paradoxically means progress, if the old ideas remain true. Verdi's old maxim *Torniamo all'antico e sarà un progresso* (Let's return to the past and it will be a step forward) was also a deeply philological sentiment.[113] While this thinker never stopped wanting revolution, philology gave him a way of waiting – and a comfortable waiting chamber of small things is important when the big things to which we devote our lives never come to pass.[114] But philology also furnished Timpanaro with a mode of intellectual struggle to try to make those things happen. His materialist philology has true enduring value only insofar as he deployed its means for ends far beyond itself and himself. That is a major correction all philologists could afford to make. And the next chapters will try to show us how Timpanaro did it.

---

113   S.T. to Grazia Cherchi, 26 August 1974, S.T. to Antonio Russi (n.d.; numbered 3 in the Timpanaro archive).
114   Timpanaro acknowledges the value of philology as escapism from political disillusionment in S.T. to Cesare Cases, 20 January 1979.

3

Enlightenment Classicists

As we saw in the last chapter, Timpanaro's programmatically 'minor' philological contributions of the first phase of his career underwent a gear-shift to something major in the 1950s and early '60s. The turn was tied to a very Pasqualian moment of self-reflective stocktaking: philology should be not just an execution of detailed interpretation of ancient texts but a thinking-through of the history of its own methods. *La filologia di Giacomo Leopardi* served that project through a sustained account of a single philologist who had not, up until Timpanaro's intervention, ever really been appreciated as a philologist. *La genesi del metodo del Lachmann* was a way of filling out the roots of that 'modern' Leopardian (and Hermannian, Pasqualian, Timpanaran) philology, casting them much further back into the past than had been done before. Both books were a very Timpanaran way of doing intellectual and cultural history – but the 'culture' with which Timpanaro was concerned in these books was a fairly specific (if important) one: that of philology. In his next phase, Timpanaro showed what else he could do with the nineteenth century beyond granulating the history of his native field.

The core of Timpanaro's cultural history of the 'enlightened' nineteenth century hardens around three main volumes, which will be the reference points for this chapter: *Classicismo e illuminismo nell'Ottocento italiano* (1965), *Aspetti e figure della cultura ottocentesca* (1980), and *Antileopardiani e neomoderati nella sinistra italiana*

(1982).[1] While the focus evolves in these works from the figures and cultural lines of the nineteenth century themselves (*Classicismo*, *Aspetti*) more to the political stake and reception of that tradition in Timpanaro's contemporary political context (*Antileopardiani*), the three share a common project: the guardianship of misunderstood, underestimated, and against-the-grain 'Enlightenment' and 'classicising' thinkers of the (mostly Italian, with nods to Germany and France) nineteenth century.[2] In these books, we find Timpanaro setting out his deepest sympathies and antipathies via exhaustively rigorous intellectual historiography, encompassing figures such as Pietro Giordani (1774–1848), Giosuè Carducci (1835–1907), Giuseppe Chiarini (1823–1897), Giacomo Leopardi (1798–1837), Carlo Cattaneo (1801–1869), Graziadio Isaia Ascoli (1829–1907), Francesco Cassi (1778–1846), Ugo Foscolo (1778–1827), Ludovico Di Breme (1780–1820), Angelo Mai (1782–1854), Domenico Comparetti (1835–1927), Theodor Gomperz (1832–1912), Alessandro Manzoni (1785–1873), the Tuscan moderates around the 'Vieusseux Group', and Carlo Bini (1806–1842). What I say below will narrow on certain particularly important strands of this material but will also bring in two non-nineteenth-century works which I argue constitute organic extensions of Timpanaro's Enlightenment project back in time, as it were: the two 'popular' Garzanti editions, Holbach's *Il buon senso* (1985) and Cicero's *On Divination* (1988). As we shall see, there are ideological through lines and turns of thought which bind all these 'Enlightenment' thinkers within Timpanaro's 'Enlightenment' filter of a mind.

In some ways, Timpanaro's entire oeuvre can be seen as a systematic attempt to furnish, and give due account of, the predecessors of his thought.[3] And, just as Giacomo Leopardi provided the counterintuitive model of philology – honest, modest, disorganic, concrete, particular – so he would also figure as the keystone for Timpanaro's next venture in laying the ideological basis for the Enlightenment, materialist, and pessimist strands of his intellectual character. The latter two are

---

1   Timpanaro also produced a later contribution in this research line: Sebastiano Timpanaro, *Nuovi studi sul nostro Ottocento*, Pisa, 1995 – also a worthy read, but less influential than the other three.

2   Timpanaro himself saw them as natural companions: *AF*, 8.

3   Extending Salvatore Settis's term to describe some of Timpanaro's work as a 'choice of his own ancestors' (*scelta dei propri antenati*) – see chapter 2 n.25.

absolutely critical to that character. I will address their connections shortly (see chapter 4), while this chapter will concentrate more on the first. For Timpanaro was compulsively drawn to the nineteenth-century figures he considered most emblematic of a kind of heroic, resistant sunset of Enlightenment in the wake of the dominant currents of romanticism seeking to dislodge it from the world.

Timpanaro considered romanticism a mostly reactionary movement sanctioning mysticism and egotistical subjectivity, and, at its worst, a breeding ground for racist ethno-nationalist ideas. Its celebration of the self and the imagination over the external world might be summed with a choice quote from a key poet and philosopher of German romanticism, Novalis (aka Georg Philipp Friedrich Freiherr von Hardenberg, 1772–1801):

> The depths of our spirit are unknown to us – the mysterious way leads inwards. Eternity with its worlds – the past and future – is in ourselves or nowhere. The external world is the world of shadows – it throws its shadow into the realm of light.[4]

As we will see in chapter 4, nothing got Timpanaro's blood up as much as the idealist's location of the world in, and subordination to, ourselves. Romanticism was another culpable manifestation of this philosophical egotism. But for Timpanaro, there was a contemporary antidote running counter, an alternative nineteenth century: 'Enlightenment classicism' – a loosely constituted group of thinkers who spurned romanticism in favour of a turning back to the past for models of inspiration, both to the Enlightenment thinkers of the previous century and to the paradigms of classical antiquity. This group would include Leopardi as protagonist, to be sure – but also a wide cast of characters parallel to him, such as Pietro Giordani (1774–1848) or Carlo Bini (1806–1842; see chapter 6), and anterior to him, luminaries such as Cicero and d'Holbach.[5] The thread common to many of these thinkers

---

4 Novalis, *Miscellaneous Observations*, in *Philosophical Writings*, ed. and trans. Margaret Mahony Stoljar, Albany, 1997; *MO*, 17.

5 Giordani: *CI*, 'Le idee di Pietro Giordani', 'Giordani, Carducci e Chiarini'; *AF*, 'Giordani e la questione della lingua', 'Il Giordani, il Montani, il Vieusseux vi risalutano caramente'; *AN*, 'Ancora su Pietro Giordani'; Bini: *AN*, appendix I; Cicero: *DD*; Holbach, *BS*.

– at least Leopardi and Giordani, the Enlightenment classicists proper
– was, for Timpanaro, their way of being apparently behind the times
as a way of being ahead of them.[6] They may have looked crusty and
classicising, but this was just a deceptive form; in terms of their scientific
knowledge and cultural politics, they were very advanced.[7] Indeed,
the non-integrated intellectuals – the *disorganici* – often end up being
more progressive than the integrated – the *organici*.[8] This stance of
being *outside* the dominant trends of one's historical period by simultaneously
harking back to the past and prefiguring the future – the stance
of the prophet – was something Timpanaro turned to as he gradually
formulated his own concept of *inattualità*, the need to be 'untimely',
'outdated', or 'irrelevant'.[9] But the strange thing about Timpanaro's
prophets is that you can understand exactly what they are saying – for
their point is to speak the truth.

Given the importance of the poet Giacomo Leopardi to Timpanaro's life
and work, his prominence in the next few chapters, and his likely total
unfamiliarity to the anglophone reader, a brief introductory digression
might be in order. Leopardi (1798–1837) remains one of the most celebrated
poets of Italy, at least *in* Italy. His stature approaches that of Dante
as a treasured 'national poet', whose career handily overlapped with a
crucial preliminary phase in the formation of modern Italy as a nation-state.
His canonicity remains a permanent fixture, sealed in the school
curriculum. But he has a much harder, darker edge than a Whitman or
a Wordsworth. His disquieting, uncompromisingly grim outlook on the

---

6   *CI*, 24, 90, S.T. to Giuseppe Petronio, 25 July 1970. On Leopardi being ahead of
his time in philology, see *FGL*, 76; on Giordani's stubborn eighteenth-century identity,
AF, 171; on Giordani's advanced views on popular education: *CI*, 208.

7   *CI*, 24–5.

8   S.T. to Marino Berengo, 7 February 1976.

9   On Timpanaro's inattualità, see Pietro Cataldi, 'Il metodo di Timpanaro', *Allegoria*
2, no. 4 (1990): 143–68; Parroni, introduction to *VA*, vii; G. F. Gianotti, 'Prima e dopo
Lachmann', in Enrico Ghidetti and Alessandro Pagnini (eds), *Sebastiano Timpanaro e la
cultura del Secondo Novecento*, Rome, 2005, 142; Perry Anderson, 'On Sebastiano
Timpanaro', *London Review of Books* 23, no. 9 (May 2001); Federico Santangelo, 'Voler
"capire tutto" ': Appunti sullo stile di Sebastiano Timpanaro', *Anabases* 20 (2014): 53;
Robert Dombroski, 'Timpanaro's Materialism: An Introduction', *Journal of the History of
Ideas* 44, no. 2 (1983): 349; S.T. to Giorgio Voghera, 11 September 1966; S.T. to Luciano
Della Mea, 10 July 1976; S.T. to Antonio La Penna (n.d.; numbered 61 in the Timpanaro
archive).

world is not quite the stuff that anglophones would associate with the wreath of the 'national poet'.

Born into a decaying aristocratic family in the small town of Recanati (near Ancona, on the east coast of central Italy), Leopardi showed preternatural gifts from an early age. He was a polymath, versed in the entirety of classical and Enlightenment knowledge, who began his intellectual adulthood beavering away in the abstruse art of philology (as we saw in chapter 2). But after around 1815, the point known as the 'literary conversion', he began to dedicate himself seriously to poetry and literature. He excelled at intensive study, but his short life was marked by a permanent cloud of a fragile constitution (perhaps spinal tuberculosis). Though we should not co-ordinate worldview and bodily condition too neatly, Leopardi's philosophy became ever more radically materialist and pessimist over the course of his life. From his early work, in which nature as an entity was roughly benevolent, or at least not outright malevolent, to his later work, in which nature became a blanket oppressive, destructive, and baleful force for humans, the philosophical direction of Leopardi almost mimicked the tendency to destruction over which he obsessed. He turned, full pelt, to the unrelieved misery of the human condition – and that is perhaps the orientation for which he is best remembered.

As the Leopardi scholar Luigi Blasucci (1924–2021) points out, there are other Leopardis – including the poet of the 'infinite' and the poet of illusion, among others – but Timpanaro is drawn to Leopardi the materialist and 'cosmic' pessimist.[10] This corresponds with Leopardi's most radical and pessimistic 'mature' phase. This was the Leopardi of the *Dialogue of Nature and an Icelander* (1824; part of the collection of *Operette morali* [Small moral works]),[11] an ironic fictional dialogue which sets out Leopardi's views on the unfairness and inscrutability of the natural world. A poor Icelander, having fled the inhospitable conditions of his home island, arrives in equatorial Africa and confronts Nature about the meaning of life and the reasons she makes humans suffer – but dies before getting any satisfying answers. This phase, too, featured the Leopardi of the *Palinodia* (1835), a comical (and obviously

---

10   Luigi Blasucci, 'Su Timpanaro Leopardista', in Nuccio Ordine (ed.), *La lezione di un maestro: Omaggio a Sebastiano Timpanaro*, Naples, 2010, 109.

11   See A. Prete, *Giacomo Leopardi, 'Operette minori'*, Milan, 2014.

tongue-in-cheek) 'disavowal' or 'retraction' of all his previous thought on the wretchedness of life and the misery of the present, in favour of an upbeat (but obviously hollow) enthusing over historical progress and the wonders of the modern age.[12] It was also the Leopardi of the *Paralipomeni* (Things passed over, 1831–37), a biting satire against a frayed pre-Risorgimento political and clerical class, angled particularly at the Florentine liberals and Neapolitan Catholics – the descendants of which targets Timpanaro himself would later line up against, mutatis mutandis. So deep was Timpanaro's saturation in this later-phase Leopardi that it is sometimes difficult to tell where the one ends and the other begins.

This moment was also, perhaps most illustratively for our purposes, the Leopardi of *La ginestra* (The broom, 1836), one of the last poems (no. 34) in the spectacular collection known as the *Canti*. The poem – an address to the yellow-flowered plant growing defiantly on the harsh slopes of Vesuvius – folds out into a cosmic meditation on the destructiveness of nature and the inevitable unhappiness of the human playthings consigned to her grim desert of a sandbox. Here, Leopardi expresses many of the sentiments that sum his poetic and philosophical identity, and that would become, for Timpanaro, the corner-stones of a Leopardian worldview: heroic and uncomfortable confrontation of bare truth, the fundamental malice of nature (*natura matrigna* – nature not as mother but as evil stepmother), and the possibility of human solidarity based on universal victimhood beneath that merciless malice. A quote from the 'solidarity stanza' of the poem can help give us a flavour:

A noble nature is one that
dares to raise its mortal eyes against
our common fate and with honest words,
detracting nothing from truth,
admits the evil that has been given us as our lot,
our low and frail state;
a nature that shows itself
brave and strong in suffering, nor with fraternal
anger and wrath, still more grievous
than other injuries, swells

---

12   See Jonathan Galassi's bilingual edition: Giacomo Leopardi, *Canti: Poems*, New York, 2014.

its miseries, reproaching mankind
for its own sorrow, but lays the blame
on *Her* who is truly guilty, who is a mother
of mortals in birth and a stepmother in Will.
He calls *Her* the enemy; and against *Her*
believing the human race to be united,
as is true, and ranked in opposition from old,
he judges as his confederates
all men, and embraces all
with true love, offering
and expecting powerful and prompt aid
in the changing dangers and hardship
of the common war. And believes it foolish
to arm one's own hand with human wounds
and set snares or traps for neighbors,
just as on the battlefield surrounded by enemy forces, in the most
    ferocious
tumult of the assault,
forgetting the enemy, to incite
bitter disputes with friends,
to scatter them in flight and strike with swords
among their own forces.
Such thoughts as these
when revealed openly, as once they were, to the crowd;
and when that horror
against malevolent Nature that first
drew men into a network of solidarity,
then partial renewal may come
from true wisdom, the honest and upright
intercourse of citizens,
and justice and piety will take another root
than foolish pride,
on which foundation the people's probity
may stand in such stability
as anything can stand that rests on error.[13]

---

13   I use Steven J. Willett's translation: 'Wild Broom Or, the Flower of the Desert',
Arion 23, no. 1 (2015): 23–32.

We might say that nature, to Leopardi, faintly resembles capitalism for the Marxist: the bringer of infinite ills, the author of humanity's collective unhappiness, but, also, the force that bonds humans in the solidarity of standing against the onslaught. However, there is one crucial difference: for Leopardi, nature cannot be overcome in the same way that capitalism can be phased out. It provides a hard limit to human aspiration and guarantees, for past, present, and future alike, a significant measure of misery. From that misery, however, emerges a very small glimmer of redemptive solidarity – precarious ('partial renewal', 'as anything can stand that rests on error'), but nevertheless there. Living in one big unhappy family beneath the iron fist of the stepmother, we are democratically 'interpellated', one might say, against a common enemy. It is this brand of powerful home truth about the human–nature relationship, delivered as straight medicine in a bitter pill, that Timpanaro will bring to Marxist materialism in chapter 4.

Two further points stand out about Leopardi's view of nature compared to that offered in the intellectual traditions behind his formation. Firstly, this kind of radical pessimism was in the minority when measured against the overall upbeat optimism of the Enlightenment thought on which Leopardi relied. Such optimism was famously parodied in Voltaire's *Candide*, and there were, of course, serious contemporary bursts of resistance to the dominant myths of progress in eighteenth-century Europe. Nevertheless, Leopardi's pessimism in the successive age stands out for its unremitting bleakness and intensity. It makes him representative of a legacy of a *certain* Enlightenment – but perhaps not the one most familiar to us, as filtered through the mainstream reception channels of anglophone liberal democracies. Secondly, the notion of nature as a callous and destructive force, anti-providential and malign, is a far cry from the overall views of a beneficent and providential nature doing the rounds in the romantic period with which Leopardi overlapped. The intellectual historiography of Timpanaro's period indeed fused Leopardi with romanticism, and he perhaps did share some stylistic and thematic common ground. Leopardi scholars of the previous generation immediately preceding Timpanaro, such as Cesare Luporini and (to a lesser extent) Walter Binni (1913–1997; a Leopardian critic of the previous generation to Timpanaro), were also keen to redeem Leopardi's progressive democratic politics and revalue his 'heroic' last poetry but could still not quite come to value the most radically pessimistic parts of the poet.[14] The ideological difference between Leopardi and the romantics, expressed neatly in this pessimistic position on nature, was cavernous. It was partly this mistaken identification of Leopardi as a romantic, and the discomfort of scholarship with his truly radical pessimism, that made Timpanaro rush in to defend the legacy of this poor, misunderstood Enlightenment classicist.

Historical periods, like any object of human study, are often subject to a brutalising reductionism. As the present is lived, it is always experienced as a swirl of contestation and contradiction, push and shove, agon and antagonism. It is only when that present recedes and becomes ossified under habits of mass remembering that 'ages' tend to congeal under certain tags as 'ages *of . . .*' It was precisely this resolving creep of a dominant historiography over the snags and outliers of actual history that fuelled Timpanaro to write his first wider book on the culture of the early nineteenth century – for that period, in Timpanaro's view, was an age particularly susceptible to the reductionism of branding under a single sign: romanticism.[15] It was time to show there were more things in heaven and earth than were dreamed of in Alessandro Manzoni's *I promessi sposi*. Indeed, that iconic novel of nineteenth-century Italy, in becoming *the* novel, was just another paradigm of romanticism which set misplaced expectations for the age.

Why did Timpanaro have it in for romanticism? Apart from the generally overappreciative context for the romantic period in the mid-'60s, which no doubt activated Timpanaro's bristly countercultural reflex, a couple of motives suggest themselves.[16] Firstly, there was an aesthetic and ideological aversion at play – if not to the entirety of

---

14   Walter Binni, *La nuova poetica leopardiana*, Florence, 1947; Cesare Luporini, *Leopardi progressivo*, Florence, 1947. See Emanuele Narducci, 'Sebastiano Timpanaro', *Belfagor* 40, no. 3 (1985): 288–9.

15   *CI*, 4–6, 36–40; cf. *AF*, xi.; S.T. to Bruno Biral, 20 April 1966, 4 May 1966, 10 May 1966, 28 May 1966; S.T. to Giuseppe Petronio, 25 July 1970; S.T. to Pino Fasano, 11 October 1971. Timpanaro's gripe about this overuse of the term 'romantic' was already evident in his 1963 review of Treves (reprinted in *AF*: see esp. 377–9), as Umberto Carpi observes ('Timpanaro e il problema del romanticismo', in Riccardo Di Donato [ed.], *Il filologo materialista*, Pisa, 2003, 138).

16   Enrico Ghidetti, 'L'Ottocento di Timpanaro tra illuminismo e classicismo', in Ghidetti and Pagnini, *Sebastiano Timpanaro*, 249; S.T. to Ermanno Circeo, 11 April 1969.

romanticism, certainly to a prevalent strain of it. Timpanaro saw romanticism as the bearer of all things irrational and mystificatory; an ideological system for advocating the obscurity of the middle ages over the clarity of Enlightenment (or antiquity for that matter); and a way of fetishising reactionary mythologies of nationalist folklore – a cultural drag which would culminate in fascism.[17] Romanticism's dubious ideological co-ordinates also corresponded to an aesthetic that Timpanaro simply could not abide: writing whose formal style – prone to crabbed or woolly expression, bouts of fabulation, and abstraction – betrayed its irritating debts to the idealist tradition. Thus, Timpanaro's scientific materialism fitted him out for deep opposition to romanticism. But it was also his inner philological splitter, as well as his pleading for the minoritarian underdog, which made him bunker down. He became fed up with attempts by lumping scholars to make Leopardi *into* a romantic – a futile task in Timpanaro's book, because it stretched the meaning of the term 'romantic' to such a flabby degree that it lost all content.[18] So it was not just a resistance to romanticism qua *romanticism* that sparked Timpanaro's defence of the counterculture of Enlightenment classicism; it was a resistance to the very idea that cultural historiography should swallow everything into the monopolising terms of its habitual periodisations. No, Leopardi was *not* a romantic, despite living contemporaneously with romanticism, and despite sophistic attempts to suck him into the same movement. At stake here was the defence of a history replete not with accommodation, conciliation, and agents of the mainstream, but with antagonism, minority, obliquity, and thinkers who *resist*.

This disaggregation of a particular thinker from their dominant cultural context was often the unspoken raison d'être of Timpanaran intellectual history from *Classicismo e illuminismo* (1965) onwards. Timpanaro started with Leopardi and Giordani, who did not fit the bill of romanticism and who stood out from their pack in their materialism and progressive Enlightenment thought, but who also could not survive a historiographical lumping-in with other 'classicists' of the period. But he then extended consideration to other favourite minor figures, such as

---

17   S.T. to Giorgio Petrocchi, 21 April 1975; *CI*, 3, 19; S.T. to Bruno Biral, 28 May 66.

18   S.T. to Giuseppe Petronio, 25 July 1970.

Ludovico Di Breme and Carlo Bini.[19] Just as Timpanaro had to step in to defend Leopardi from attempts to domesticate him to romanticism, so too did he have to save Holbach from scholarly bids to twist him from a materialist into a romantic vitalist.[20] Again, Timpanaro's feel for the philological particular put him on the lookout against sloppy historio-graphical conflations leading to all-out distortions. The minoritarian tradition was always on the cusp of being swallowed by the majoritar-ian, but, with care, the intellectual line could be drawn, and the content saved from the threat of reducing or resolving it into the oblivion of coherence with the dominant periodisation.[21]

While rescuing Enlightenment classicism from the all-embracing clutches of romanticism is one of Timpanaro's most trenchantly argued ideological positions, his antipathy to all forms of 'conceptual creep' or 'definitional sag' runs deep in his work. Several terms, stretched beyond their limits, come in for a Timpanaran cutting down to size over the course of his career. He criticised the historian Piero Treves (1911–1992) for a too capacious definition of not just romanticism but 'Neo-Guelphism', a nineteenth-century Italian political movement aiming to unite Italy under the pope as king. Timpanaro thought that Treves's use of this term ended up bunching hugely disparate thinkers such as Goethe, Foscolo, Leopardi, Heine, and Cattaneo in the same box.[22] Likewise, he scorned Benedetto Croce's tendency to sophistically stretch out the concept of the lyric merely by asserting that 'all poetry is lyric',[23] just as Walter Binni came under fire for using 'idylls' as a designator for Leopardian poems which should not bear the name.[24] Timpanaro took the Swiss linguist Ferdinand de Saussure (1857–1913) to task for a slip-page in his use of the term 'sign' to mean simply 'signifier', when strictly it should (within Saussure's own system) mean the *unity* of signifier and signified.[25] The glottologist Paolo Ramat's (1936–) use of the term 'dialectic' came under fire for its excessive breadth tipping it over into

---

19   On Di Breme combining mixed Enlightenment-romanticism positions: *AF*, 143; on Bini's early strand of romanticism, distinct from the *Antologia* group: *AN*, 206; on Bini's old-school polemic and Enlightenment style: *AN*, 234, 239.

20   *BS*, xxxiv.

21   S.T. to Romano Luperini, 19 April 1968.

22   *CI*, 36–7; for Timpanaro's separation of Cattaneo from romanticism: *CI*, 233.

23   S.T. to Bruno Biral, 10 May 1966.

24   S.T. to Walter Binni, 6 April 1963.

25   S.T. to Giulio Lepschy, 18 April 1963.

the generic.[26] The historian of classical philology Rudolf Pfeiffer was singled out for putting everything under the banner of 'Winckelmannism' (after the influential German classical art historian Johann Joachim Winckelmann, 1717–1768), and neglecting whatever failed to fit the scheme.[27] Even a concept closer to home, like the Marxist notion of totality, came in for a Timpanaran specification, with our splitter pointing out to the Germanist and comrade Cesare Cases that reality features not just one form of blending, but many: systems, aggregates, composites, mixtures.[28] Timpanaro was well aware of the hermeneutic violence these broad-brush terms committed, categorising the world into single dominant classes and epistemically exiling the misfits. The intellectual trauma in the background here, so to speak, is the tendency of Italian idealism to make predictable argumentative moves that collapse distinction into higher unities: the idealist philosopher of Italian fascism Giovanni Gentile, for example, asserting that everything was philosophy, or everything was spirit.[29] Timpanaro's feel for the inassimilable and irreducible in experience, as well as his heterodox pluralism, made him resist these idealist habits of thought that teeter over into fully fledged monism. For Timpanaran philosophy, the world is never one, but many – and the job of intellectual history is to write up those at risk of drowning in the illusory hyper-inclusiveness of the Imaginary One.

While our materialist, then, maintained a need for the finite over against the idealising infinite across many terms and concepts, he was especially sensitive to the abuse of overextended tags in the writing of history. Misrepresented historical periods were a Timpanaran obsession. This applies to the contemporary world: he singled out the philologist and historian of the Italian language Alfredo Stussi's biased selection of certain ideological currents to characterise modernity, at the expense of others. Stussi chose to elevate structuralism and psychoanalysis as the definers of the contemporary, rather than Trotsky, Lenin,

---

26   S.T. to Enrico Rambaldi, 4 December 1978.

27   S.T. to Silvia Rizzo, 6 April 1979.

28   S.T. to Cesare Cases, 12 October 1970.

29   Higher unities: *SLO*, 159–60; Timpanaro also accused Gianni Sofri and Lucio Colletti of a Giovanni Gentile–style sleight of hand in collapsing the Marxist distinction between base and superstructure into a unity (S.T. to Gianni Sofri, 10 April 1969). Everything is philosophy: see Sebastiano Timpanaro, *La morte di Spinoza*, in Michele Feo (ed.), 'La morte di Spinoza: Scritti di e su Sebastiano Timpanaro', *Il Ponte* 10–11 (2004): 9–16. Everything is spirit: S.T. to Enrico Rambaldi, 7 January 1979.

and Einstein.[30] But it also applies to the nineteenth century, in which Timpanaro felt most at home. Nor was it just that a more rationed distribution of attention needed to be given to competing cultural movements like romanticism versus Enlightenment. The terms *themselves* needed to be sufficiently split into their various components. Romanticism was not one movement, and its various camps contained good and ill.[31] Likewise for the Enlightenment: Timpanaro complained to Cases about the Frankfurt school ossification of this movement, their tendency to make *di ogni erba un fascio*, 'a bundle of every blade of grass'.[32] Instead, we need a campaign of intellectual-historical disentanglement, an attempt to weed the elements of Enlightenment such as proto-repressive reason and capitalist scientism out of the good bits, such as liberation from myth and dissolution of dogma.[33] For Timpanaro, intellectual historiography required an attentiveness not only to culture as a site of conflict but to the conflicts *within* those conflicts, the bumps within bumps. Terminological subtlety and suppleness was necessary to nail down the complexity of clashing culture.[34]

Timpanaro often seized on a split at the level of the individual thinker to make sense of a bigger historical conflict. In a reminiscence of his separation of Leopardi the poet from Leopardi the philologist, Timpanaro made one of his ancient 'Enlightenment' thinkers, Cicero, into a kind of walking paradox, perfectly capable of inhabiting very different positions depending on the context: the same person, after all, could simultaneously be a member of the college of augurs (Roman priests who interpreted bird signs) in his official capacity, and also suspect that same system of augury as a philosopher.[35] That did not necessarily mean that Cicero was living in a majority-religious or majority-sceptical intellectual age; it simply meant that those strands were

---

30   S.T. to Alfredo Stussi, 16 May 1975.

31   Timpanaro's fine-grained prising apart of different romanticisms: *CI*, 4-6; *AF*, 142–3. Timpanaro's complex/contradictory attitude to romanticism: Carpi, 'Timpanaro e il problema', 147–9.

32   Timpanaro was also keen to separate Leopardi from bundling alongside Frankfurt school pessimism, as he was to quarantine Leopardi from Freudian and neo-Gramscian distortions: see Luca Bufarale, *Sebastiano Timpanaro: L'inquietudine della ricerca*, Pistoia, 2022, 66.

33   *AN*, 168–9.

34   *CI*, 40.

35   *NC*, 262.

rubbing up against each other, sometimes even in the same person. Pietro Giordani, too, seemed to embody these partial clusters of sympathy and antipathy around certain historical moments: Timpanaro pointed out his split view on Dante, combining aesthetic-stylistic veneration with reservations towards his religiosity, just as Giordani liked the style of certain Jesuits while abhorring their reactionary politics.[36] His anti-eighteenth-century position from linguistic and literary angles was counterbalanced by his alignment with the period from an ideological standpoint.[37] What is more, just as Giordani bounced between attraction towards and repulsion from different elements in the historical mix, so his own mode of historical periodisation did justice to complexity: for Giordani, the 1300s were no flat, even keel but a bouncing mess of variation.[38] Timpanaro was drawn to these figures who showed, in their many ways, the dynamism and contestation of history itself.

Timpanaro was also attracted to characters not only out of joint with their historical moment (and so expanding our very notion of that historical moment), or out of sync with themselves, but those clashing with the lazily inherited categories we deploy to make sense of the world. On the famous crux moment of Socrates' condemnation, Timpanaro pointed to the interesting and productive way this situation upsets our standard associations of political and philosophical orientation: Socrates was an anti-democratic rationalist as well as an anti-traditionalist; his opponents were democratic obscurantists and traditionalists.[39] Such a strange line-up of ideological teams challenges our own habitual identification of democracy and rationalism, showing that the two do not necessarily go together. This is a central point of Timpanaro's work on Enlightenment classicism: that sometimes, politics, philosophy, and intellectual/artistic style join up or face off in unexpected ways. Intellectual profiles are never clean, never packaged. And in drawing up our terms, camps, and periods, we should take nothing for granted.

The principle of illuminating the counterculture – or the cultural losers of the nineteenth century, as it were – applies to many of Timpanaro's

---

36   *AF*, 181–2; *AF*, 209.
37   *AF*, 222–3.
38   *AF*, 183.
39   *AF*, 431.

subjects in *Classicismo* and *Aspetti*.[40] A long survey of Pietro Giordani's ideas opens *Classicismo*. Timpanaro was attracted to this classicist partly because of his formative role in the cultivation of Leopardi's genius; partly for his radical ideas on education, pitched as he was against the quaint and pointless humanist traditions of Latin composition, and in favour of reforms to popular education (e.g., the institution of the *asilo*, nursery school or kindergarten); partly because of his anti-clericalism and disappointment in the nobility; partly for his constitutional opposition to all forms of obscurantism; and partly because he had posed the important Timpanaran problem of the writer's position vis-à-vis political power.[41] But perhaps just as much as Timpanaro was charmed by the content of Giordani's ideas, he was also drawn in by his position relative to the world: isolated, anxious, spectatorial; distant from the mainstream group of the 'Tuscan moderates' (bourgeois liberals in the circle of the review *L'Antologia*, such as Giovan Pietro Vieusseux and Gino Capponi) in being open to the revolution of Risorgimento, and a 'passionate admirer' of it – but also feeling detached from the motors of that big historical moment, a man too *fuori del suo tempo* – 'outside his own time' – to truly partake in it.[42] In the later *Aspetti*, Timpanaro added to the usual suspects of Giordani and Leopardi figures like Ludovico Di Breme, a supposed romantic thinker who is difficult to digest fully into romanticism pure and simple. According to Timpanaro, the Enlightenment quality of his thought became ever more important over time; and on some issues, such as the language question, his position was clearly an Enlightenment one.[43] A few years later, Timpanaro devoted a lengthy and deeply resonant appendix of his *Antileopardiani* to the Livornese writer Carlo Bini (see chapter 7), trimming him from the climate of the Florentine political moderates around *L'Antologia*, both in his differently accentuated romanticism and his distinct flavour of religiosity.[44] Timpanaro's work on nineteenth-century cultural figures is powered by this taste for the unorthodox, the thinkers who do not quite fit the mould.

---

40   Timpanaro often takes issue with a historiography of the winners, for instance, S.T. to Antonio Piromalli, 25 March 1982.

41   S.T. to Carlo Galante Garrone, 10 January 1984; *CI*, 97, 81, 101, 148; S.T. to Carlo Dionisotti, 10 November 1971.

42   *CI*, 80.

43   *AF*, 143.

44   *AN*, 204–7.

The feel for this brand of intellectual or social misfit cuts across the Timpanaran corpus – in philology, for example, he also had a tendency to point out buckers of trends such as Ulrich von Wilamowitz-Moellendorf and Friedrich Leo, who were themselves (like Timpanaro) looking back to the early eighteenth century for their live models.[45] The myth of the dignified misfit is indeed so powerful for Timpanaro that he applied it even in cases of pure speculation. Gossiping to his philologist friend Scevola Mariotti about the snobbiness of eminent UK-based Latinist Otto Skutsch towards his rival Australian Ennius-interpreter Harry Jocelyn, Timpanaro suspected that Skutsch's contempt for Jocelyn was partly down to a form of centre–periphery dynamic: Skutsch the old Mitteleuropean intellectual thinking Jocelyn the Australian was presumptuously planting his flag in the 'sacred citadels of European philology', where he did not belong.[46] The way that Timpanaro latched on to the 'outsider' explanation gives us a glimpse, in a moment of pure projection based on absolutely no evidence, at Timpanaro's deepest habits of dividing the world into those with and against the grain. Timpanaro was partly rooting for Jocelyn because his 'outsiderness' reminded him of Leopardi, who reminded him . . . of himself.

The symbol and lodestone of Timpanaro's against-the-grain nineteenth century is, of course, Leopardi; and he does come across in *Classicismo* as the perfect realisation of Giordani's 'outside of his own time' figure in maintaining the concept of 'disagreement with one's own century' (*dissidio col proprio secolo*).[47] But in true, unpredictable Timpanaro fashion, the project of Leopardian recuperation stretching across *Classicismo*, *Aspetti*, and *Antileopardiani* is also about *downplaying* the isolation of Leopardi, at least insofar as that 'isolation' had been instrumentalised against Leopardi as a way of relativising and disqualifying his thought.[48] In *Alcune osservazioni sul pensiero del Leopardi*, one of the outstanding pieces from *Classicismo*, some of the most beautiful pages are given to the famous question of the role of illness and deformity in the genesis of Leopardian pessimism. Leopardi protested the way people wrote off his pessimism as the outgrowth of

---

45   S.T. to Eduard Fraenkel, 27 December 1955.
46   S.T. to Scevola Mariotti, 26 November 1973, 16 January 1974.
47   *CI*, 138–9.
48   CL, 29; see also Narducci, 'Sebastiano Timpanaro', 302. Timpanaro reasserts Leopardi's lack of isolation at *VR*, 176.

a pathological condition and 'deprived it of any general validity' in the process – a line of dismissal running all the way to Timpanaro's idealist bugbear Benedetto Croce.[49] The scholar of Italian literature Vanna Gazzola Stacchini's Freudian reading of Leopardi did the same thing, performing a controversial 'analysis at a distance' to defang the poet's thought by reducing it to the reflex of a generic Oedipal complex.[50] A dual psychic and physical malady, in this case, was deployed against Leopardi as a means of isolating him from the shared, default standard of healthy humanity. But Timpanaro elegantly showed that this disability was not just a biographical determinant of Leopardian whining; it was a 'cognitive instrument' giving the poet access to a particular truth about the oppressive power of nature over humanity.[51] Timpanaro's attempt to redeem Leopardi's physical limitations as *enabling* special access to profound truths about the vulnerability of the human condition anticipates recent work in disability studies – and has even been metabolised into it.[52] Just as the experience of the alienating relations of labour allows a member of the proletariat access to a crystalline class consciousness, so illness gave Leopardi a particularly privileged window onto a fundamental truth about the human–nature relationship.[53] That truth is not an isolable or relative quirk of an individual's subjectivity but the grasping of an absolute that can stand as the basis for a universal solidarity of humans against nature.[54] Leopardi may have been isolated socially, culturally, and intellectually vis-à-vis his dominant contemporary context – but in apprehending a higher truth that wriggles free from the limiting concerns of that context, he was the least isolated of all, laying down a way for us to follow suit several centuries in his train.

---

49   CL, 156–7; see also S.T. to Francesco Orlando, 27 December 1976. Timpanaro notes this form of dismissal happening for his and Leopardi's soulmate, Carlo Bini, too: *AN*, 282.

50   *AN*, 155, on Vanna Gazzola Stacchini, *Alle origini del sentimento leopardiano*, Naples, 1974. Cf. S.T. to Vanna Gazzola Stacchini, 11 February 1976.

51   *AN*, 157; S.T. to Giorgio Voghera, 31 October 1965.

52   See, for example, Nicolò Bellanca, Mario Biggeri, and Francesca Marchetta, 'An Extension of the Capability Approach: Towards a Theory of Dis-capability', *Alter* 5, no. 3 (2011): 163. Thanks to Francesca Bellei for pointing me in this direction.

53   Luigi Blasucci, 'Sugli studi Leopardiani di Timpanaro', in Di Donato, *Il filologo materialista*, 120.

54   *CI*, 172, *LF*, 171; see also Bufarale, *Sebastiano Timpanaro*, 68.

However, if Timpanaro's work on the Enlightenment classicists and their relatives was an attempt at recuperating those isolated at their time of writing and giving them a kind of 'vertical' company *across* time, he was also squarely invested in defending the value of marginal positions *as* marginal. The pressing conceptual bête noire of Timpanaro's Enlightenment classicists trilogy was Gramsci's idea of the 'organic intellectual' – or at least its abuse within the political context of the Italian left in the 1960s, '70s, and '80s.[55] Gramsci's original use of the term was not value laden but, rather, descriptive: it was designed to capture a particular kind of intellectual rooted within, emergent from and bound to a particular social class, but there was nothing inherently virtuous about being 'organic' per se.[56] From the 1960s onwards, Timpanaro saw that the concept was becoming bastardised: now the mere fact of being 'organic' was what was important, no matter the class or the ideology to which one was organic. In that climate of emerging 'historic compromise' and rampant accommodationism within the ranks of the PCI, Timpanaro saw what was being done with new 'justificationist' historiography.[57] PCI readers such as Umberto Carpi were validating their own reformist 'participation' by slighting the isolated and irrelevant Leopardi.[58]

The *Antileopardiani* confronted the problem head on. Timpanaro accounted for the recent turn against Leopardi in leftist circles with an

----

55   Timpanaro's polemic against the 'organic intellectual' concept was certainly in full swing by the late '70s and early '80s: it is present in the preface to *AF* (xii–iii), with Timpanaro having to hold the rant back, and also dominates the end of Timpanaro's review of La Penna's Marchesi ('Il "Marchesi" di Antonio La Penna', *Belfagor* 35, no. 6 [1980]: 669). But then it was all over the *AN* (indeed opposition to it is almost the unifying principle); see for instance, 18–19, 51, 88–9, 145, 294, 300–1. Timpanaro noted Gramsci's evolution of thought here: apparently, he was more tolerant of the inorganic intellectual in his earlier phase (S.T. to Rocco Mario Morano, 22 July 1983; reprinted in *VR* as chapter 11). Timpanaro sometimes differentiated the Gramscian concept from its bastardised reception on the contemporary Italian left, where 'organic' was translated into 'must represent the winner in a given historical moment': see, for instance, S.T. to Bruno Biral, 22 July 1976. At other times, the dichotomy between organic and traditional intellectual had risks of its own, with no one to blame but Gramsci: *AN*, 88. Cf. Timpanaro, 'Il "Marchesi" ', 669.

56   Thanks to Ramsey McGlazer for helping articulate this.

57   On the connection between the 'new manzonianism' and the historic compromise: *AN*, 18–19.

58   Luigi Blasucci to S.T., 21 January 1976; S.T. to Luigi Blasucci, 3 January 1979.

over-insistence on the exclusive value of thought from 'organic intellectuals'. Gramsci's concept was being leveraged more and more to focus solely on those figures fully *embedded in* and *representative of* social classes, but also organically connected to the dominant strains of culture.[59] The dichotomy between organic and traditional intellectual leaves oddballs like Leopardi unrecognised, falling between the cracks, because they belong to neither.[60] Leopardi and Co were devalued merely because they belonged to the losing side and were isolated from the corridors of cultural power, a sort of deracinated intellectual aristocracy without public context, making it hard for their ideas to 'stick'; celebrated instead were the culture warriors with real power, whatever their politics, such as the Tuscan moderates.[61] Even if their ideas were regressive compared to the advanced atheism and materialism of a Leopardi, they were cast as *progressive* purely because they emerged from thinkers with cultural power.[62]

Timpanaro rightly points out the self-serving politics of this irritating counterintuitive manoeuvre, which indirectly justifies the PCI's selling out to the forces of capital for the sake of wielding mainstream parliamentary influence.[63] Privileging the *form* of the 'organic intellectual' at all costs over the *content* of what those intellectuals were actually saying was a textbook reactionary move taking place to Timpanaro's immediate right flank, and his vigorous defence of Leopardi was a way of combatting this closet 'justificationism'.[64] As Timpanaro says, it produces a strange effect when the 'organic bond' of the intellectual is not to the proletariat but to the bourgeoisie.[65] In the supercharged intellectual wing of the Italian left in this era, such cultural politics mattered: the debate over Leopardi was, in its way, a proxy war over the wisdom of 'integration' and compromise as political strategies.[66] For Timpanaro, it was the historical losers who mattered the most because they were the

59   *AN*, 88.

60   *AN*, 300.

61   *CI*, 17–18.

62   On the advanced nature of Leopardi's materialism with respect to the *Antologia* crowd, see *AN*, 171.

63   *AN*, 18–19.

64   On anti-justificationism as a linchpin of Timpanaran popular philosophy, see Bufarale, *Sebastiano Timpanaro*, 73.

65   *AF*, xii–xiii.

66   *AN*, 83.

ones courageous enough to tend the untimely flame of truth which would finally blaze up under socialism. When the dominant culture was *wrong*, an object for correction, there was only one politically responsible position: isolation.[67] And it was a Stalinist mistake to think that politics should have such an intense governing sway over culture in the first place.[68]

We have already seen the obvious isomorphism between Timpanaro and Leopardi with respect to their stubbornly out-of-time ideological positions. Many scholars have noted that when Timpanaro talks of Leopardi, he is usually, at some level, talking of himself.[69] Without risking too great a flourish of the pop Freudianism Timpanaro so despised, when it comes to a thinker such as Timpanaro – so shy with the 'I' – the best way to gain a sense of their priorities is to observe the factors common to the personalities they study, or at least the factors they tend to showcase. But we can also test for the convergence between the things Timpanaro tends to repeat about himself and the things he tends to repeat about his major cast of characters.

Pietro Giordani's anachronistic outsider status makes him an interesting case here. At one time or another, Timpanaro noted Giordani's feeling of being prematurely old, his failure to write a big organic work, and his position as a kind of 'spectator of life' rather than an agent in it.[70] All of these are traits accumulating to Timpanaro himself across his correspondence: he often confessed himself older than his 'anagraphic' age and a trafficker in the bitty and the disorganic.[71] In a rare direct reflection on his political life, Timpanaro picked a metaphor similar to spectatorship to describe his relation with contemporary greats of the Italian left. As we saw at the beginning of this book, when Antonio Perin asked him to write an autobiography for the political instruction of the new generation, Timpanaro characteristically declined to write of

---

67   *AN*, 145.

68   On the possible relationship between Timpanaro's resentment of the organic intellectual and his distaste for Stalinism, see Narducci, 'Sebastiano Timpanaro', 302.

69   Piergiorgio Parroni, 'Timpanaro e la filologia', in Ordine, *La lezione di un maestro*, 60–1, quoting Mordenti: 'Raul Mordenti, il quale sospetta . . . che Timpanaro 'parli spesso di se parlando di Leopardi'; cf. Blasucci, 'Sugli studi', 8.

70   S.T. to Carlo Galante Garrone, 10 January 1984; *CI*, 80.

71   Timpanaro complained of premature ageing even as early as 1972 – when he was only forty-nine (S.T. to Arnaldo Momigliano, 12 December 1972). See chapter 2 on 'scrittarelli molto aridi e disorganici' (S.T. to Piero Treves, 6 March 1979).

himself, letting that self in only as a kind of 'bit part' or 'extra'.[72] This gleaming pearl of a moment in which Timpanaro felt permitted – if only for a second – to lay out an autobiographical vista shows us that his self-conception was not so far from that of Giordani in contemporary political life. Perhaps not so distant as to be a pure observer, perhaps just making the cut to appear on stage – but certainly *only* as a minor player.

Timpanaro's main Enlightenment classicists are, like their twentieth-century sympathiser, both marginal and not. Timpanaro defended the value of a Giordani's or a Leopardi's isolation, at the same time as he limited that isolation insofar as it was leveraged to relativise the validity of their thought. Over time, Timpanaro's self-positioning acquired complicated hues from both of these camps. His usual script was to claim an isolation within all his various life contexts: to the scholar of French literature Francesco Orlando (1934–2010), he claimed he had no authority in Marxist camps and was simply treated as a vulgar materialist spoilsport.[73] To the philosopher Girolamo De Liguori (1933–2022), he claimed no sway at either his workplace, La Nuova Italia, or in the fields of nineteenth-century studies, Italian literature, and history of ideas, or in the university.[74] And to his younger correspondent Rinantonio Viani, he offered himself up as an avowed non-organic intellectual on the left, a Leopardian and non-dogmatic Marxist thought of as reactionary by the 1968ers for failing to appreciate Mao, and a complete dinosaur because of his hewing to the straight line of Marx and Lenin.[75] But come the *Antileopardiani*, Timpanaro – just as he had done and will do for Leopardi – also felt the need to pedal back on that isolation. No, Timpanaro could not be called isolated in the strict sense; for evidence, one need simply look at his history of committed political engagement, and at the longer shifts he had put in at political meetings and rallies relative to study time.[76] Timpanaro's dual, shifting declaration of marginality and embeddedness gets to the heart of his paradigmatic non-organic intellectuals, the Enlightenment classicists. Their

---

72   See the introduction of this book.

73   S.T. to Francesco Orlando, 30 June 1974; Orlando thought Timpanaro was underestimating his prestige in Marxist circles (Francesco Orlando to S.T., 9 July 1974).

74   S.T. to Girolamo De Liguori, 13 May 1981; S.T. to Girolamo De Liguori, 14 April 1984.

75   S.T. to Rinantonio Viani, 30 August 1992.

76   *AN*, 11–12. Cf. *VR*, 122.

isolation was part of a context of thinking against the grain. That context, although small, is not quite the same as isolation. The minor player is still part of something, and maybe one day that something will be major again.

The reduction of the size of the observer, and the turning of the self to the world, is partly what Timpanaro identified as the Enlightenment pose – and it is also what connected him to another object of trans-historical identification, in the philosopher and classical philologist Theodor Gomperz (1832–1912). Timpanaro's portrait of Gomperz reveals many of the classic features of the ideal Timpanaran intellectual: 'extravagant' in the sense of ranging freely through disciplines, isolated in his contemporary context, and a philological commitment to handling all thinkers great and small with the same egalitarian interest.[77] But Gomperz also compressed elegantly within himself two further desiderata of Timpanaro's Enlightenment-classicist tradition, both to do with the self and its relation to the world (the big question of idealism versus materialism after all). Firstly, Gomperz represented for Timpanaro the 'rediscovery', or at least reappreciation, of the Greek philosophical tradition of atomism – a turning of philosophy towards the investigation of nature and away from contemplation of the self, at a historical moment (the late nineteenth century) in which the latter was preponderating over the former.[78] But then again, Timpanaro knew that the self could not be extinguished entirely, and that any science worth its salt acknowledged the position of the observer as a crucial factor in the process of observation. This is where Gomperz came in handy. One of the reasons Gomperz was so unpopular in his heavily historicising moment is that he strove to make ancient thinkers speak to the present, to bring them up to date – in Timpanaro's loaded vocabulary, *attualizzare*. For Gomperz, there was an inevitable importation of the self in that process of *making relevant*. Gomperz himself updated the imagery of Homer *Odyssey* book 11, where Odysseus made the shades of the underworld drink sacrificial animal blood to speak to him, to reflect on this process. It is also an eerie premature updating of Wilamowitz's *subsequent* use of the same imagery, which he went on to deploy for the opposite purpose:

77   *AF*, 392, 394; *AF*, 319.
78   *AF*, 405.

to show that even if we must animate ghosts by giving them our own contemporary blood, we should do whatever we can to drain the alien part of the transfusion away again:

> The tradition yields us only ruins. The more closely we test and examine them, the more clearly we see how ruinous they are; and out of ruins no whole can be built. The tradition is dead; our task is to revivify life that has passed away. We know that ghosts cannot speak until they have drunk blood; and the spirits which we evoke demand the blood of our hearts. We give it to them gladly; but if they then abide our question, something from us has entered them; something alien, that must be cast out, cast out in the name of truth![79]

Gomperz, however, had had a different idea:

> The blood that we infuse in the shades of the past so that they speak to us is drawn from our own veins. The historian, to resuscitate before himself and others that which is dead, has no other means than analogy.[80]

In the process of bringing life to a dead past, there was nothing we could do *but* transfuse some of our own blood. The necessary price of historical work was in fact animation of that past with a part of the present. When that past spoke, it was a form of ventriloquism – but partial ventriloquism was not the same as pure projection. Ventriloquism could also speak the truth, if the voices were in chorus.

For Timpanaro, these Enlightenment classicists (broadly conceived) were models of such intellectual communion across time. This communion was always, at base, possible for Timpanaro and his classicists because similar biological conditions of humans across time enabled affinities: nervous temperaments could provide tunnels between

---

79   Ulrich von Wilamowitz-Moellendorf, *Greek Historical Writing, and Apollo: Two Lectures Delivered before the University of Oxford, June 3 and 4, 1908*, trans. Gilbert Murray, Oxford, 1908, 25. See also Robert Fowler, 'Blood for the Ghosts: Wilamowitz in Oxford', *Syllecta Classica* 20 (2009): 171–213. Fowler (n61) also points out the commonness of the trope in contemporary German philology.

80   Theodor Gomperz, *Essays und Erinnerungen*, Stuttgart, 1905, 139; discussed by Timpanaro at *AF*, 432.

temporally disconnected figures; the biological continuity of humans across time enabled us moderns to still communicate with Homer.[81] But the classicists also converged with their objects of study in other ways. They all ported with them what contemporary scholars might write off as heavy ideological 'bias'. But that bias was the cognitive instrument allowing them to receive and impart truths in the world. Gomperz was one of the first to see the Enlightenment elements inherent in early Greek culture, only because he was an Enlightenment thinker himself.[82] Leopardi's illness and frailty did not give him reason for unnecessary pessimism; rather, they clued him in to pessimism as the only reasonable worldview to tackle the inevitability of decline and death. As Timpanaro said in his exchange with Girolamo De Liguori, ideological sympathy with Leopardi did not mean distorting him, but appreciating what was new in him. A similar ideological slant keyed you into Leopardi's truth and novelty, just as a positioning on the official left like Umberto Carpi's, or an ideological reserve like that of literary critic Mario Fubini (1900-1977), disqualified them from truly 'getting' Leopardi.[83] In fact, in Timpanaro's scheme, an encompassing passion for an author was absolutely necessary for good scholarship on them: if you wanted to appreciate a Leopardi, you could not be too mysticising, like the obscurantist and modish literary critic Franco Fortini; nor could you be too professorial, like PCI literary critics such as Carpi and Alberto Asor Rosa.[84] Timpanaro also allowed for this truth to operate even in scholarship proper: he took great interest in Arnaldo Momigliano's point about contemporary interests of the historian enabling (rather than blocking) discoveries about the past.[85] As Timpanaro said of the French Marxist and philosopher Jean Fallot's take on his favourite ancient philosopher Epicurus, 'Enthusiasm indeed sharpens rather than dulls the interpreter's gaze.'[86] Academic distance was a lie. In order to see what was there, one had to invest, to disagree, to engage.

---

81   *OM*, 50; *OM*, 52.

82   *AF*, 432.

83   S.T. to Girolamo De Liguori, 1 July 1973; S.T. to Liana Cellerina, 23 October 1975; S.T. to Giuseppe Pacella, 13 June 1978; S.T. to Sergio Solmi, 12 January 1967.

84   S.T. to Romano Luperini, 5 February 1976; S.T. to Girolamo De Liguori, 1 February 1981.

85   S.T. to Arnaldo Momigliano, 12 December 1972.

86   *VR*, 92.

It is this deep emotional and intellectual investment that forms the backbone of Timpanaro's best scholarship on 'Enlightenment classicism' – and the tool enabling his generation of two other spiritual forebears predating the nineteenth century. Relatively late in his career, Timpanaro applied his own Enlightenment commitment to accessible learning and broad diffusion of ideas by producing two 'divulgatory' editions of crucial texts in the *illuminismo* tradition. The first was from the Enlightenment proper: the Baron d'Holbach's *Il buon senso* (*Good Sense*), a popular work articulating a radical version of atheism and materialism. The second was from antiquity: Cicero's *On Divination*, a two-book philosophical dialogue containing a defence and repudiation of the practice of interpreting the future from various kinds of natural portent. We often get the sense that for Timpanaro, as for his mother, staking out an anti-clerical fury was as important an element of social-ism as anything – and in these two works, Timpanaro fully bulked out his case against religion through translation and interpretation of pioneers in that struggle.[87] But these later works of Timpanaran Enlightenment pushed the cause forward in other ways too.

Timpanaro was drawn to Holbach in general as a thinker encapsulat-ing and inspiring many of his own political and ethical convictions, both in the content of his thought and the way he disseminated it. Holbach often removed himself from any possibility of contemporary fame in preference for a posthumous truth, by publishing anonymously and ascribing false publication dates (making himself, in some sense, artificially 'fuori del suo tempo'); his modest packaging of ideas – a 'renunciation of individualism' – was also about caring solely for the content of those ideas and removing the ego invested in them.[88] That mode of course resonated with Timpanaro's self-minimising and world-focussing ways. But the content itself was the proper ideological catnip: Timpanaro relished, for example, Holbach's exposition of human knowl-edge as involving a significant level of passivity, of response to external stimuli, oppositional grist against any idealist delusions about the trium-phant supremacy of the human mind to apprehend the world.[89] But, apart from this general and extensive meeting of minds between these

---

87   S.T. to Grazia Cherchi, 13 January 1979.
88   *BS*, xxii–xxiii.
89   *BS*, xxxviii.

authors, Timpanaro felt especially close to *Il buon senso* as a special case. This was not only because it was an undervalued work, with no edition produced since the nineteenth century – Timpanaro, as we have seen, was an aficionado of the underdogs of intellectual history – but also because it was a tract programmatically lacking *originality*.[90] It was a rehashing and refining – in Timpanaro's opinion, a much more rigorous and clear version – of Holbach's more 'academic' magnum opus, *The System of Nature*.[91] *Il buon senso* was a kind of radical articulation of the atheism and materialism of *The System*, but designed to be intelligible to a much broader audience. For Timpanaro, as we have seen, originality meant little. The value of *Il buon senso* lay more in its Enlightenment content, but also in its accessible framing thereof. Transparency and truth mattered more than innovation – a philological principle if ever there was one.

A similar pattern of general and particular sympathy holds for Timpanaro when it comes to Cicero and the *On Divination*. Timpanaro pointed to Cicero's *illuminismo neoaccademico* (neoacademic Enlightenment) obtaining at a cultural moment receptive to attacks on superstition.[92] He singled out his anti-dogmatism, his respect for opposing arguments, his romanisation of Greek thought as essentially a way of sending it in an Enlightenment direction, his dug-in position as a rationalising antagonist against the mystical elements in Stoicism.[93] But the *On Divination* is also a particularly forceful embodiment of those principles. In fact, it models very elegantly the mode of open-minded, honest, and firm disagreement which Timpanaro both inherited from Pasqualian philology and located in the Enlightenment.[94] In the first book of *On Divination*, Cicero ascribed the apology for divination practices to his brother; in the second, the case against it comes straight from the mouth of Cicero himself. For Timpanaro, this is a crucial ethical balance: permitting airtime to a dialectic opponent, representing their views honestly,

---

90 *BS*, xviii, xxvi; S.T. to Fabio Minazzi, 5 August 1985.
91 *BS*, xvii.
92 *DD*, lxxiv.
93 *DD*, xxiii, lxxxiii; *NC*, 261–2.
94 As, for instance, in the harsh critical voice of the later Holbach (*BS*, xxii). The culture of dialogue also came from the Florentine Faculty of Letters environment: see Antonio Rotondò, 'Sebastiano Timpanaro e la cultura universitaria fiorentina della seconda metà del Novecento', in Ghidetti and Pagnini, *Sebastiano Timpanaro*, 35.

but also not being afraid to tear them apart. Timpanaro invested so heavily in this proto-Enlightenment version of Cicero that he scythed through
a set of recent anglophone scholarship on the dialogue locating a post-
modern erosion of certainty in its ideological orientation (or disorienta-
tion) – did Cicero balance the for and against with equal weight, and thus
opt for neither? No, said Timpanaro: there was a clear Enlightenment
position here. Cicero meant what he said, disagreed with views he
opposed, without ever straying into the dogmatic.[95]

A striking common thread connecting these Enlightenment classicist precursors to the real deal (Leopardi, Giordani, etc.) expounded by
Timpanaro earlier in his career is not just ideological stance, though
they do all share rough compositions of atheism, materialism, anti-
superstition, and democratic or divulgating modes of presentation. It is
also the fact that these ideological stances have been written off in intellectual history by dubious biographical sleights of hand, psychologising
tricks to corner uncomfortable truths about the world into individual
eccentricities. The trick with Leopardi, as we saw above, was to think of
his worldview as arising from limiting ill health. But Timpanaro noted
similar processes at play for both Holbach and Cicero.[96] For Holbach,
intense grief at the loss of his wife was used to curtail the validity of his
theoretical system – if *Il buon senso* was just the bleakness of a man in
mourning speaking, could it really be taken seriously at an abstract
scientific or philosophical level?[97] Likewise, Cicero's renunciation of
consolation in *On Divination* could have had a prompt in the loss of his
beloved daughter Tulliola immediately before writing.[98] For Timpanaro,
again, these experiences were not grounds for qualifying or relativising
the respective rejections of every foolish philosophical comfort (*ogni
conforto stolto*) found in both Holbach and Cicero.[99] Rather, they were

---

95   See Timpanaro's chapter on *DD* in *NC*.
96   See also Paolo Cristofolini, 'Materialismo e dolore. Appunti sul Leopardismo
filosofico di Sebastiano Timpanaro', in Ghidetti and Pagnini, *Sebastiano Timpanaro*, 354–5.
97   *BS*, lxiv.
98   Preface to *DD*, xxi; see also Cristofolini, 'Materialismo e dolore', 355.
99   *BS*, lxv. This refusal of comfort is an important component of philosophical
pessimism for Timpanaro: see S.T. to Antonio La Penna, 9 January 1981; Cristofolini,
'Materialismo e dolore', 358; cf. Timpanaro's refusal of consolation in Epicurus (Paolo
Mastandrea, '*La filologia di Giacomo Leopardi* (1955)', in Ghidetti and Pagnini,
Sebastiano Timpanaro, 273–4). It is also an element connecting Leopardi and Marx, in
Timpanaro's scheme: see Bufarale, *Sebastiano Timpanaro*, 65.

cognition-enhancing moments, points at which these authors were granted special access to the truth: that there were no other things in heaven and earth to take the pain away, and that the pain should not be thought away, but thought *with* and thought *about*. Thinkers confronting such pain were not blinded by it; their vision was augmented by the ache.

I said above that transparency and truth mattered to Timpanaro, and it is these things that he looked to in his ideological defence of the Enlightenment classicists. But at one point relatively late in his Enlightenment classicists' career, Timpanaro had to intervene more directly on behalf of such principles. I close this chapter with a vignette of Timpanaro putting Enlightenment in action to come to the aid of the poet with whom we opened. It turned out that Leopardi's legacy was being materially threatened by his own biological ancestors. Fortunately, other forms of filiation could save him from his own.

At the end of the 1960s, the National Centre for Leopardi Studies – Italy's big public institution for protecting the Leopardian legacy, based in Leopardi's hometown of Recanati – settled on an ambitious initiative. The plan was to make a new Leopardi shine by publishing ten solid volumes of hitherto-unpublished and rare material. The series was under the directorship of two seasoned Leopardians, Umberto Bosco and Antonio La Penna – the latter, at this stage of their careers, one of Timpanaro's closest companions. Timpanaro and Giuseppe Pacella were entrusted with one of the volumes, the *Scritti filologici*, which came out in 1969 to rave reviews. But Timpanaro and his wife Maria Augusta were charged with another one: the *Dissertazioni filosofiche* and the *Dialogo sull'analisi dell'idee*, both juvenilia, but important pieces to have circulating easily in the public domain, especially for Leopardi scholars interested in the poet's early life and thought. Maria Augusta had worked on and published the only *dissertazione* then available in print.[100] Thus, things were well set up for this marital collaboration to render another big service to their national treasure. With all the other volumes on track to be published sooner rather than later, it was looking like Leopardi would hit a long stride of scholarly attention over the 1970s and beyond.

---

100   S.T. to Umberto Bosco, 28 June 1983.

By 1983, only three out of the ten assigned volumes had been published. Even considering the glacial pace of scholarly time, better tracked in geological ages than calendar years, this was slow. What was blocking the traffic? Timpanaro, bursting with frustration, finally cracked, writing an expose in *Il Ponte* (a key journal of the Tuscan intelligentsia) about how things had gone wrong with the project.[101] We were not talking scholarly lassitude or over-subscription. In fact, the problem was a rather more sordid affair of private profit being put above public benefit. The first two volumes in the series had been entrusted to Walter Binni, due to produce the *Puerilia poetici* and the *Discorsi sacri*, and the Timpanaros, due for their *Dissertazioni filosofiche* and *Dialogo sull'analisi dell'idee*. It turned out that the Leopardi family – still actively invested in exploiting their distant forebear for personal gain, long after he was no longer around to be sickened by their cynical profiteering – still owned autographed copies of all of those works. Even though the family had made a commitment to the Centre to allow those writings to be published for the first time under the agreed, official plan, they also agreed *another* publication separately, with the private publisher Bompiani, under the editorship of Maria Corti. This private deal no doubt put money directly in the pocket of the Leopardi family; whereas the public deal under the aegis of the Centre would not have earned them anything at all. The private arrangement was looking like it would upstream the public one, because Corti was set to publish before Binni and the Timpanaros could reasonably finish their projects. This also rendered the later publication a less attractive prospect, both for the editors – why publish something that's just been published? – and for the publisher – would the duplicate sell? It seemed that Corti and Bompiani would get the finders' fee, and this old aristocratic family would see some money in the bank – and in the end, what did a small act of pocket-lining matter, if the result of publication was the same?

But the result was not the same. Corti only published the *Puerilia poetici* and *Discorsi sacri*; she did not get to the Timpanaros' domain. But by the time that had become clear, it was too late. Years had passed. The Timpanaros' scholarly schedule was full with other matters – and

---

101   Sebastiano Timpanaro, 'Come nel 1983 si può impedire la pubblicazione di importanti inediti leopardiani', *Il Ponte* 39 (1983): 340–5.

the momentum had been sapped.[102] But the work still had to be done, even if the Timpanaros no longer had the zest for it. The series editor Umberto Bosco kept nudging the Timpanaros to finish the project after the *Il Ponte* piece came out, but Timpanaro demurred, citing lack of motivation. Interestingly, however, the *Il Ponte* piece had done its job as a call to arms. The PCI newspaper *L'Unità* announced in July 1983 that it would publish the missing writings, thanks to the help of an 'enterprising collaborator' who leaked the relevant text. Timpanaro chased this up quickly by writing to Bosco and assuaging his suspicions – Timpanaro would never resort to underhand ways, and what was more, he would never collaborate with the PCI and its rag.[103] But for Timpanaro, the quick publication of these long-overdue pieces was now the point. He said as much in another piece in *Panorama* dated 5 September 1983, in which he called for other takers to publish the writings in a timely fashion.[104] Bosco still tried to inveigle Timpanaro to publish with the Centre at the end of October, and encouraged him to find a younger collaborator if Maria Augusta was now too occupied with other things.[105] But the last-ditch request fell on deaf ears. Timpanaro had used the best of the press's harsh glare to flush these words out into the open, even if he would not be the one to finish the job.

The affair dragged on and got uglier. The Leopardi family took umbrage at Timpanaro's 'calumnies' about profiteering. In their version, there was no legal impediment to Timpanaro or anyone else publishing the material. All they owned were the autographs, not the copyright.[106] Timpanaro hit back with a final dig at them: even if they did not own the copyright, they *did* use their presence on the directors' committee of the Centre to issue a veto and divert the rights of publication to Bompiani and Maria Corti. And it was hard to see why they would do that, save for financial motives.[107] But, apart from restating the case against the Leopardi family, this final reply of Timpanaro's is valuable for showing the intellectual

102   S.T. to Umberto Bosco, 1 October 1983.

103   S.T. to Umberto Bosco, 28 July 1983.

104   In the Timpanaro archive, this is attached to the letter S.T. to Umberto Bosco, 1 October 1983.

105   Umberto Bosco to S.T., 28 October 1983.

106   Sebastiano Timpanaro, 'Prosaiche meschinità attorno a Giacomo Leopardi', *Belfagor* 39 (1984): 104–5.

107   Ibid., 108.

stakes of the affair. He ended it not with a final spray of asperity but a gesture of thanks to Margherita Hack, director of the Trieste Astronomical Observatory, for showing what the publication of these writings actually meant for our view of Leopardi. Commenting on Leopardi's *Dissertazione sopra l'astronomia*, written when the poet was thirteen, Hack marvelled at the sophistication of the ideas, and the fact that they were completely up to date with, and on top of, the latest science on the stars. That astronomical knowledge would later become a source of poetic inspiration to Leopardi; and Timpanaro doffed his hat to Hack for apprehending better than many more literary scholars a key feature of his Leopardi, 'the union, free from contradictions, between an Enlightenment search for the truth and a high and tragic poetic and moral inspiration'.[108] In other words, what these earliest works revealed was a precocious Enlightenment poet in the making. They were a tool in the struggle for the scientific, rationalist, progressive essence of Leopardi, a cause behind which Timpanaro had put his entire being. They needed to be in the world to defend that essence and the principles behind those adjectives.

Ultimately, this affair with the Leopardi family tripped a nerve for Timpanaro, not just because of his protectiveness of the poet, nor because of scholarly ego and direct investment in the issue, nor gall at the high-handed treatment by snooty old money; he was piqued because this behaviour was a threat to the Enlightenment project he held so dear. The threat concerned access to and ownership of knowledge: writings like this should not be the property of, nor subject to the mildest interventions or vetoes of, a private family. They should belong to the public domain of scholarship. They should be out in the open and available for discussion, unobstructed by back room deals. Enlightenment meant knowledge should be visible and *public*. But this type of intrigue was also a threat to Timpanaro's Enlightenment principles because of the *content* it concealed. It kept us from seeing the first fruits of the young Leopardi, himself so obviously and essentially a *product* of Enlightenment in these early writings. They were another point for a Timpanaran Leopardi deeply infused with science – the science of the stars, no less. The world needed to know that Leopardi had been turned towards it from a very early age.

~

---

108   Ibid., 111.

Timpanaro's intervention in the Leopardi family affair shows just how much he cared for the ongoing exposure and reception of these Enlightenment classicists. Timpanaro got many things from this nineteenth-century tradition, or recognised many of its bearers' qualities as his own: an uncomfortable, slanted relationship to dominant thought – no organic intellectuals they; a way of accessing the friction in intellectual history, rather than systematising it into oblivion; a standing outside of time, and a rejection of an idea's contemporary palatability coming at the cost of truth and honesty; a way of being both ahead of the curve and behind the times simultaneously; a prioritisation of the clear diffusion of ideas in accessible prose; a stand against religion and superstition, and a push for a lean materialism wherever possible; and active intervention through the press to defend those principles and patrimony where necessary. The next chapter will drill deeper into the materialist-pessimist legacy Timpanaro claimed from Leopardi and the rest of this enlightened crowd.

4

A Material Boy

Timpanaro's name pricked up the ears of the English left via two relatively famous polemics written in the political foment of the late 1960s and early '70s. The first, this chapter's subject, was *On Materialism*;[1] the second, subject of the next chapter, was *The Freudian Slip*. These two works are, in certain ways, very different: the first a spirited defence of scientific materialism originally penned for an 'in-group' of the radical left, the second a bestselling evisceration of Freudian psychoanalysis aimed at a popular audience. But together, they form the beating heart of a unified project at the dead centre of Timpanaro's career: nothing short of an attempt to put the 'materialism' back into 'historical materialism'. We saw in the introduction that Timpanaro was profoundly allergic to idealism, the philosophical view of the world which at best equated consciousness with reality, and at worst elevated the former above the latter. Timpanaro's allegiance was, contrarily, to philosophical materialism, which privileged physical matter as the most fundamental layer of the world and treated the phenomena of consciousness as dependent on material (biological and physical) processes, not the other way round. As we saw of the classic gesture opening the book, in which ego was subordinated to the world, for Timpanaro it was always a case of matter over mind.

---

1   Chapters 1, 2, and 3 of *Sul materialismo* first published in *Quaderni Piacentini* 28 (1966): 76–97; 32 (1967): 115–26; *Nuovo Impegno* 2 (1967–68): 54–66.

So where had the world's materialism gone? In Timpanaro's view, leftist organisations both Old and New had lost their materialist bearings by the mid-1960s.[2] Western Marxism had split into two major camps, neither of which Timpanaro was particularly comfortable with, and both of which served to condition his energetic apology for materialism. On the one side, to the right, the PCI were pegged to toeing the line of Moscow and rapidly dissolving into a state-capitalist contingent of cheerleading reformists, and to using anti-materialist logic of so-called 'dialectic' to mask the embarrassing truth.[3] I will expand on this below: Timpanaro's attack on the dialectic is one of the things that makes him most heterodox, not to say heretical, as a Marxist thinker. On the other side, the organisations of the radical left were starting to dilute intellectually certain components of Marxism that were unreceptive to their wishful thinking, and yoking Marxism to certain theoretical systems alien to it: Freudian psychoanalysis, structuralism, and phenomenology, to name a few.[4] Timpanaro viewed this double-dip dilution of Marxism as a betrayal of the non-negotiable essence of Marxism, namely materialism, by subbing in a concomitant helping of idealist guff.[5] Timpanaro's work on materialism was thus another attempt at a major correction: a

---

2 Timpanaro pointed out that anti-materialism actually joined Stalinism to Western Marxism (Domenico Losurdo, 'Materialismo della prima e materialismo della seconda natura. Rileggendo Timpanaro che legge Marx e Engels', in Nuccio Ordine [ed.], *La lezione di un maestro: Omaggio a Sebastiano Timpanaro*, Naples, 2010, 120). On the lack of materialism in any of the various Italian brands of Marxism by the mid-1960s: S.T. to Cesare Cases, 24 January 1963. On Timpanaro's minoritarian left position defending a non-dogmatic Leninism against the *PCI* on one side, voluntaristic avant-garde on the other: Emanuele Narducci, 'Sebastiano Timpanaro', *Belfagor* 40, no. 3 (1985): 291.

3 Gian Mario Cazzaniga, 'Timpanaro fra Marx e Leopardi', in Riccardo Di Donato (ed.), *Il filologo materialista. Studi per Sebastiano Timpanaro*, Pisa, 2003, 166; Narducci, 'Sebastiano Timpanaro', 305. The irony in the reception of Timpanaro's materialism work was that it seemed to gain more traction in PCI circles than anywhere else on the left, because it ended up chiming with the PCI vision of Lenin as sober 'professor of physics': see S.T. to Valentino Gerratana, 9 June 1971; S.T. to Attilio Chitarin, 13 May 1972; S.T. to Luciano Della Mea, 15 July 1973.

4 *LF*, 181.

5 On Timpanaro's vision of a general anti-materialist contemporary Italian left, which extended effectively to the larger anti-materialist bias of the entire twentieth century, see Luca Bufarale, *Sebastiano Timpanaro: L'inquietudine della ricerca*, Pistoia, 2022, 85–6.

philosophical realignment of a tradition he believed to be going astray.

In some ways, as we shall see, this materialism was something fairly new and strange – a distinctively Timpanaran philosophical system. But it was also a kind of philological return to the *old*. Timpanaro lived his Verdi motto about returning to the past as progress when he came to construct his materialist brand: as he said at the end of *On Materialism*, the renovation of socialism should rest on a vision of the originals and the best – Marx, Engels, Lenin, and Trotsky.[6] Timpanaro remained sceptical of any talk of 'reinventing socialism wholly anew'. Such back-to-the-drawing-board principles had the stench of reformism about them. As we have seen, his elegant quip at the end of *On Materialism* is that those who talk of reinventing socialism anew wind up inventing something very old: capitalism.[7] As ever for Timpanaro the materialist philologist, progress was not about invention from scratch. It was about dusting off and restoring the spirit of the original. So, what did Timpanaro's version thereof look like?

The core of Timpanaran materialism was the assertion that there was indeed a *core*: a hard aspect of external reality irreducible to the human mind processing (*not* 'creating') it. The left, according to Timpanaro, was plagued either by the spectre of 'vulgar materialism' or the need to demonstrate one's commitment to avoiding it.[8] One was either stuck with the unimaginative PCI crew piping pieties about the absolute determining power of the economic base over the cultural superstructure; or one was trying to appear intelligent to fellow bourgeois intellectuals by saying it was not that simple, that ideology played a huge role, that human praxis had the power to transform reality. Timpanaro sided with neither. For him, Marxism needed to be supplemented with a strong shot of Leopardian pessimism, a system of thought which took into account not just humanity's conflictual and exploitative economic relationships with each other, but humanity's relationship with a nature

---

6   *OM*, 261.

7   *OM*, 261.

8   *OM*, 29. Cf. Paolo Cristofolini, 'Materialismo e dolore. Appunti sul Leopardismo filosofico di Sebastiano Timpanaro', in Enrico Ghidetti and Alessandro Pagnini (eds), *Sebastiano Timpanaro e la cultura del Secondo Novecento*, Rome, 2005, 348–9; Giulio Lepschy's introduction to *SLO*, 7–8; Bufarale, *Sebastiano Timpanaro*, 74–5.

engineered to stymie it.[9] There was another order of human conditioning completely missed by Western Marxism. Of course, there was a
cultural superstructure determined by the economic base. Timpanaro
often defended this as an Engelsian sine qua non, invoking the famous
passage in the *Anti-Dühring*:

> The economic structure of society always forms the real basis from
> which, in the last analysis, is to be explained the whole superstructure
> of legal and political institutions, as well as of the religious, philo-
> sophical, and other conceptions of each historical period.[10]

Timpanaro's twist was to add a third, complicating and constraining,
term. For the base *and* superstructure also had the cold hard limits of
nature to contend with. Humanity was not just an assemblage of social-
ity but a biological being with a very significant animal part.[11] In a letter
to the palliative physician Franco Toscani, Timpanaro listed the many
forces in the world conditioning us beyond the productive ones: family
and cultural formation, work environment, union experiences, inter-
personal relations, and our physical organism.[12] No matter how high
utopian Marxism could aim in its delivery of full human happiness,
there were certain things simply beyond its grasp: old age, illness, death.
All of these ills resulting from humanity's oppression by nature were
ineliminable for Timpanaro, despite other Marxists protesting that
their number was readily shrinking.[13] So a key job of any Marxism
worth the name should be not to will those things away or pretend they
did not exist, but to accept their ineliminability and predicate a form of
human solidarity on the resistance to the merciless limitations of

---

9   On Timpanaro's Marx-Leopardi combination: S.T. to Giorgio Voghera, 27
December 1969; S.T. to Luciano Della Mea, 1 June 1973; S.T. to Cesare Cases, 28 March
1979. On Leopardi as a way of completing rather than substituting for Marx in
Timpanaro, see Bufarale, *Sebastiano Timpanaro*, 69; cf. Cortesi, introduction to *VR*, xii.
10   Friedrich Engels, introduction to *Anti-Dühring*; Timpanaro's discussion at S.T.
to Antonio Carlo, 14 April 1972; S.T. to Gianni Sofri, 10 April 1969. Timpanaro was
generally critical of anti-materialist sleights of hand in pushing for a non-deterministic
Marx based on unpublished rather than published material (S.T. to Dario Faucci, 13 July
1979).
11   S.T. to Edo Cecconi, 8 March 1993; Cristofolini, 'Materialismo e dolore', 349.
12   S.T. to Franco Toscani, 6 October 1976, 27 October 1976.
13   S.T. to Cesare Cases, 18 December 1964.

nature.[14] Marx needed Leopardi to round out a view of the world that should theoretically seek to eradicate all economically incurred types of suffering, and to philosophically square up to the inevitability of everything else.[15]

This version of Leopardi-enhanced Marxism immediately met with some resistance among Timpanaro's comrades on the left. One of the more controversial points was Timpanaro's separation of the social-economic and the biological planes, which seemed to grate awkwardly with the Marxist truism about the former as ultimate determinant of everything else.[16] The letters feature many attempts, in effect, to re-acquire the territory that Timpanaro had portioned off: the German classical philologist and Marxist Rudolf Führer made the reasonable point that the biological ills that formed the Timpanaran platform, i.e., things like death and disease, were no absolutes; their meaning and impact changed under different social conditions. The scholar of Marxism Valentino Gerratana, too, insisted that these biological problems had a social dimension. Cesare Cases even went one further to take a kind of proto-techno-fixer position and claimed that science had already cured three-quarters of the ills Timpanaro was so worried about, and would continue to do so – the problem under capitalism was the proper distribution of those fixes. All of these objections – if predictable examples of what Timpanaro questioned as the Colletti-style Marxist tendency to reduce the biological to the social – did have some force. But Timpanaro obstinately batted them away.[17] Humans were bumping up against hard limits in the progress of the medical sciences, particularly against degenerative disease; and no matter how much the social inflected the meaning of the biological, the biological would continue to exert its own irremovable weight; the social mediated the biological, yes, but could never completely cancel or transform it.[18] There really was nothing to be done. We might question, with Gerratana, why there was

---

14   *CI*, 178–9; cf. 407.

15   Enrico Ghidetti, 'L'Ottocento di Timpanaro tra illuminismo e classicismo', in Ghidetti and Pagnini, *Sebastiano Timpanaro*, 254.

16   See also Bufarale, *Sebastiano Timpanaro*, 76.

17   See S.T. to Domenico Settembrini, 2 July 1970; Narducci, 'Sebastiano Timpanaro', 290–1.

18   S.T. to Cesare Cases, 12 May 1970; S.T. to Rudolf Führer, 7 October 1971; S.T. to Liana Cellerina, 19 March 1977.

even a need to talk about this. Should not socialism just fix on what was soluble through socio-economic transformation, and ignore what was not?[19] But for Timpanaro, that was not the point: as a philosophy of truth, Marxism had to engage with the whole picture and build into itself a vision of the parts of the world it could not touch.

Of course, it was also matter of debate as to how whole this Timpanaran rounding-out of Marxism and the world actually was. Raymond Williams's thoughtful response to *On Materialism* pointed out that Timpanaro's vision of the world was perhaps too heavily weighted towards the negative and limiting forces acting on human flourishing – there were also, after all, youth, the love of children, health, and sexual love and pleasure, all unalloyed goods of human life ever in operation, countervailing Timpanaro's constants of old age, illness, and death.[20] Williams also took issue with the flattening of 'nature' in *On Materialism* as a kind of 'humanist personification' signifying everything that was not human – bundling together the complex relationships between the external 'nature' that conditions us (the solar system, the atmosphere) and the internal 'nature' that composes us (our bodies, organs, genes).[21] In fact, Timpanaro's reductive Leopardian concept of nature inverted the slightly embarrassing Marxist insistence on human conquest over the natural world. But in Timpanaro's materialist-pessimist view, a dark mirror reversed relations.[22] It was now *us* groaning under the oppression of nature.

For Timpanaro, then, the most broadly determining elements of human existence were the unavoidable forces he gathered beneath the broad-brush 'nature'. Such nature circumscribed human action. A true philosophy of reality had always to factor in the passivity factor in human experience, the situation imposed from without[23] – in Perry Anderson's eloquent paraphrase, 'all that was suffered rather than done'.[24] The conditioning and passivity inherent to human existence

---

19   S.T. to Valentino Gerratana, 26 July 1975.

20   Raymond Williams, 'Problems of Materialism', *New Left Review* 109 (1978): 7, 12.

21   Ibid., 6.

22   Ibid., 8–9.

23   *OM*, 34; cf. S.T. to Giorgio Voghera, 6 February 1967, 28 February 1967.

24   Perry Anderson, 'On Sebastiano Timpanaro', *London Review of Books* 23, no. 9 (May 2001).

might seem somewhat obvious to us, standing as we do in the midst of a wishfully titled late capitalism which shows no real sign of senescence, let alone death. But we should bear in mind the very different political context in which Timpanaro was working in the mid- to late 1960s (when he was writing his first interventions on materialism), and the crucible in which he had been formed. By his own admission, Timpanaro had cut his political teeth in a post-war frenzy of an ascendant left, at which time the realisation of socialism was never for a second in doubt – the only thing in debate was how long that would take.[25] As a committed Marxist with a deeply felt pessimism, then, Timpanaro's job was not to pour cold water over the aspirations of Marxism as a path to communism.[26] On the contrary, his convictions remained, till the very end, firmly anti-capitalist, Leninist, and revolutionary. He rather thought of his ideological correction to and towards materialism as a way of truthfully inscribing the *limits* of Marxism: an honest admission of what Marxism could and could not promise in this world, and a clear articulation of the contents of both categories. Socialism would furnish the economic conditions for full human flourishing, no doubt; communism even more so; but that flourishing would always itself be conditioned by humanity's non-negotiable biological lot, pitched *outside* the remit of political and economic life. To give that biological lot its dues would be not just a way of circumscribing the potential of Marxism but a means of completing it.[27]

In its stripping of the determinants of human existence one stage further back, as it were, Timpanaran materialism was constantly making the variables of life confront and *stand apart* from the non-variables. The method was applied to many different philosophical outlooks on the world. Firstly, Timpanaro's Marx–Leopardi combination tried to correct some of the hardened pieties of Marxist materialism itself, or at least a contemporary version filtered through the Marxist philosopher Lucio

---

25   S.T. to Della Mea, 2 June 1967, 8 December 1968.
26   Timpanaro was drawn to an anti-idealist pessimism from the earliest phase of his formation, even as early as 1948; see Bufarale, *Sebastiano Timpanaro*, 23.
27   S.T. to Sergio Solmi, 3 January 1970; S.T. to Raffaella Solmi, 18 May 1987; S.T. to Edo Cecconi, 8 March 1993. On Timpanaro expanding the conception of Marxism, see S.T. to Claudio Del Bello, 18 March 1971.

Colletti (1924–2001).[28] Timpanaro acknowledged the determining power of economic relationships but added to this the even more fundamental relationship between humans and nature. The economic relationship was a variable that could be removed with the destruction of capitalism; the relationship with nature characterised by illness, old age, and death was an *invariable*, a constant over time, the given which could not be toyed with no matter what Silicon Valley gurus might nowadays claim for the future.[29] Secondly, Timpanaran materialism was in combat with the idealist tradition that would make the world a mere epiphenomenon of the human mind or self. No, Timpanaro said – there was a core of external reality which was irreducible to the mind making sense of it. The mind did not invent this given but passively apprehended it.[30] Now we can fully comprehend the philosophical import of Timpanaro's modesty. For him, the subjectivity of the individual was small fry compared to the vast natural forces conditioning it – so best attend to the things in the world rather than ruminate on the tiny grey matter humming inside one's skull.

Such disregard for the individual self is paired, also, with a scorn for all anthropocentric views of the world, including those within Marxism.[31] Timpanaro never lost his 'cosmic' optics: the universe existed for most of its time very happily without human beings.[32] And, after the final explosion of the sun, in a cosmically brief time scheme, the universe would return to its blessed human-less state. Timpanaro's dramatic pick to illustrate the point was a passage from Engels's *Dialectic of Nature*, in which Engels dwelt with a 'calmly tragic' sense on this crux for life on earth:

> Millions of years may elapse, hundreds of thousands of generations
> be born and die, but inexorably the time will come when the declin-
> ing warmth of the sun will no longer suffice to melt the ice thrusting

28   Narducci, 'Sebastiano Timpanaro', 290–1; Cortesi, introduction to *VR*, xvi–ii.

29   Cf. Anderson, 'On Sebastiano Timpanaro'.

30   This is a point of absolute certainty for Timpanaro's Marxism: objective reality is not a product of human thought (Timpanaro to Gabriella Sica, 23 May 1975).

31   S.T. to Gian Paolo Marchi, 25 October 1985.

32   *OM* 37; Romano Luperini, 'Testimonianza per Timpanaro: Il dibattito sul materialismo e altri ricordi degli anni sessanta e settanta', in Ghidetti and Pagnini, *Sebastiano Timpanaro*, 367.

itself forward from the poles; when the human race, crowding more
and more about the equator, will finally no longer find even there
enough heat for life; when gradually even the last trace of organic
life will vanish; and the earth, an extinct frozen globe like the moon,
will circle in deepest darkness and in an ever narrower orbit about
the equally extinct sun, and at last fall into it. Other planets will have
preceded it, others will follow it; instead of the bright, warm solar
system with its harmonious arrangement of members, only a cold,
dead sphere will still pursue its lonely path through universal space.
And what will happen to our solar system will happen sooner or
later to all the other systems of our island universe; it will happen to
all the other innumerable island universes, even to those the light of
which will never reach the earth while there is a living human eye to
receive it.[33]

This strangely poetic passage (in fact Timpanaro immediately compares
similar phraseology in a contemporary passage of the nineteenth-
century classicising poet Giosuè Carducci) is a prime example of where
Timpanaro went to expunge anthropocentrism from the Marxist tradition. The long view on our solar system, and our universe, was that it is
– like us – earmarked for destruction. And it would happen indepen-
dently of whether a 'living human eye' is there to receive the vision or
not. Though Timpanaro did not comment explicitly on that final flourish, we can infer that the minimised and passive (note the verb 'to
receive') role of human subjectivity spoke volumes to him. This passage
must have given to Timpanaro nothing short of a knowing what was
already known, a philological discovery of Timpanaran materialism
already there, *given*, in Engels.

It is precisely this cosmic view, the dismantling of all things anthropocentric and providential, that Timpanaro saw as Leopardi's gift to
Marxism.[34] When, in the *Antileopardiani*, Timpanaro came to clearly
state the relationship between Leopardi's materialist pessimism and
Marxism itself, he claimed that the productive difference between them
is what made the one work for the other. We should not mildly

33   *OM*, 98–9.
34   Leopardi's refutation of anthropocentrism: *OM*, 20; *CI*, 160. See also Bufarale,
Sebastiano Timpanaro, 61–2.

'reconcile' the two philosophies – again, the rough incompatibilities must be respected – by forcing Leopardi to bear some kind of Marxist message *avant la lettre*. Indeed, Timpanaro resisted importing Marx to Leopardi, as he did in demurring to put his politics into his philology (see this book's conclusion). Leopardi was not a Marxist but a thinker whose philosophy was helpful for nudging Marxism towards a hard-nosed, scientific worldview stripped of any misconceptions that humans were at the core of the cosmos or that history was working for us. Both philosophies should converge on their honest refutation of such comforting lies.[35]

If Timpanaro's materialism sought to point out the invariables beyond the economic sphere, beyond the human self, and beyond humanity as a collective entity stretched across time and space, it also strove to spotlight the world beyond one of the most treasured concepts of historical materialism: the dialectic. This idea – of history as *process*, working itself out through the progressive resolution of contradictions (the most important of which is class struggle) – is something dear to Marxism. Indeed, many thinkers within the Marxist tradition would say that there is no Marxism *without* the dialectic. But to Timpanaro, self-proclaimed advocate of an 'adialectical' and 'vulgar' materialism, the dialectic was a kind of Hegelian cancer which Marxism could and should happily remove, or at least shrink.[36] After the operation, it should feel more itself than ever.

Timpanaro's problems with the dialectic were manifold: for one, he hated the way it implied a providential conception of history, always angling that history towards an ultimate progress.[37] He also resented the abuse of the dialectic as a way of justifying a political

---

35   *AN*, 196.

36   See S.T. to Gian Paolo Marchi, 25 October 1985. According to Cristofolini, 'Materialismo e dolore', 352, Timpanaro thought there was no such thing as a true materialist dialectic – the only possibility was Hegelian – but there are also signs that he considered the worst sense of the dialectic in Marxism a Hegelian 'inheritance', while entertaining the value of other ways in which Marx and Engels used the term, for instance, the historicity of nature, the polemic against social Darwinism, and so on: see *OM*, 91–3, 251; S.T. to Luciano Della Mea, 14 July 1971. Timpanaro also claimed he did not want to get rid of the dialectic altogether but merely to entertain the possibility of other kinds of relationship in reality (S.T. to Lucio Colletti, 25 January 1975).

37   S.T. to Antonio La Penna, 13 December 1975; cf. Bufarale, *Sebastiano Timpanaro*, 80. See also *VR*, 210–11.

stance of 'historic compromise' – making a pact with capitalism as simply one more dialectical stage in the ultimate triumph of socialism, a closet providentialist way of justifying inaction and going with the flow by making a historical moment a necessary phase in a grander scheme.[38] The Hegelian dialectic was essentially a form of 'theodicy' (Luca Bufarale's apt term) for Timpanaro: a piece of metaphysical machinery allowing endless justification of ills by reason of their grander scheme servicing of the Good.[39] The dialectic was like a piece of intellectual elastic allowing one to bend with history in any direction, even when it turned to the right.[40] Timpanaro also bristled at other ways in which the concept was used as a vague and generic evasion, for instance, as an illusory solution to get rid of human unhappiness (for Timpanaro's Leopardian worldview, unriddable), or as a form of intellectual gymnastics used to generate irritating counterintuitive conclusions, as in Adorno's reading of Ugo Foscolo's *Grazie* to argue that the most profound way of doing politics was by *not* doing politics.[41]

But Timpanaro's main gripe with the dialectic was again a branch of his general hostility to 'methodological overreach'. Just as the economic relationships privileged by Marxism could not account for, nor resolve, humanity's hard-wired biological immiseration, so the dialectic could not apply to or explain every single relationship of opposing forces.[42] Nor could dialectical leaps be used as a general rule to chart all patterns of history. Some historical patterns involved non-dialectical destruction, in which the previous element is not swallowed and transformed into something else in its next phase, but eliminated entirely and definitively.[43] One dramatic example would be that end of the solar system,

---

38   Cazzaniga, 'Timpanaro fra Marx e Leopardi', 166; Narducci, 'Sebastiano Timpanaro', 305. On the inherent idealist providentialism of the dialectic: S.T. to Franco Arato, 25 June 1984; S.T. to Fabio Minazzi, 5 August 1985.

39   Bufarale, *Sebastiano Timpanaro*, 80–1.

40   S.T. to Sergio Landucci, 10 July 1963.

41   On the vagueness of the term: S.T. to Christine Buci-Glucksmann, 18 October 1971; S.T. to Enrico Rambaldi, 4 December 1978. Illusory solution to happiness: *CI*, 180–1. Adorno on Foscolo: S.T. to Vigilio Masiello, 10 May 1969.

42   Timpanaro sets out further nuances on some of these different relationships of 'real opposites' in his letter to Lucio Colletti of 25 January 1975, discussed at Bufarale, *Sebastiano Timpanaro*, 81–2.

43   S.T. to Cesare Cases, 15 August 1958; S.T. to Sergio Landucci, July 1962.

which Timpanaro threw up as a challenge to Engels's dialectical thought, something he apparently never properly accounted for.[44] Another would be the number of classical texts we have genuinely lost without a trace, gaping lacunae particularly visible to Timpanaro as a philologist.[45] Timpanaro borrowed an economic term to capture these absolute cases of non-dialectical destruction: *perdità secche* (deadweight losses), that is, market losses which are to the detriment of both consumer and producer, where nobody wins.[46] The evolution of language, too, was a historical pattern that refused to obey the dialectic – and to apply it in this case would simply be an invalid process of anthropomorphising (and politicising) the cosmos.[47] The dialectic was something that only functioned in very optimal conditions; in fact, much of history and reality functioned non-dialectically. As a posited system, it was a little like Lachmann's method: heuristically useful, even fully functional in certain rare cases – but mostly unable to straighten out the mess of a Pasqualian universe characterised by constant 'contamination'.

The dialectic was not the only beloved Marxist hobby horse Timpanaro took to task. Ever the splitter over the lumper, his thinking on the notion of 'totality' is broadly comparable. Totality has a long and complex life in Marxist (particularly Western Marxist) discourse, but for Timpanaro it had the Hegelian ring of picturing the world and consciousness as a unified whole.[48] In an exchange with his comrade and Germanist Cesare Cases, Timpanaro questioned the utility of a totalising imposition *of totality* across the board. Reality had to be granulated into its various relationships: there were systems that looked like totalities, but there were also aggregates, composites, mixtures. Some systems featured parts which were bound together strictly and followed the logic of totality. Others had parts loosely tied.[49] Whether in nature or human institutions, there were differing degrees of cohesion and independence among individual elements. It was arbitrary to privilege

44   Losurdo, 'Materialismo', 123–4.

45   S.T. to Enrico Rambaldi, 7 January 1979.

46   *VR*, 211; Cortesi, introduction to *VR*, xliii–iv.

47   S.T. to Sergio Landucci, July 1962.

48   On the history of the concept, see Martin Jay, *Marxism and Totality: The Adventures of a Concept from Lukács to Habermas*, Berkeley, CA, 1986.

49   S.T. to Cesare Cases, 12 October 1970.

the organic or systematic over the 'atomistic' as models of natural relationship. Sometimes, things held together in tension and had an impact on one another as they bumped around. Sometimes, they roamed freely in blissful ignorance of the others' presence. As usual with Timpanaro, a commitment to case-by-case empiricism toppled a Marxist article of faith, however piously observed it may have been. There was no reason to opt for totality a priori over other models of system operative in reality – just as there were patterns of time and history left unexplained by the dialectic.

Next in the firing line of load-bearing Marxist concepts squared up by Timpanaran materialism might be that of superstructure. As we saw above, Timpanaro agreed with the determining power of economic base over cultural superstructure, even as he outflanked both by the introduction of a higher- (or lower-) level determinant: the human–nature relationship. But he also took issue with the idea of a superstructure *solely* set by the economic base. Timpanaro – standing deep in a long Italian tradition of dialogue with the whole of European intellectual history – asserted, quite rightly, that it was not just political economy deciding the shape of culture but also the past. Ideas generate ideas.[50] Present culture was also a product of past antecedents. Timpanaro was sensitive to critiques from the left which accused him of deploying a sort of 'parthenogenetic' type of intellectual history insufficiently attentive to historical and economic determinants. When Antonio La Penna put this problem to him, Timpanaro pointed to several moments in his work when he did play up such determinants – for instance, on romanticism's role as a bourgeois block to revolution, or the economic context of *mezzadria* (sharecropping) behind the *Anthology* moderates in the *Antileopardiani* (or, we might add, the critique of Freud as a mere historical reflex of bourgeois anxieties; see chapter 5).[51] But with Timpanaro, one did not have to go far to see the 'cultural' causes of culture working just as efficiently as the economic. Timpanaro himself embodied that truth as a thinker: his thought was just as vividly determined by eighteenth-century Enlightenment or its nineteenth-century

---

50   Timpanaro showed this to be an Engelsian position: *OM*, 115. Cf. S.T. to Antonio La Penna, 13 December 1975.
51   S.T. to Antonio La Penna, 13 December 1975; cf. S.T. to Romano Luperini, 29 April 1968.

continuators as it was by the particular historical-political juncture of anti-capitalist struggle in post-war Italy.[52] To privilege one or the other context would be to underrepresent the complexities of intellectual genesis. And, if a single brain could have so many determinants both material and intellectual, spanning so many centuries, one struggles to imagine what it is to fully account for the multi-level cultural assemblage we call 'superstructure'.

The last important Marxist category subjected to Timpanaran scrutiny might be ideology. Timpanaro's circles, as well as European Marxism in general in the 1960s and '70s, were full of unreflective critiques of science as a mere reflex and reproducer of bourgeois capitalist ideology.[53] Science was too often invoked as just another way of naturalising and servicing capitalism. Such critiques had special pungency in Italy, where the predominance of idealism and humanism in the educational tradition already inscribed a certain level of suspicion towards science into the general intellectual culture.[54] Timpanaro thought that these critiques were senseless, especially now that they had become automated and parrot-like. Again, he drew a hard line: science was not reducible to pure ideology.[55] Scientific results were independent of the ideological orientation of the humans that arrived at them or deploy them. They were external to ideology; they held *no matter what*. Marx and Engels, Timpanaro claimed, knew this well: they themselves made a distinction between the evolutionary theories of Darwin – indisputably, scientifically *true* as long as they continued to fit the evidence – and the ideological perversions of *social* Darwinism made to inflect the theories into reactionary politics.[56] It was of the highest importance to Timpanaro that science be protected from the empty pot-shots of so-called Marxist ideology critique. Again, any Marxism worth its name would need to be

---

52   On Timpanaro's vivid and immediate engagement with past thinkers, see Anderson, 'On Sebastiano Timpanaro'.

53   *SM*, xxv; *LF*, 149; *AN*, 173. Timpanaro appreciates Lenin's clear distinction between science and ideology (Bufarale, *Sebastiano Timpanaro*, 84).

54   See Glenn Most's introduction to *GLM*; S.T. to Giulio Bollati, 3 May 1950; S.T. to Calogero Randazzo, 18 January 1997.

55   S.T. to Paolo Flores d'Arcais, 20 April 1972; S.T. to Emilio Bigi, 13 July 1975; S.T. to Luciano Canfora, 16 September 1976; S.T. to Giulio Maccacaro, 26 June 1976.

56   S.T. to Valentino Gerratana, 14 March 1971.

founded on the principles of science.[57] And any socialist society worth its name would make as generous a space for doctors, engineers, and scientists as it would for Frankfurt school critics. As Timpanaro wrote at the end of the preface to the first edition of *Sul materialismo*, if the Canadian communist doctor Norman Bethune had told his sick Chinese comrades that they were unwell because of imperialism, and if he thought his revolutionary activity could be enhanced by withdrawing from medicine, his value to the cause of revolution would have been immeasurably less.[58]

All of these Timpanaran ripostes carved out the limits of theory to explain the world: where political economy breaks down and biology takes over; where the human self, and the human in general, ends and the dominant forces of external reality begin; what historical patterns the dialectic cannot capture, or what kinds of relationships the totality cannot figure; what generates the superstructure beyond its economic base; and the core of science unimpeachable by, unyielding to, ideology. All of these things add up to the assertion, in Timpanaran materialism, of what we might call the *autonomy* of reality: the huge, indeed preponderating proportion of the world that is irreducible to human relationships, behaviour, and thought.[59] For Timpanaro, any theory of the world, any description of reality, had to take all of this into account. Marxism, as the best explanatory theory we have, had to expand itself to take notice.

If Timpanaran materialism has so far come across as negative or antagonistic – variously taking issue with Marxism itself *and* the idealistic elements infiltrating its twentieth-century evolution – that is because it is. But antagonism and polemic, as we have seen, were not just unnecessary spice in the mix, or unavoidable flavours of the political and intellectual cultures in which Timpanaro moved; they were absolutely vital ingredients of a worldview seeking, programmatically, to preserve *conflict* as an antidote to the pallid accommodations of political compromise, which had betrayed revolutionary politics within Timpanaro's

---

57   Timpanaro aimed to restore the severed link between praxis and science; hence the danger of combining anti-scientific psychoanalysis with anti-scientific Marxism (*LF*, 9).

58   *SM*, xxix.

59   Cf. S.T. to Vigilio Masiello, 10 May 1969.

living generation. Timpanaro's antagonism sought to preserve a sense of cultural history as a venue of struggle. It was a reprising, too, of the originally antagonistic spirit of Leopardian pessimism: a kind of constitutional resistance to any accommodations with the world as it was, a striving 'non-acceptance of reality'.[60] Just as Timpanaro found it urgent to keep alive the alternatives and challenges to romanticism, so he always fought to maintain a sense of contradiction within history's individuals. As we saw, and as we will see again, Timpanaro was tickled by culture and individuals as sites of conflict: he was piqued, for instance, by the tonal variations in Carlo Bini's prison manuscript, rolling between vehement, ironic, and stringently reasoned; and these variations represented burs in the Binian personality that should not be smoothed over (see chapter 7). Contradiction, for Timpanaro, was not a target for resolution but a motive force acting within all of us, at all periods of history. As we saw in the introduction (and will return to in the conclusion), Timpanaro himself self-identified as a 'non-integrated' personality, whose various aspects sat together not as organic totality but in mild tension at worst, mutual indifference at best. Timpanaro identified *On Materialism* itself as born from one of these generative conflicts, namely the need to reconcile and synthesise two imperfectly juxtaposed elements in his philosophical make-up – Marxism and Leopardism.[61] Yet, if Timpanaro was up front about the contradictions within, he was also remarkably consistent about the things *out there* that his materialism vehemently opposed. As Leopardi and Giordani stood aloof and against their dominant intellectual culture of romanticism, so Timpanaro and his materialism defined themselves against related phenomena: idealism in the philosophical tradition, and voluntarism, its reflex in the political sphere.[62]

Timpanaro's gripes with idealism were deeply felt. His stake against it was almost Oedipal, though he would surely cringe at this bastardised Freudianism. Timpanaro's father had been a card-carrying idealist, believing in the possibility of reaching happiness by transcending the empirical ego. Timpanaro often talked of long debates with his father

---

60   S.T. to Silvano Piccoli, 28 April 1989; this attraction to agonistic pessimism also explains Timpanaro's love for Holbach: Narducci, 'Sebastiano Timpanaro', 311.

61   S.T. to Scevola Mariotti, 11 September 1971.

62   On the close relationship between the two, see Bufarale, *Sebastiano Timpanaro*, 79.

along these lines when asked to trace his intellectual genealogy.[63] As we saw in the introduction, the Timpanaro family also benefitted materially (if not willingly) from the idealist-fascist philosophical–political axis of the 1930s: Timpanaro Sr owed his appointment to a position at the Domus Galilaeana in Pisa to the direct intervention of Giovanni Gentile. There was thus a fairly hefty score of guilt to settle against this philosophical tradition, when the materialist finally found his colours.[64] It was perhaps this recent personal history of convergence between Fascism and idealism that made Timpanaro invest so heavily in the inherent ideological valences of idealism versus materialism: when Cesare Cases objected that these philosophies did not have necessary political content, Timpanaro was quick to disagree.[65] For Timpanaro, materialism was the *only* possible basis for the right kind of Marxism. An idealist Marxism did not compute.

Timpanaro's problems with idealism were several, and regularly revisited. First, there was the annoyance – common to structuralism, too – of what we might call idealism's argumentative defect: the way it denied the separability of phenomena, wiped away distinctions between things, and dissolved the fine-grained world into unwieldy (and meaningless) overarching categories and concepts.[66] Timpanaro's joke with Cesare Cases about teeth had structuralism as its target, but it could equally be levelled at idealism: a structuralist approach to dentistry would be to say that you could not just extract the problematic tooth; you have to extract them all because all teeth are connected.[67] A joke it is, but, in essence, it captured one of Timpanaro's central problems with this mode of thinking. Second, there was the objection we might call historical: idealism posited the spirit (or mind, perception, or sensation) as primary, but how could it account for the fact that these things could

---

63   S.T. to Remo Ceserani, 25 May 1979; S.T. to Giuseppe Cambiano, 5 July 1979; S.T. to Luigi Blasucci, 10 July 1987; cf. S.T. to Giorgio Voghera, 27 December 1969; and cf. Bufarale, *Sebastiano Timpanaro*, 22, who points out the role of Timpanaro's father, but also early encounters with anti-idealist philosophers like Giuseppe Rensi.

64   S.T. to Giovanni Lista, 29 October 1983; S.T. to Pietro Polito, 31 March 1994; S.T. to Antonio Russi (n.d., numbered 3 in the Timpanaro archive).

65   S.T. to Cesare Cases, 5 February 1970, on which see Bufarale, *Sebastiano Timpanaro*, 77; cf. S.T. to Giulio Lepschy, 14 May 1971.

66   Sebastiano Timpanaro, 'Giorgio Fano', *Belfagor* 19, no. 4 (1964); S.T. to Luciano Canfora, 16 September 1976.

67   S.T. to Cesare Cases, 26 July 1970.

never be chronologically or *historically* primary, since inorganic matter occupied the world long before the human mind started pumping it through the processor?[68] Third, the cognitive objection: idealism did not account for the passive aspect of knowledge, the 'given' that is arranged by our consciousness but not created by it. Objective limits quite quickly overpowered idealism's expansive sense of human freedom.[69] Knowledge was not merely a subsidiary of praxis; it was also a passivity, a getting to grips with everything which is not dependent on us or created by us.[70] For Timpanaro, idealism was flawed insofar as it clumped the universe together arbitrarily and claimed an unworkable priority of the human mind, not just in making sense of the world but in creating it ex nihilo. As we have seen, Timpanaro had no truck with such anthropocentrism. The world was mostly beyond us. Lastly, Timpanaro also experienced a kind of aesthetic repulsion to what we might call the general *snobbery* of idealism. He criticised his doyen Giorgio Pasquali for his idealist blind spot in only recognising cultural traffic going one way, trickling down from high culture to the people, rather than entertaining the possibility that cultural transfer also went the opposite way.[71] Idealism tended to skew the world towards the high, the ethereal – but the low and the everyday needed their dues too.

These frustrations with idealism played out visibly in Timpanaro's critique of Gramsci. While Timpanaro was full of praise for Gramsci as a historical and political thinker, he made no bones pointing out his limitations, insofar as he served as a bridge to the recent excesses of Western Marxism, and as a type of vessel for the smuggling of an idealism into the ranks of the left.[72] Unlike the worst of the idealists, Gramsci, according to Timpanaro, did not deny the existence of external reality; but he did make that reality into a passive object of human

---

68   S.T. to Giorgio Fano, 17 August 1955, 27 April 1957.

69   S.T. to Giorgio Voghera, 6 February 1967.

70   S.T. to Anna Fano, 7 February 1967; S.T. to Franco Toscani, 23 August 1977. See also Timpanaro's response to the accusation that he was simply espousing a philosophy of passivity: *OM*, 55, 57; cf. S.T. to Luciano Della Mea, 29 April 1969, 27 March 1976.

71   *AF*, 360.

72   *OM*, 236–8, *VR*, 217; S.T. to Rosario Romeo, 30 October 1956; S.T. to Girolamo De Liguori, 17 May 1980, 1 February 1981; S.T. to Rocco Mario Morano, 22 July 1983 (reprinted in *VR* as chapter 11). For the originality of Timpanaro's position on Gramsci, see Cortesi's introduction to *VR*, xx–xxi.

knowledge–praxis.[73] Reality was real only insofar as it became a property of the human working on it.[74] For Timpanaro, Gramsci's philosophical problem was effectively to colonise Crocean idealism and exploit it for revolutionary purposes.[75] Gramsci took it over by hypostasising the moment of 'praxis', and swelling that praxis as the active human principle over everything: nature was not just a passive object of active human knowledge as it was in Crocean terms, but still, it was no better than an object of transformation under human work.[76] Gramsci put such an accent on the human–active over the nature–passive that he even prognosticated vulcanology would sort out the problem of volcanoes.[77] Timpanaro's Leopardian materialism found this absolutely, unforgivably absurd. Volcanoes could never be fixed by rolling up the sleeves of the human mind and getting down to a good bit of creative problem-solving deep in the earth's crust. Nature remained the resistance point at which humans encountered the sum of their objective limits, met the definitive riposte to the overestimated abilities of their imaginations, hit the wall of objectivity. But this wall could also be a source of cohesive struggle. Gusts of hot ash and torrents of lava would always trump our capacity to understand, act on, and transform them – but in defeat, there was solidarity.[78]

The political manifestation of this idealist current seeping into the left, for Timpanaro, would be *voluntarism*: the idea that the human will is always the dominant factor at both individual and universal levels.[79] Timpanaro thought that idealism had taken Marxism hostage due to the recession of revolutionary expectations. As the objective conditions of revolution fizzled out in the motor of post-war capitalist growth, so the intellectual frontliners of Western Marxism began to take refuge in abstract concepts of 'revolutionary will', and started stalling purely at the

---

73   *OM*, 236.

74   S.T. to Rodolfo Montuoro, 15 February 1981.

75   *AN*, 301; *RV*, 136; cf. Cristofolini, 'Materialismo e dolore', 353.

76   *AN*, 301.

77   *AN*, 308. Timpanaro also criticised Gramsci for insufficient materialism in defining the human solely as an assemblage of social relationships and underestimating its animal part: see *VR*, 138–9; Cortesi, introduction to *VR*, xxiv.

78   *AN*, 309; *CI*, 172, 407.

79   Timpanaro's attacks on voluntarism: S.T. to Domenico Settembrini, 29 January 1969; S.T. to Cesare Cases, 5 February 1970; S.T. to Gian Mario Cazzaniga (n.d., numbered 7 in the Timpanaro archive).

level of superstructural change.[80] Such voluntarism Timpanaro traced back to Gramsci and drew as a through line all the way to vanguard organisations like Lotta Continua: according to this position, we should have faith in the ability of the working class to effect revolution as a pure act of will.[81] For Timpanaro, again, that was nonsense. Lenin himself knew that there would be no revolution without the conditions of economic crisis to precipitate it.[82] There was a reason the working classes were resistant to revolution at this historical moment: relatively prosperous material conditions were blunting their antagonistic edge.[83] Human will, whether individual or collective, was a mere drop in the ocean compared to the vast swells of economy and biology actuating and restricting it.

It was not only at the political level that Timpanaro was opposed to this fetish for free will; his objection was also philosophical and personal. Philosophically, his prose returned several times to the illusion of free will involved in silly historical counterfactuals. For Timpanaro, you could not blame a terrible poet for not writing like Dante.[84] For the same reasons, the moralising castigation of Hitler or the Italian right did not make any sense; if you wanted to haul something over the coals, one should take political *systems* to task, not individuals.[85] Holbach's exposure of the absurdity of free will also resonated with Timpanaro: moral decision-making was not an act of freedom or an unweighted choice, but the result of several impulses warring in our psyches and only, inevitably, the strongest prevailing.[86] This notion of free will as a mere temporary triumph of an internal faction was preserved by Timpanaro right up to one of his very last articles, on Agamemnon's 'choice' to sacrifice Iphigeneia in Aeschylus's *Agamemnon*.[87] Even Freud, as we shall

---

80   S.T. to Domenico Settembrini, 14 December 1969.

81   Voluntarism in Gramsci: S.T. to Rocco Mario Morano, 22 July 1983. Voluntarism in Lotta Continua: S.T. to Luciano Della Mea, 28 November 1970, 3 February 1971; S.T. to Grazia Cherchi, 3 March 1971; S.T. to Giulio Maccacaro, 26 June 1976.

82   S.T. to Domenico Settembrini, 29 January 1969.

83   S.T. to Luciano Della Mea, 6 November 1967, 30 July 1976; S.T. to Giulio Maccacaro, 26 June 1976.

84   Arguments against free will: S.T. to Luciano Della Mea, 28 July 1967; S.T. to Giulio Maccacaro, 26 June 1976.

85   *AN*, 318–19, 325.

86   *BS*, xlii–xliii.

87   Sebastiano Timpanaro, 'Antinomie nell'*Agamennone* di Eschilo', *Giornale Italiano di Filologia*, 1998: 163–6.

see, put the nail in the coffin of free will as a structuring principle of the psyche.[88] But for Timpanaran materialism, there was no time to trumpet our will as a displacement of the divine right of *prima causa* onto ourselves.[89] We were the moved, not the mover.

So much for the philosophical. The personal motive, or perhaps reflex, of Timpanaran antipathy to the will was that he felt his own life to be an embodiment of the will's ultimate subordination. Recall that Timpanaro never worked in or at a university, despite all of his talents and networks of cultural capital weighting him in that direction. As we saw in the introduction, many people read this fact from the outside and creatively aligned it with Timpanaro's politics to make of him a species of honourable refusenik, a man too pure and resistant to be sullied by the inevitable compromises of Italian academia. In other words, people were quick to ascribe Timpanaro's 'outsiderness' to a noble act of *will*. But for Timpanaro himself, this was an alien ascription of intention to a condition that was emphatically *not* of his own choosing: it was merely the result of his prohibitive neurosis forcing him to seek a more introverted career path. In some ways, then, Timpanaro's very life direction became a guarantor to the materialism he had worked up both politically and philosophically:[90] a testament to what was suffered rather than done, a plaque commemorating the weakness of the human will against the natural forces supervening, and then superseding it.

In his correspondence with Ludovico Geymonat (1908–1991; a mathematician, historian of science, and PCI member), Timpanaro reacted in typical style to a too restrictive typology of humankind's relations with the world. According to Geymonat, humans could either know the world or work on it. Timpanaro added a third: to suffer it, be conditioned by it, be obstructed by it. Humanity – grammatically, politically – was both agent and object. Anything else was denial. But, according to Timpanaro, admitting this and knowing it in our bones should not make us abandon the struggle; it should, rather, help us form a vision unvarnished, a necessary basis for struggle: 'If we're

---

88   S.T. to Luciano Della Mea, 9 June 1976.

89   *AN*, 318.

90   On the physical–psychological roots of Timpanaro's materialism: S.T. to Piero Treves, 10 April 1972. Cf. Narducci, 'Sebastiano Timpanaro', 295–6.

materialists, we have to take note of [human passivity], not to discourage ourselves and abandon the struggle, but to have a vision of our human reality not masked by 'panglossisms' [naive optimism].[91] Only a truly materialist, pessimist Marxism could give us the right vision of reality. Only that can keep our vision straight. Socialism had to be built on this sobering truth.

5
Freud's Slips

Timpanaro's identity as a philologist may have sometimes made him blush on the dock of his political commitments. It may have pushed him into the double life of unresolved contradiction, grumpy and anti-dialectical. But he wrote one classic where his status as a qualified nitpicker was out there in full force for the world to see, *in action*. *The Freudian Slip* still stands as a bracing moment in intellectual history when the vocation of the classical philologist – a details-based, micro-focussed, empirical human science – finally came up against a relative it did not know it had: Freudian psychoanalysis. The contretemps had never really happened before, but *The Freudian Slip* is a book that makes you wonder why it had not.[1] It took the unique background, training,

---

1   Apart from a hint in a footnote of Pasquali's ('Congettura e probabilità diplomatica', *Annali della Scuola Normale Superiore di Pisa. Lettere, storie e filosofia*, series II, 17, no. 3/4 (1948): 220–3, reprinted in the second edition of *Storia della tradizione*, 481–6) – which Timpanaro, ever scrupulous on matters of intellectual priority, openly acknowledged as playing a role in the genesis of *The Freudian Slip* (*LF*, 16; S.T. to Scevola Mariotti, 16 August 1973; S.T. to Vincenzo Tandoi, 31 December 1973). (Timpanaro liked to attribute the genesis of his bigger works to a throwaway or marginal moment in Pasquali; see also *GLM*, 37.) Timpanaro noted that Caretti and Rossi had called for more of an encounter between textual critics and Freud's psychopathology (*LF*, 18). The book also grew out of ideas earlier formulated in Timpanaro's correspondence, especially with Carlo Ginzburg and Francesco Orlando (see, e.g., S.T. to Francesco Orlando, 31 March 1971); on the latter, see Luca Bufarale, *Sebastiano Timpanaro: L'inquietudine della ricerca*, Pistoia, 2022, 90.

and sheer polemical chutzpah of a Timpanaro to put the two together. What came out is a compulsively readable critique of Freud using the weapons no one had ever thought to throw at him: the arts of textual criticism, one of the most technical subfields of classical philology.

The confrontation made sense in so many ways. In *The Psychopathology of Everyday Life*, Freud dealt with the psychoanalytic roots of common everyday mistakes made in cognitive life: errors in speech, slips of the tongue, mistakes in recollection.[2] These lapsus – now famous under the folk concept of the Freudian slip – were not innocent. They were supposedly revelatory of the deep workings of unconscious repression, and their emergences were allegedly susceptible to a Freudian uncovering of the psychic mechanisms leading to the lapsus. Psychoanalysis gravitated to error because of its revelatory power, enabling access to certain flashes of the behaviour of the unconscious. But linguistic error was also the more humdrum business of textual criticism. In this field of philology, charged with producing an edition of an ancient text sanded down to be as close as possible to what the ancient author wrote, slips of the pen in the manuscript tradition were both a crucial diagnostic tool used to reconstruct the family tree of a given text's manuscripts (*recensio*), *and* an object of thought themselves, a target for correction (*emendatio*). Textual criticism had its own way of identifying errors, and part of the process of weeding them out involved a sort of implicit theorising about the *causes* of those errors.[3] For example, sometimes the wrong word might be substituted because of phonic similarity, for instance 'Anaxagoras' for 'Protagoras'. On the one hand, psychoanalysis was gathering a dataset of slips which it was parading as further evidence for the validity of unconscious repression as the motive force behind human psychology; on the other, textual criticism had already gathered a huge evidence base, in its reams and reams of corrupt manuscripts, of how the human mind in general tended to make mistakes, and of what kind. If the philologist might get possessive about any territory, it would be the study of error. Now the psychoanalyst was butting in. Maybe it was time to strike back.

---

2   First published as Sigmund Freud, *Zur Psychopathologie des Alltagsleben*, Berlin, 1901; the more recent Penguin English edition: Sigmund Freud, *The Psychopathology of Everyday Life*, trans. Anthea Bell, London, 2002.

3   As Fabio Stok points out, Timpanaro wanted to restore 'superficial' causes of lapsus as possibilities: Fabio Stok, introduction to *LF*, xxiii–xxiv.

What motivated Timpanaro to write *The Freudian Slip*, however, was not really the perception of a boundary violation on the part of an aggrieved philology; it was the more severe and consequential encroachment of Freud into the political sphere. This explosion of *marxismo freudiano* was a craze Timpanaro recoiled from both at home (among friends and comrades such as Cesare Cases, Cesare Luporini, and Francesco Orlando) and abroad (particularly in France, as iconised by Althusser).[4] Timpanaro found the increasing popularity of Freud on the European left of the 1960s a symptom of its intellectually bankrupt abandonment of materialism.[5] Whether Timpanaro was right about the percolation of Freud into Italian intellectual culture beyond the relatively niche radical left is an open question. Recent work has suggested that Freud's influence in Italy has always been limited, and resistance to him widespread.[6] The long march of time has perhaps shown Timpanaro to be less isolated in his Freud-scepticism than we might conclude purely from reading Timpanaro.

However, Timpanaro was worried not about the Italian reception of Freud in general but, in particular, the psychoanalyst's increasing pervasiveness in the subculture of the New Left. Instead of following the lead of a scientific and empirical materialism, an influential swathe of that New Left was getting sidetracked with the vagaries of the human mind, focussing on individual psychology rather than social and economic liberation. But it was also the type of thinking represented by Freud that provoked Timpanaro qua materialist. In Timpanaro's view, Freud was part of the general culture of abstract idealism infecting the leftist intelligentsia around him: like Lévi-Strauss and the poison of structuralism, Freud was simply sneaking in everywhere, from forced interpretations of Leopardi or Ennius to day-to-day equations of psychoanalytic and

---

    4   S.T. to Francesco Orlando, 30 June 1974; on contemporary Western Marxists admiring Freud more than Marx: *FR*, 193.

    5   Freud as non-materialist: *LF*, 160–1, 165; as Fabio Stok points out, Timpanaro's interest in Freud grew from his work on materialism (Stok introduction to *LF*, viii). The years in which Timpanaro was working on the *LF* overlapped with a period of great political crisis (Mario De Nonno, 'Timpanaro tra filologia e storia della lingua latina', in Enrico Ghidetti and Alessandro Pagnini [eds], *Sebastiano Timpanaro e la cultura del Secondo Novecento*, Rome, 2005, 112–13).

    6   See Pierluigi Barrotta and Laura Lepschy with Emma Bond (eds), *Freud and Italian Culture*, New York, 2009.

sociopolitical 'repression'.[7] The psychologisation of Marxism was producing a series of incompatible solderings, gluings-together of frameworks which were, to Timpanaro, mutually exclusive at best, sworn enemies at worst.[8] Timpanaro did not want his Marxism being led astray thus. So, the best way of getting to Marxism–Freudianism was to aim at the weaker partner and attack Freud directly.[9]

We could say, then, that *The Freudian Slip* was the philologist's riposte to Freud, driven by the Marxist's grievance. In fact, it contains a critique of Freud on both levels and from both perspectives.[10] The book's reception has featured a split judgement according to these two different levels.[11] The first level is the book's bread and butter: a critique of Freud's method in *The Psychopathology of Everyday Life*, using the principles of textual criticism to account for errors which, in Timpanaro's view, had much simpler and more workaday explanations than the uneconomical, self-serving back-narratives tacked on by Freud. One of the most important conceptual tools Timpanaro used here was the idea of 'banalisation' or 'trivialisation': in the copying of manuscripts of high Latin literature, medieval scribes tended to make unconscious errors which pushed words in the direction of easier, more familiar alternatives, often closer to the vernacular language of the copyists themselves in terms of vocabulary, grammar, and syntax. Their errors tended to make the text more in tune with their everyday linguistic lives, more 'banal' or trivial. Timpanaro applied this principle in a stunning opening salvo against Freud's first example in *The Psychopathology*, a young Austrian man's

---

7   Leopardi: S.T. to Vanna Gazzola Stacchini, 11 February 1976; *AN*, 155. Ennius: S.T. to Mario Martino, 20 April 1978. 'Repression': *AN*, 10.

8   On these incompatible solderings: *LF*, 181; cf. S.T. to Giorgio Voghera, 1 May 1975. Another example of incompatibility was Marxism and Catholicism, stridently opposed by Timpanaro (S.T. to Luciano Paolicchi, 19 September 1959; numbered 16 under 'PSI' in the Timpanaro archive).

9   As Stok points out, this 'straight to the source' directness was a habit for Timpanaro: he also tackled structuralism itself in *SM*, rather than confining his critique to structuralist Marxism (Stok, introduction to *LF*, xi).

10   In fact, Timpanaro called the two strands of critique in the book 'political' and 'scientific' – and derived both of them from the brand of Marxism to which he was committed (S.T. to Francesco Orlando, 30 June 1974).

11   See Giovanni Jervis, 'Timpanaro e la psicoanalisi', in Nuccio Ordine (ed.), *La lezione di un maestro: Omaggio a Sebastiano Timpanaro*, Naples, 2010, 30; on the general reception of the book in the anglophone world, see Adolf Grünbaum to S.T., 17 November 1981.

misquotation of a line of Virgil's *Aeneid*.[12] Through a series of subtle analytic twists and turns, Freud ended up arguing that the omission of the Latin word *aliquis* (someone) from this quotation revealed the young man's anxiety about a possible unintended pregnancy. Timpanaro's philological solution to the conundrum, by contrast, cut through the alembicated Gordian knot of the Freudian interpretation. No, Timpanaro said, it was not repression rearing its head; it was, rather, a common mistake of omission and reordering that tends to happen (to all of us) when we are recalling a quotation of a foreign language, which we tend to 'banalise' into a form closer to our native tongue.[13] There are certain things about Virgil's word order, for example, that seem strange to a German speaker. And so, the young Austrian had just committed a text-book error caused by the natural assimilation of a chunk of foreign language into one's 'everyday' communication system. A similar process was at play for Freud's second cited example, a patient's substitution of Botticelli for Signorelli,[14] with the reason of homophony (i.e., the words sounding similar) adding to the confusion. Such slips were absolutely par for the course in the history of manuscript transmission. Nothing to write home about.

This philological critique does end up folding out into bigger and bigger issues (more on that in a moment), but for now, a quick word on the second stratum of critique: Timpanaro the Marxist's feud with Freud. The book also features a kind of historicising attack on basic Freudian concepts such as the Oedipus complex, relativising these psychoanalytic paradigms as a mere reflexive outgrowth of the fin de siècle Viennese bourgeoisie. Timpanaro argued that many interpretive structures of psychoanalysis were far from universal but, rather, represent particular quirks, obsessions, and pathologies of a certain social class corrupted by a higher-than-usual degree of sexual constraint and bodily reserve.[15] There were also parts of Freud which were personal issues of Freud himself dressed up as valid across the board, such as the

---

12   *LF*, 19–20.

13   *LF*, 20.

14   *LF*, chapter 6.

15   *LF*, 90–1. This kind of criticism was familiar to thinkers on the New Left, ironically even those to whom Timpanaro was somewhat allergic, for instance, to Herbert Marcuse's *Eros and Civilisation* (New York, 1955; thanks to Bufarale, *Sebastiano Timpanaro*, 91, for pointing this out).

inherent conflict between father and son. Freud was notoriously control-
ling and authoritarian with his acolytes (a trait to which Timpanaro, as
a trained liberal-minded Pasqualian, particularly despised), so he was
essentially projecting his own power-hungry 'angry father' model onto
the entirety of human society. Strictly, then, the book contains a Marxist
critique ('Freud the neurotic bourgeois'), ironically working alongside a
kind of pop-psychologising critique ('Freud the megalomaniac').[16] The
latter is perhaps perilously close to the mode of argumentation often
used to discredit Leopardi's ideas ('pessimism because he was crippled
and depressed'), a move that Timpanaro could never abide.[17] This
strand of the book, then, comes across as a bit more amateur and
elementary than the philological side. Timpanaro himself understood
the imperfect combination of these two strands as emerging from his
particular Marxism: revolutionary and scientific.[18] Yet again, we have
another strike for the practice of a divided self.[19] But it is important to
remember that Timpanaro's objections to Freud went well beyond the
gripes of the philologist. These more political critiques have the ongoing
function of showing the urgency of the political impulse driving *The
Freudian Slip* in the first place: to paraphrase slightly flippantly, Freud,
to Timpanaro, was not just an intellectual charlatan but a walking case
of the psychological deformations of the ruling class.[20] He was not a
good partner for a Marxist to hyphenate with.

The anglophone reception of *The Freudian Slip* responded differently
to these different levels of critique. The British psychoanalyst Charles
Rycroft found much to commend in book overall. He was sympathetic
to Timpanaro's first task, to show Freud's methods in this case did not
hold up under scrutiny. He even added some unacknowledged evidence
from Freud himself, who squeezed a footnote into the 1920 edition of
The Psychopathology of Everyday Life explaining that associative chains
could lead to the revelation of the unconscious's preoccupation *no*

---

16   See RF, 77; S.T. to Luigi Blasucci, 10 August 1974. Timpanaro was of course
worried about freedom of speech in his political culture. Führer points out the analogy
(Rudolf Führer to S.T., 18 July 1992).

17   See chapter 3.

18   S.T. to Francesco Orlando, 30 June 1974.

19   See introduction and chapter 2.

20   See *LF*, chapters 4 and 6; on Freud the reactionary and conservative beloved of
Mussolini, see S.T. to Alessandro Pagnini, 27 August 1986.

matter what the prompt – it could be a slip, or it could be any word, picture, or number presented to the patient.[21] Rycroft was less sympathetic, however, to Timpanaro's points about the irreconcilability of Marxism and Freudianism, which were based on a very outdated notion of what psychoanalysis had become since Freud.[22] Timpanaro was, indeed, far removed from the day-to-day realities of psychoanalytic practice, particularly in the anglophone heartlands of the UK and US. It was also the 'critique of Freudian method' side of *The Freudian Slip* that was fully taken up in the philosopher of science Adolf Grünbaum's exhaustive challenge to the methods and reasoning underlying the entire Freudian system in his 1985 book *The Foundations of Psychoanalysis: A Philosophical Critique*. Grünbaum largely validated Timpanaro's alternative causal explanations, with some qualifications. His fourth chapter on slips of memory, tongue, ear, and pen is in close dialogue with Timpanaro throughout. The more critical reaction to the original extract of *The Freudian Slip* published in the *New Left Review* under the same name – a series of well-made counterarguments to chapters 3 and 4 of the book by Jacqueline Rose, Juliet Mitchell and Lucien Rey, Alan Beckett and John Howe, and David Rumney – was also mainly taken with the problems in Timpanaro's argument from the perspective of psychoanalytic method.[23] Of course, these authors were responding to a section of *The Freudian Slip* that was rich in the philologist's critique, but not the Marxist's. But this is all to say that the splash made in the anglophone world in the wake of *The Freudian Slip* found more of substance in philology's riposte to psychoanalysis than it did in the frustrated materialist's.

So much for these two basic faces of Timpanaro's picked fight with Freud. If we zoom out a little, we can see the nature of the critique informed by a number of deeply held intellectual principles. The critique allows us to get still closer to answering the question: What drove Timpanaro? Freudian psychoanalysis was so deeply offensive to Timpanaro because it seemingly transgressed a number of systemic boundaries that were close to his heart – not just philological, not just

---

21   Charles Rycroft, 'Timpanaro and *The Freudian Slip*', *New Left Review* 118 (1979): 84.

22   Ibid., 86.

23   'Four Comments on *The Freudian Slip*', *New Left Review* 94 (1975): 74–84.

political, but methodological, scientific, biological, even philosophical. So, what did Timpanaro's polemical *against*, in the case of Freud, show him to be *for*?

The first point of method which discomfited Timpanaro about the Freudian system was its over-complicated approach to interpreting and narrativising the problem.[24] In some of the most entertaining (and most criticised) parts of *The Freudian Slip*, Timpanaro indulged himself in a kind of satirical mode of presenting Freud's argumentation: he came up with imaginary explanations for slips which followed the same unbridled Freudian logic but whose artificiality was engineered to show the ridiculous leaps and long-shot conclusions of the analytic method.[25] That method was almost *aesthetically* objectionable, an offence to Timpanaro's philological sensibility, which itself privileged a kind of Occam's razor approach to interpretative issues: the most economical and elegant explanation, more often than not, is the best.[26] In the historian of philosophy Alessandro Pagnini's terms, Timpanaro was an 'epistemological minimalist'.[27] In this sense, 'banalisation' was not just a principle of explaining verbal error but a Timpanaran philosophical conviction: the ordinary, material, unremarkable solution – unsexy, but statistically probable – was often the *right* one.[28] Again and again, across his long career and disciplinary expansions, we see Timpanaro opt for the simple explanation over the 'brilliant' rationalisation of a given phenomenon. He was, as we saw in chapter 2, deeply suspicious of the 'brilliant' conjectures of cocky English philologists like A. E. Housman, who changed the text partly to peacock their own virtuosity. On the issue of editing Senecan tragedy, Timpanaro backed the more conservative scholar Giancarlo Giardina over the more radical editor Otto Zwierlein, partly because the former is sober with the intellectual

---

24   On Timpanaro's critique of Freudian hyper-interpretivity: Jervis, 'Timpanaro e la psicoanalisi', 29.

25   *LF*, 33–4.

26   *LF*, chapter 3, is called 'pedestrian (but true) explanation of a lacunose citation'; for the banality of truth, cf. conclusion. At the beginning of chapter 4, Timpanaro says his explanation may not have the brilliance of Freud, but it's the simplest and most economical.

27   Alessandro Pagnini, 'Timpanaro, la filologia, la medicina, la psicanalisi: Per un'epistemologia delle "scienze inesatte" ', in Ordine, *La lezione di un maestro*, 50.

28   See *LF*, 30.

exhibitionism. In dialogue with the historian Carlo Ginzburg (1939–), Timpanaro pitted his minimalist explanation above Ginzburg's 'brilliance' when talking of the first example in Freud's *Psychopathology*.[29] Timpanaro's hostility to the sinologist and Maoist Edoarda Masi (1927–2011) played out against her ingenious dialectical readings that turned night into day.[30] He was unrepentant about giving Cesare Cases an unoriginal account of the *Oedipus Rex*, if the truth was (as usual) banal.[31] Whatever the issue, Timpanaro's eye *banalised* the phenomenon down to earth to reduce the importance of the subjectivity interpreting it. Just as he thought of his own limited creativity, so he thought of the general capacities of the human mind: average.[32]

Timpanaro's next suite of problems with Freudian psychoanalysis revolved around what we might call its non- or anti-scientific nature. One of the major issues, for Timpanaro, was that Freud offered a method without much method: the number and kind of Freudian interpretations allowable is virtually infinite. As a materialist, Timpanaro was deeply invested in, and adhered strictly to, the concept of *limit*. Any good science has to articulate and be aware of its own limits. There need to be 'constraints' (*vincoli*) which place a brake on the speculation of the human brain, and there need to be 'prohibitions' (*divieti*) which rule certain things beyond the bounds of possibility.[33] Just as the law of gravity makes it impossible for an object to float upwards into the air, so there need to be some regulations placed on the unconscious and its analysis.[34] And, just as the art of textual conjecture cannot be left to willy-nilly, heavy-handed intervention, because the philologist must remain accountable to the limits imposed by a vast knowledge of the literary, historical, and linguistic situation of a given moment – the

29   See S.T. to Carlo Ginzburg, 5 March 1971; Pagnini, 'Timpanaro, la filologia', 45.

30   S.T. to Grazia Cherchi, November–December 1976 (n.d., numbered 10 in the Timpanaro archive), March 1972 (n.d., numbered 26 in the Timpanaro archive), 7 September 1973.

31   S.T. to Cesare Cases, 2 March 1963.

32   As Timpanaro shows at *LF*, 136, a lapsus can stabilise as wrong knowledge even in very learned minds; that is to say, intellectuals are nothing special. Cf. Timpanaro's bracing remarks on our tendency to overestimate the mental capacities of ancient authors: *NC*, 305–7.

33   *LF*, 193; Pagnini, 'Timpanaro, la filologia', 50; Pagnini, introduction to *FR*, 19–21.

34   S.T. to Carlo Alberto Madrignani, 14 July 1974.

limits of the thinkable and writable – so the psychoanalyst must be bound to something, anything. If the unconscious is a language, there need to be some boundaries set to the apparently limitless signifying power of each term (conditions under which language, in fact, is itself impossible).[35] A minimal requirement for the validity of a scientific theory is to articulate *how* and *when* it is falsified – and there can be no way of showing a Freudian interpretation to be false.[36] The Freudian principle of attendance to the singular conditions of each individual's psyche renders the 'theory' beyond criticism. Its security as a method is guaranteed by its evasion into the non-methodical. In this way, it resembles little more than a kind of magic.[37]

So there is a problem, for Timpanaro, with Freud's 'methodological overreach' at the minor level: it is so individualising as to be unfalsifiable. But then this problem also scales up, in a different form, to a much higher level. It is not only too individualising; it also tends to revert to extremely generic or reductive explanations, all-resolving principles on which the analyst can always rely, and whose frequent 'success' as analytic tools then end up being leveraged as yet more 'empirical' evidence for the validity of the principle itself, a vicious circle of self-validation. Concepts like the Oedipus complex, in Timpanaro's contemptuous terms, are *bonnes à tout faire* – working in any scenario, for whatever you want to do with them.[38] The unconscious itself is almost a religious concept, an equivalent of the 'will of God' which furnishes an ultimate, ever-reliable platform in the chain of causality.[39] Such tools are blunt instruments: they reduce phenomena to a couple of treasured causal mechanisms and produce the same patterns every time. In chapter 4, we saw Timpanaro show the same impatience with the twinned methods of the 'dialectic' and 'structuralism': arguments within these

---

35   *LF*, 193; S.T. to Luigi Blasucci, 10 August 1974; cf. *FR*, 90–1. On the capacity of each item in the Freudian language to be interpreted as its opposite: *LF*, 44–5; *FR*, 209–14; S.T. to Remo Ceserani, 3 May 1974; S.T. to Alfredo Stussi, 16 May 1965; S.T. to Carlo Alberto Madrignani, 14 July 1974.

36   *LF*, 35, 190–1. On Timpanaro's appeal to the Popperian notion of falsifiability: Stok, introduction to *LF*, xxiv; Alessandro Pagnini, 'Sebastiano Timpanaro su psicoanalisi e scienza', in Ghidetti and Pagnini, *Sebastiano Timpanaro*, 306.

37   *LF*, 69.

38   See *LF*, 92; *FR*, 103, 105; Pagnini, introduction to *FR*, 23; S.T. to Vanna Gazzola Stacchini, 11 February 1976.

39   *LF*, 79.

frameworks always end in the same conclusion, that X and Y, as opposites, are actually two sides of the same coin, and that you cannot have
the one without the other. Timpanaro found this kind of thinking
predictable and somewhat mechanical, an affront to the principles of
empiricism and historical particularity absorbed in his philological
training.[40] Any method which allows for such interpretative flexibility
made him cringe – and in the case of *The Freudian Slip*, even drove him
to spoof the method itself.

Another anti-philological trait about Freudian psychoanalysis is a
cardinal sin for Timpanaro: a priori thinking. Timpanaro's ideal of
philology – at least in principle – was the empiricism overseeing its
individual acts of interpretation. The philological method keeps all
possibilities on the table, without prior commitment one way or the
other. Like a good materialism, it attends only to 'the thing itself' and
brings in no prejudices or investments of the external observer. That is,
of course, a theoretical ideal unreachable in practice – but it was always
something operating in the back of Timpanaro's mind, informing his
judgement of Freud. For Timpanaro, Freud's implausible flights of
interpretative fancy happen because they are designed to generate a
preset conclusion: the validity of Oedipus, the workings of unconscious
repression, the id furnishing the ultimate instinctual truth.[41] The
Freudian method has committed to these things in advance, and so
each case of analysis is inevitably bound up with demonstrating the
very things the method takes as read. In Timpanaro's terms, Freud is
plagued by an *amor di tesi* – a need 'to just make a point' which already
stacks the decks in favour of a certain interpretation. Timpanaro was
particularly sensitive to these aprioristic weights throughout his work:
he took the ancient historian Luciano Canfora to task for his 'amor di
tesi' which forced him into all sorts of 'sophistries', argumentative
contortions and deformations made to twist the evidence to fit the
prefabricated theory that Giorgio Pasquali, in his *Idea di Roma*, was
showing problematic leanings towards the Fascist ideology of *roman-
ità*.[42] Timpanaro was repelled by what he saw as so much tendentious

---

40   See chapter 2.

41   *LF*, 99. On psychoanalysis reducing phenomena to a few standard explanations:
S.T. to Cesare Cases, 12 March 1975. On the id as Freud's touchstone of human reality:
LF, 107.

42   S.T. to Cesare Questa, 15 July 1981; cf. *LF*, 99.

point-scoring, tantamount to a kind of 'inquisitorial moralism'. Philology, a field characterised by constant intellectual splitting, was supposedly immune to such sophistry because it never posited a theory to save; it reconstructed the world inductively rather than deductively. Again, this was the philologist's fantasy. But it was an ideal to which Timpanaro was always tending.

The Freudian Slip draws attention to this defect of tendentiousness not just in the Freudian mode of interpretation after the fact but also on the very process of teasing out the initial problem itself. Timpanaro was convinced that Freud employs a twisted Socratic method in the therapy room: a way of asking leading questions to move the analysis in a particular direction on which the therapist has already settled.[43] Freud's questions are anything but innocent. They have something in mind, and they set the analysand on a particular track from which it is impossible to escape. Commenting on Freud's subtly manipulative interventions in bringing the young Austrian back to certain names of saints and their associations, like Origen, Augustine, and Gennaro, Timpanaro pointed to the process of analyst coercion:

> So far from Freud's attention being 'suspended', we have a series of explicit interventions, thanks to which the analysis becomes not unlike the 'maieutic' Socratic or Platonic dialogue. It is, of course, well known that the function of maieutics is to allow the pupil-patient to arrive 'by himself' at precisely the conclusion that the investigator of souls intends that he should: they induce the disciple to recollect from among the host of things which he sees in the world of Ideas or has buried in his own unconscious, exactly that which confirms an already established doctrine.[44]

While this process purports to be a form of 'free association' and driven by the patient, this method is actually far from free. It is in fact a system of subtle promptings to constrain the patient's account of their own psychic life and harmonise it with the principle Freud wished to demonstrate in the first place. Even if the patient appears to 'get there themselves', they have actually done so under the influence of a manipulative,

---

43   See *LF*, 40; S.T. to Antonio Alberto Semi, 18 September 1975.
44   *FS*, 40.

maieutic enabler. Evidence produced under these conditions should not count.

Timpanaro's final objection to Freud was his violation of materialism – not just in a Marxist sense but in the biological sense deeply entwined with Timpanaro's faith in science.[45] Like the contemporary anti-materialist Marxism with which Timpanaro was sparring on the left, Freud also underestimated biological fragility as a cause of lapsus.[46] Freud, too, could have learned from Leopardi's emphasis on humanity's pathetic subjection to nature (or from Pavlov's more physical and biological approach to neurology, as Timpanaro kept saying).[47] One problem with Freud's picture of the unconscious is that it posits a force much too active, and not, at the same time, also passive.[48] In Timpanaro's hands, whatever is left of the unconscious should be fashioned more in the image of a Leopardian human rather than a god.[49]

Interestingly, Timpanaro's 'real' thinking on the psychology of forgetting – what *really* makes information fall from our mind's grasp – comes out in his correspondence when he explains the memory problems of the two people to whom he is closest: himself, and his mother. His letters are laced – increasingly as he ages – with apologies for forgetting crucial material, which he invariably attributes to 'arteriosclerosis' – the thickening of artery walls in old age, causing attendant memory loss.[50] So a very material, medical explanation is offered in his own case, just as it is for other friends' psychological problems: he is convinced that editor and comrade Luciano Della Mea's depression, for example, is more curable with drugs than therapy.[51] For his mother, the mechanics are slightly different. When pressed to explain why his mother had forgotten most of her early youth among the avant-garde of a particular poetic circle in Naples, Timpanaro offered two possibilities: either it was some unspecified psychic mechanisms of repression, or it was a *conscious* devaluing of a certain intellectual phase of her life, an attempt to get

---

45   Cf. Bufarale, *Sebastiano Timpanaro*, 94.
46   *LF*, 95–6, 100, 171.
47   *LF*, 168; S.T. to Cesare Cases, 26 March 1971.
48   *LF*, 168.
49   The unconscious should also be subject to mechanical processes: *LF*, 171.
50   As Federico Santangelo points out to me, the invocation of 'arteriosclerosis' is very common in colloquial Italian (equivalent to English 'having a senior's moment') – but it is interesting that Timpanaro tended to invoke it so often.
51   S.T. to Luciano Della Mea, 26 January 1974.

beyond a slightly embarrassing (because tied to a pro–World War I stance) and misguided moment.[52] For Timpanaro, it was not just that Freud makes no space for workaday processes of forgetting that were familiar in philology, or for forgetting caused by biological prompts. Rather, he does not allow for our mind's *conscious* attempt to get rid of unpleasant past experiences. No coincidence, then, that the Freudian slips for which Timpanaro had the most time were the 'gaffe' types, which are made because the speaker is conscious of the unpleasant memory or feeling they are repressing.[53] In a sense, Timpanaro presented the possibility of a mind that works exactly like a hedonistic human being: it seeks pleasure, and avoids pain and discomfort.[54] To that end, he saved the concept of repression – but made it into something *conscious* over unconscious, Italian *repressione* (the active attempt to suppress something, in politics or psychology) rather than *rimozione* (the unconscious repression of a thought or memory).[55]

Both Timpanaro and Freud were – each in their own way – enemies of free will, and Timpanaro acknowledged Freud's contribution in helping bury the pernicious misconceptions of human behaviour that are moralism and voluntarism.[56] This means an investment in unconscious processes for both of them. Indeed, *The Freudian Slip* could be read as an attempt to introduce a competing and alternative unconscious, a Timpanaran unconscious, which functions not through mysterious and complicated mechanisms of repression, but according to much more quotidian patterns.[57] Timpanaro would never argue that the slips he covered in *The Freudian Slip* were made *on purpose*. But in the two examples above, he interestingly added to the repertoire of possible

---

52   S.T. to Carlo De Matteis, 29 October 1977.

53   *LF*, 106.

54   Hedonism and the search for happiness is in fact an important, if understated, thread connecting Timpanaro's politics and philosophy: see Bufarale, *Sebastiano Timpanaro*, 97.

55   For the distinction: S.T. to Francesco Orlando, 8 September 1971; *AN*, 10.

56   *LF*, 173; cf. S.T. to Luciano Della Mea, 9 June 1976. Despite this, Timpanaro also criticised the anthropomorphisation of the unconscious, and Freud's ascription of will to it: at *LF*, 171; and S.T. to Francesco Orlando, 30 June 1974.

57   Timpanaro's mentor Pasquali was, interestingly, much more open-minded about the role of the Freudian unconscious in generating lapsus: see appendix 2 in the second edition of *Storia della tradizione* (thanks to Alessandro Schiesaro for pointing this out).

causes for forgetting by making a small space for the will's role too. The 'arteriosclerosis' model is another kind of unconscious materialist forgetting we might add to the pile built up in *The Freudian Slip*: sometimes we forget through biological causation far beyond our control, which is often a by-product of the very Leopardian bind of old age. But at other times, like Timpanaro's mother, we forget because, at some level, *we want to.* We would rather not remember, because remembering causes pain.[58] Whether the forgetting is intentional or not, in no case do we really need a Freudian capital-*U* Unconscious gambolling away in the shadows, pulling the strings for our slips. The explanation lies closer to hand, up front, out there, in the light. It's the material world, or it's a theory of pleasure. Leopardi's Enlightenment materialism is usually more than enough, even to grasp the workings of our own mind.

Timpanaro did not discount many thinkers tout court. Unless the contempt was all encompassing – which it was in cases like Lévi-Strauss or Lacan – he usually made some attempt to sort the wheat from the chaff.[59] As with ideology, so with the variety of human thought: there is usually a core contribution that can be salvaged, even from the wreckage of a scientifically flawed system. We have seen the sizeable amount Timpanaro threw overboard of Freud's legacy. What items did he want to save?

First, there was the 'general' contribution, which allowed Timpanaro to row back a little from what could be construed – not without reason – as a wholesale condemnation of Freudianism. For Timpanaro, Freud's reception committed a category error, taking the wrong things from his memory. Instead of being treated as a science with a valid body of knowledge, and a therapeutic method yielding reliable results, Freud's work should be moved to the realm of fiction: a profound novelistic insight into the human mind, after the manner of a great artist like

---

58   Ironically, Silvia Rizzo points out that Timpanaro strategically forgot about certain passages in the *Psychopathology* where Freud dealt with uncomfortable topics like death and illness as reasons for forgetting (S.T. to Silvia Rizzo, 1 October 1976).

59   Lévi-Strauss: *VR*, 84, 220; S.T. to Cesare Cases, 5 February 1970; S.T. to Antonio La Penna, 9 January 1981. Lacan: S.T. to Gabriella Sica, 23 May 175. As Perry Anderson says, the Saussure–Lévi-Strauss–Lacan–Althusser front of French structuralism was one of Timpanaro's main (negatively) orienting axes ('Timpanaro among the Anglo-Saxons', in Riccardo Di Donato [ed.], *Il filologo materialista: Studi per Sebastiano Timpanaro*, Pisa, 2003, 177).

Proust.[60] That more creative or humanistic addition to the human repertoire was not to be sneezed at – indeed, Timpanaro did study and value literature for a living, and took it very seriously (see chapter 7) – but nor should it be placed in the same league as the great leaps forward in science.[61] The insights gained were capped by the ceiling of a single human subjectivity – which, as we have seen, cannot quite bear comparison with the sum of the world outside it.

While Timpanaro's hostility to Freud was unquestionable, we should also bear in mind that *The Freudian Slip* was an explicitly circumscribed work. Timpanaro was always careful to reiterate that he was trying to destroy not the whole Freudian system, but merely a part of *The Psychopathology of Everyday Life* concerned with lapsus.[62] Nor was he claiming that lapsus are never caused by Freudian motors; he argued only that they are *not always* caused by them.[63] With those qualifications in mind, it follows that Timpanaro sometimes showed himself more open to Freud than we might expect. In his unguarded and generous correspondence with Antonio Perin (with which we opened this book), for example, Timpanaro and his mentee Perin dove deeper into the possible reasons for Timpanaro's ongoing neurosis – and here, Timpanaro did say the unconscious must be playing some part:

> In part there's anger not so much for my personal circumstances as for the damn world in which we have to live; in part, it's about a constitutional neurosis from which I've always suffered (anxious states even without a specific reason, phobias of various kinds etc); as happens to all neurotics, there are periods in which it goes better and those in which it goes worse; and often even these alternations don't depend on specific reasons (or: a Freudian would say, these reasons are there,

60   Timpanaro also found such support for a 'literary' Freud in Trotsky: *LF*, 180–2. While this might sound like damning by faint praise, we should bear in mind that Timpanaro was a genuine admirer of Proust (see Bufarale, *Sebastiano Timpanaro*, 22).

61   S.T. to Luigi Blasucci, 10 August 1974; cf. S.T. to Vanna Gazzola Stacchini, 11 February 1976; S.T. to Adolf Grünbaum, 6 March 1982; and see Stok, introduction to *LF*, xxvii.

62   S.T. to Renato Badali, 10 April 1975.

63   Cf. Stok, introduction to *LF*, xxiii–xxiv. Francesco Orlando posits that the big contribution of the *LF* is to specify the boundary between Freudian and non-Freudian slips (Francesco Orlando to S.T., 22 June 1974). Timpanaro admits the possibility of a genuinely Freudian slip at S.T. to Elvio Fachinelli, 6 November 1976.

but they're concealed in the unconscious; and it might be true: I, as you know, don't believe in many essential points of Freud's doctrine, but that the unconscious has a big part in neuroses and so many other behaviours of ours, especially in those apparently 'without a reason', I believe it.[64]

Despite his intellectual convictions otherwise, embodied psychological experience forced him to concede something to Freud – even if he remained markedly vague on what that something might be. There is a melancholy softening in moments like this, where Timpanaro reflects on his own lifelong psychological disorder as an element more or less unresponsive to and impenetrable by his reasoning mind. Sometimes, Timpanaro even identified the things blocking him from sympathy for psychoanalysis as typical resistances.[65] Timpanaro acknowledged his own failure to understand or improve his own psychological problems. In this, there was almost an oblique admission that Freud may have managed to help, were Timpanaro merely open to it.

As well as conceding this general ongoing value to Freud, and the rueful possibility of a benefit in a personal road not taken, Timpanaro cited a couple of other specific elements of Freud's corpus which we might also want to take with us on the ark. It is safe to say that Timpanaro liked Freud's earlier work better than his later texts.[66] The working out of large-scale collective myths, as in *Totem and Taboo* or *Moses and Monotheism*, paired with a ramp-up in arbitrary interpretations, rendered the late Freud especially beyond repair. Timpanaro predictably opted for an early Freud still freighted with a good weight of Enlightenment and materialism – not the author of books and books of interpretation, but the author of *scientific studies*. Of this Freud, Timpanaro singled out the three essays on the theory of sexuality, identifying the choicest contribution to be Freud's distinction between hidden sexuality and the genital phase (although he also criticised the implicit normativity of this), as well as his explanation of 'perversions' as

---

64   S.T. to Antonio Perin, 30 December 1983.
65   S.T. to Francesco Orlando, 30 June 1974.
66   The need to distinguish various historical phases of an individual's thought is one of the first rules of Timpanaran intellectual history: regarding Marx, see S.T. to Aldo Rostagno (n.d., numbered 1 in the Timpanaro archive); regarding Aristotle, S.T. to Arnaldo Momigliano, 23 March 1972.

infantile erotic tendencies.[67] Again, a core of hard scientific value is still extractable from a compromised system. But Timpanaro read Freud overall as a figure embodying one of his favourite historical and intellectual conflicts: that between the materialist-scientific and the humanistic-cultural – a version, that is, of the main conflict Timpanaro read into recent Italian intellectual history, that of the eternal war between materialism and idealism. Timpanaro acknowledged that *both* of these formations were operative in Freud, and that the work on infant sexuality was towards the best end of the materialist-scientific side.[68] But this work is historically isolated in Freud's early phase. In Timpanaro's scheme, Freud's humanistic-cultural side eventually gets the upper hand, seeing him gravitate more and more to literature and the figurative arts as evidentiary documents, and to the most poetic and mythic philosophers like Nietzsche.[69] Timpanaro mapped a general move in the Freudian intellectual biography towards anti-materialist, anti-scientific, and anti-Enlightenment ends.[70] So he found in Freud a very familiar pattern of cultural conflict, and a kind of horrific spectacle of what happens when a depreciation of science, and a drift towards the 'mythic' humanities, are introduced into a system, with real consequences for the myriad human beings on the couch. It is this sense of Freud as a thinker who encapsulated both Enlightenment and mysticism within him that made *some* of him salvageable for Timpanaro. But also, it is the sense that Freud abandoned the former for the latter that made him so desperately disappointing, even dangerous, for our Enlightenment philologist. If Freud had stayed on the empirical track, Timpanaro implied, it could have been otherwise.

So there is some minimal redemption of Freud even within the very resistant *Freudian Slip* – but Timpanaro saved the true appreciation for a few years down the track.[71] His lengthy essay on Freud's 'Roman phobia' – Freud's famed inability to travel to Rome despite many attempts, due to an inhibiting and mysterious neurotic block – was far

---

67   S.T. to Carlo Alberto Madrignani, 14 July 1974; *LF*, 156.

68   *LF*, 156.

69   *LF*, 159.

70   *LF*, 171; however, Timpanaro attributed to Freud a species of Enlightenment 'Jewish' thought in the *FR* (S.T. to Giulio Lepschy, 10 April 1985).

71   For the very different political exigencies motivating the *FR* versus the *LF*, see Bufarale, *Sebastiano Timpanaro*, 96.

from a rehabilitation of Freud.[72] But it was an attempt to show that Freud could be right sometimes – and could be right precisely by offering a *non-Freudian* account of a psychological phenomenon. For Timpanaro, Freud became defensible precisely at the moment he was least Freudian, just as Timpanaro would clear space for literary scholars like Francesco Orlando who called themselves Freudian but, in reality, did not feature much of Freud.[73] This later work of Timpanaro's was perhaps an attempt to show that there *were* some very faint tones of Enlightenment Freud left, and that we should listen to those above the Freudian din drowning it out.

The problem of the Roman phobia was quite simple: Freud was overwhelmed by a psychic obstacle preventing him on several occasions from reaching Rome. Speculating about its sources, he offered the plausible (to Timpanaro) theory that it had something to do with an early identification with Hannibal,[74] and a fear of the Catholic Church based on its structural anti-Semitism. This explanation offered everything a Timpanaro could want: a political account of a psychological disorder based on the very material fear of oppression by the powerful, in this case not the bourgeoisie but Timpanaro's other most despised sector of the social order, the Catholic Church. The moment is precious because it is as if Timpanaro catches Freud reading his own psyche as a Timpanaro would: a psyche embedded in the world and driven by concrete fears

---

72   The article was first published as 'Freud's Roman Phobia', *New Left Review* 147 (1984): 4–31. Timpanaro was responding to the article of Cesare Musatti, 'Freud e l'ebraismo', *Belfagor* 35 (1980): 687–96, and originally tried to publish this response in the same journal, but its editor Carlo Russo encouraged Timpanaro to send it elsewhere for fear of getting the valued collaborator Musatti offside (see Pagnini's introduction to *FR*, 24–5). The article was finally published in Italian in 1992 as the first part of *FR*, 54–110.

73   S.T. to Francesco Orlando, 8 September 1971. Timpanaro included Madrignani, Muscetta, Luperini, and Mineo in this list (*AN*, 10). Orlando and Timpanaro bonded over a common Enlightenment aesthetic that seemed to transcend their very different views on psychoanalysis (Francesco Orlando to S.T., 11 May 1975; S.T. to Francesco Orlando, 21 June 1975; cf. S.T. to Emilio Bigi, 13 July 1975). Indeed, it was precisely Orlando's written lucidity that made him, for Timpanaro, such a tough nut to crack (thanks to Alessandro Schiesaro for this point).

74   Interestingly, Timpanaro admitted to sharing a pro-Hannibal position in his early youth (S.T. to Arnaldo Momigliano, 14 July 1976). As Federico Santangelo pointed out to me, many anti-fascists called their sons 'Annibale' in the 1930s – so the celebration of Hannibal as a kind of proto-resistance figure was certainly shared.

brokered by the particular constraints of the social order. Freud did not always have to be Freudian.

The bigger problem, and the source of the intellectual perversity to which Timpanaro gravitated, occurred when the issue passed from the hands of Freud to those of the *Freudians*. Timpanaro showed how Freud's acolytes and epigones systematically ignored Freud's own account of the neurosis, preferring to move it onto a more textbook 'Freudian' plane: of course it was sexual conflict; of course Rome had to represent the mother in some way (as 'alma mater').[75] This put the constitutionally daddy-deferential Freudians in the strange position of overruling the father on a particular to save the father's general system. This allowed again for some borderline satirical presentation of Freudian modes of analysis, but this time, displaced from Freud himself onto what was, for Timpanaro, the even more egregious parroting of the acolytes.[76] It is another pattern in Timpanaran intellectual history that theories go particularly astray not in the hands of their makers but in those of their over-mechanical transmitters: it happened with Johann Friedrich Herbart (1776–1841) in linguistics, with Darwin in evolutionary biology, with the Austrian physicist Ernst Mach (1838–1916) and his successors on materialism, with Giordani vis-à-vis his follower Carducci, with Lachmann in philology, and with Marx and Engels (along with Richard Bentley and A. E. Housman too).[77] Just as in philology, texts start to get messed up the very minute the original is copied, so too in intellectual history ideas go haywire as they replicate uncontrollably via the contributions of those who fancy themselves faithful to the original. Timpanaro aimed to show that in this case, Freud, for once, had it right the first time, and that it took a certain kind of intellectual chicanery to completely ignore the patient's self-analysis just because the conclusion did not look very Freudian. Particularly when that patient was . . . Freud.

Here we see Timpanaro going up against the same aprioristic thinking he had originally pulled up in Freud himself: ignoring more

---

75 *FR*, 89.

76 *FR*, 105.

77 Herbart: *SLO*, 176. Darwin: *SLO*, 194. Mach: *OM*, 231. Giordani: *CI*, 125. Lachmann: Glenn Most's introduction to *GLM*, 25. Bentley and Housman: Federico Santangelo, 'Voler "capire tutto" '. Appunti sullo stile di Sebastiano Timpanaro', *Anabases* 20 (2014): 64–5.

convincing explanations merely because you want to validate the theory you have subscribed to in advance, even when that means dismissing the claims of the theory's founder *about his own psychology*. There is something interesting and heavy at stake for Timpanaro in this general dynamic of an individual offering an account of themselves, only to be overwritten by the powerful a priori myths held by others. As we have seen, Timpanaro experienced this process first hand with the myths of political virtue that came to circulate around him later in his career: that the reason he never held a university post was a result of his high-minded choice not to sully himself with the compromises of institutional politics. In actual fact, it was not a choice; it was merely his neurosis preventing him from speaking in front of a big group of students. In that case, the myth of the refusenik intellectual overrode Timpanaro's alternative explanation *about himself*. There was something analogous in the way the Freudians denied Freud's own self-explanation.

But there was also something bigger at stake in this defence of Freud from the Freudians. It got to the heart of a treasured philological principle: the attempt to understand the author on their own terms, the injunction to strip back to the original and get to 'what the author wrote'.[78] Textual criticism in classical philology has that very object in mind, and in 'The Roman Phobia', Timpanaro applied it to the world of ideas. The project was to clear away the later, deforming encrustations of the Freudian 'tradition' and get back to the core of what Freud himself wrote. Of course, it helped that Timpanaro was invested in the content of the originary hypothesis, because it accorded with his worldview. But he would have observed the principle no matter the content of Freud's initial explanation. If *The Freudian Slip*'s philological side was about leveraging working principles of textual criticism towards rescuing the phenomena of linguistic errors from the grip of Freudian interpretation, here Timpanaro did the same for Freud himself – but this time, the underlying principle was a philological faith in attending to what the author wrote.

So, Timpanaro continued to pit philology against psychoanalysis, even in 'The Roman Phobia', by insisting on principles of interpretation that would look very out of place in the analytic tradition: that people

---

78   Cf. Rudolf Führer to S.T., 18 July 1992.

can often understand and articulate for themselves what is going on for them, and that the author can have the final word on the author. But if 'The Roman Phobia' was about correcting and curating a small part of the Freudian tradition, the other half of Timpanaro's Freud-adjacent work – now collected in the same volume as *The Roman Phobia* – was dedicated to another very sacred principle of Timpanaran philology: correcting and curating one's own intellectual tradition. We discussed in chapter 2 the paradigmatic sublime experience of philology for Timpanaro: to find one's work already completed in a part of the tradition one had overlooked. Losing priority was not a case of failing to get there first but a beautiful confirmation of one's views the second they become transhistorical and shared. Timpanaro's last and perhaps greatest experience of this was in his late discovery of Rudolf Meringer (1859–1931), an Indo-European philologist whose critiques of Freud foreshadowed many of Timpanaro's in *The Freudian Slip*.[79] After Timpanaro's long disappointment at the silence of the intellectual universe greeting that book (a silence perhaps a little overplayed by Timpanaro's chronically self-minimising paranoia),[80] he finally found an interlocutor who fully agreed with him: but in the past, not the present. With Meringer, Timpanaro had found his anti-Freudian equivalent of a Leopardi – the precursor for good company, the generator of further grist for the anti-Freud mill.

As we have seen, across his entire corpus Timpanaro was invariably scrupulous about the attribution of priority in intellectual history. This time, he took it as absolutely incumbent upon himself to produce an Italian translation (with commentary) of Meringer's critique of Freud as a way of righting the record – and of supplying an intellectual tradition to scaffold his thoughts on Freud, which he felt, post–*Freudian Slip*, to be a voice in the wilderness.[81] In the case of Meringer, this

---

79 Pointed out to Timpanaro in Rudolf Führer to S.T., 15 January 1981.

80 On the reception of the *LF*, see the introduction to this volume. The book actually sold very well in Italy, but Timpanaro again self-deprecatingly attributed this to the mere fact of Freud's name in the title: S.T. to Antonio Carlini, 14 May 1975. Even a cursory glance at the reams of Italian reviews that greeted the book (comparable in number to *SM* and *CI*) – collected conveniently at Michele Feo, 'L'opera di Sebastiano Timpanaro', in Di Donato, *Il filologo materialista*, 226–7 – puts the lie to Timpanaro's downbeat self-evaluation.

81 *FR*, 162; S.T. to Rudolf Führer, 1 January 1977; S.T. to Cesare Cases, 20 January 1979; S.T. to Antonio Perin, 30 December 1983.

philological impulse to acknowledge predecessors and supply origins dovetailed with another deeply held egalitarian ethic of Timpanaran Enlightenment philology: to give publicity to the unacknowledged, to make the unknown known.[82] Meringer, an intellectual dwarf to Freud's giant, needed some scaling up.[83] Timpanaro was drawn to these acts of retrospective justice in intellectual history. Indeed, he not only performed them, as here, but narrated *others* performing them. As we shall see in the next chapter, one of Timpanaro's favourite linguists, Graziadio Ascoli (1829–1907), gradually came to see that he had been anticipated in many things by the linguistic work of a thinker who preceded him by a generation, Carlo Cattaneo (1801–1869).[84] This process of delayed recognition and subsequent repairing of the record, a kind of paying of intellectual reparations for former neglect (as well as a bolstering of one's argument through the invocation of a discovered authority), became Timpanaro's model to follow in his belated acknowledgement of Meringer. The ethical ideal of a Timpanaran intellectual meant excavating, with philological attention, precisely where and how one was *not* original. But that loss of originality did not compromise one's contribution; it simply fortified its content through concordance across time.

We see, then, the tools of the philologist cutting across Timpanaro's long onslaught on Freud. The basics of textual criticism helped supplant Freud's overwrought accounts of lapsus in *The Psychopathology of Everyday Life*; attendance to the words of the original helped save Freud from the Freudians; and, with Meringer, Timpanaro did the same for himself that he did with Lachmann, spotlighting the people who got there first but whose contributions had fallen out of circulation. However, we should remember always the ends to which this philological thinking was put. Taking Freud down a peg was not just an intellectual game or an abstract exercise in polemic for Timpanaro. It had political implications: the dominance of Freud was standing in the way of the scientific, properly materialist Marxism that Timpanaro saw as the solution to the wayward turns of the contemporary Western left. But

82   See Anderson, 'On Sebastiano Timpanaro' for these 'acts of retrospective justice'; and cf. chapter 2.

83   Timpanaro took issue with the automatic ascription of greater truth to the major over the minor thinker, merely by virtue of name recognition: *FR*, 169.

84   *CI*, 342–4.

it also had consequences for the vast swathes of humanity stuck in what was, for Timpanaro, the dead end of psychoanalytic therapy. For some illnesses, such as the heavy and worsening neurosis experienced over the course of his life, Timpanaro thought there were no psychological fixes. There was liberation in the insistence that things happen outside the human will, that not everything lies within the power of the self to repair. In this admission of defeat before his own neurological reality, Timpanaro was actually closer than he thought to Freudian psycho-analysis, which also refuses to traffic in easy 'fixes'; the analytic process was often interminable, the 'liberation' from neurosis elusive, the cure not the end goal.[85]

If Timpanaro's belief in the ineliminability of such neurosis accorded with Freudian psychoanalysis on the personal level, in biographical time, it also formed an eerie double of it at the cultural level, in histori-cal time. Freud's famous *Civilization and Its Discontents* was, among other things, an attempt to mark out the irreducible dissatisfaction of humans *no matter what* vast changes in the social and economic order they managed to secure.[86] Set against that Freudian project, Timpanaran materialism was a competing and parallel means of accounting for the *permanence* of human misery even after the revolution. If we picture Timpanaro's anti-Freudianism in continuity with the materialism discussed in the last chapter, we can perhaps understand it as a means of displacing a Freudian pessimism from Marxism, only to work Timpanaro's own Leopardian version into the breach. Timpanaro's mirroring of Freud on both these 'individual' and 'cultural' levels was a recognition that Marxism needed supplements. For Timpanaro, Freud was identifying a real lack in the Marxist system. He was only filling it badly. Both the materialist and the psychoanalyst, then, felt the profound need to acknowledge the ongoing nature of human misery independent of curative therapeutic interventions or seismic shifts in political economy. But the content of those acknowledge-ments, and the reasoning behind them, ended up looking very differ-ent indeed.

---

85   Sigmund Freud, 'Analysis Terminable and Interminable', *International Journal of Psychoanalysis* 18 (1937): 373–405.

86   On the persistence of human unhappiness and antagonism in Freud despite the acknowledged drive to political change, see Anna Kornbluh, *The Order of Forms: Realism, Formalism, and Social Space*, Chicago, 2019, 163–4.

Timpanaro never found out whether analysis would have helped him, even a little. He continued to resist. A part of him dignified that resistance with the tools of philology; another part with those of the Marxist. For minor slips, philology did the job. For bigger ones, requiring major corrections, the real answer from Timpanaro's perspective was not more therapists and more sessions but the abolition of capitalism.[87] Even then, the job would never be finished.

87   *LF*, 183; S.T. to Carlo Alberto Madrignani, 14 July 1974.

6
Language and Linguistics

The histories of philology, materialism, and linguistics are all mixed up. It thus makes intuitive sense that Timpanaro would be drawn to this latter area of intellectual history, especially its evolution in the nineteenth century, which was both directly adjacent to, and deeply intertwined with, the contemporary evolution of classical philology. Timpanaro's philological approach was itself often a kind of historical linguistics, deploying his wide knowledge of Greek and Latin usage and its development to illuminate single passages of ancient texts.[1] His earlier works on the history of philology always made sure to dovetail contextually with developments in the wider sciences of language, such as those in Indo-European linguistics.[2] The elongation of Timpanaro's interests in this direction in the 1960s and '70s, then, seems so organic as to require very little rationalising.[3]

---

1   See, for instance, *ut vidi, ut perii* – *CF*, 219–87. For the heavily linguistic component of Timpanaro's philology, see Tullio De Mauro, 'Timpanaro e la linguistica', in Riccardo Di Donato (ed.), *Il filologo materialista*, Pisa, 2003, 91–103.

2   De Mauro, 'Timpanaro e la linguistica', shows this interest in comparative and historical linguistics to be a Pasqualian inheritance – but Timpanaro went much further in reflecting on the tools and concepts of linguistics itself.

3   The material treated in this chapter is drawn from the following: Sebastiano Timpanaro, 'Le idee linguistiche ed etnografiche di Carlo Cattaneo' and 'L'influsso del Cattaneo sulla formazione culturale e sulla linguistica ascoliana' (1965), in *CI*, 229–357; Timpanaro's various chapters in G. Grana (ed.), *Letteratura italiana. I critici*, Milan, 1969 ('Graziadio Isaia Ascoli' [vol. 1, 303–21], 'Domenico Comparetti' [vol. 1, 491–504,

But there are also more deeply felt reasons for Timpanaro's attraction to linguistics that transcend the proximity of the discipline to his home turf, speaking in terms of intellectual history. Just as in the anti-Freud work of the mid-1970s and later, the expertise and content came from philology (but, in this case, more the history of philology) and the prompt to fire from a political urgency (pushing back against the encroachment of Freud on the left), so here, philology was the fuel, politics the spark. Timpanaro capped *On Materialism* with a long essay taking structuralism apart.[4] And his correspondence is full of assaults on a system he had come to identify with the worst kinds of intellectual misstep on the Italian left. Structuralist linguistics, infused with that same nefarious idealism, was for Timpanaro a bankrupt way of arranging the world as a kind of abstract snapshot of a particular moment in time, rather than an attempt to understand where it came from and how it changed. As we shall see below, Timpanaro did not care for the synchronic (rather than diachronic) orientation of structuralist linguistics. In fact, structuralism, for Timpanaro, became a threat on the level of Freud.[5] It was perhaps this disgust for the wrong-headedness of contemporary structuralist linguistics – and its tendency to infect disproportionately other spheres of intellectual life – that pushed Timpanaro to want to understand where things had gone wrong. And so, Timpanaro being Timpanaro, this begged for a historical compensation: an excavation of structuralism's deep roots going back to his beloved nineteenth century. Contrary to the static interests of structuralism, which seek to explain the system of language as it is rather than where it came from, Timpanaro's work on linguistics is about the history

---

508–10], 'Giorgio Pasquali' [vol. 3, 1803–25, 1831–3], 'Nicola Terzaghi' [vol. 4, 2513–23]); 'Il primo cinquantennio della *Rivista di filologia e di istruzione classica*', *Rivista di filologia e di istruzione classica* 100 (1972): 387–441; 'Graziadio Ascoli', *Belfagor* 27 (1972): 149–76; 'Friedrich Schlegel e gli inizi della linguistica indeuropea in Germania', *Critica storica* 9 (1972): 72–105; 'Il contrasto tra i fratelli Schlegel e Franz Bopp sulla struttura e la genesi delle lingue indeuropee', *Critica storica* 10 (1973): 553–90; 'Giacomo Lignana e i rapporti tra filologia, filosofia, linguistica e darwinismo nell'Italia del secondo Ottocento', *Critica storica* 15 (1979): 406–503. The three articles of 1972 and those of 1973 and 1979 are republished in *SLO*.

4   *OM*, chapter 4.

5   On structuralism's essential idealism: S.T. to Giulio Lepschy, 6 June 1967; *OM*, 53. On structuralism's over-estimation of the synchronic: S.T. to Giulio Lepschy, 31 July 1966? (year unclear; numbered 4 in the Timpanaro archive); S.T. to Paolo Ramat, 10 July 1966; *OM*, 144–5.

of its history: it deals mainly with intellectuals thinking out the big questions about where language came from and how it evolved over time.

Given the slightly technical aspects of Timpanaro's forays into linguistics, it might be useful to pause a second to furnish a brief account of the history of the field in the nineteenth century – the period in which Timpanaro was most interested.[6] The nineteenth century was the age of what became known as comparative and historical linguistics. In the eighteenth century, work had been done on the historical relationships between European language families and their respective relationships in turn to Latin. But just as in classical philology, where there was an explosion in systematic methods in the nineteenth century, with German universities at their centre, so also in linguistics. This was the moment of the European discovery of Sanskrit – a huge leap for historical linguistics because it allowed connections to be made between languages over vast tracts of space and time. Sanskrit was so important to this nascent science of historical linguistics that many of its early scholars were Sanskritists by trade: August Wilhelm Schlegel (1767–1845), his younger brother Friedrich Schlegel (1772–1829), Franz Bopp (1791–1867), and August Friedrich Pott (1802–1887). The first three were favourite subjects of Timpanaro's, and will feature prominently in what follows. Friedrich Schlegel was one of the first to use the term 'comparative grammar' (in fact not the first, as Timpanaro spotted with his keen eye). He focussed mainly on comparing the morphology (i.e., the study of the internal structure of words and their parts) of Sanskrit with other Indo-European languages such as Latin and Greek. The Danish linguist Rasmus Rask (1787–1832) and the German linguist and folklorist Jacob Grimm (1785–1863) continued this work into wider comparative and historical study of the Indo-European family. Together with Bopp, Rask and Grimm are now thought of as founders of historical linguistics as a scientific discipline.

The next step forward – again remarkably parallel to developments in nineteenth-century philology – was to try to reconstruct the lost hypothetical ancestor of the great mother language, today known as

---

6   I am reliant in this section on R.H. Robins's effective summary of nineteenth-century European linguistics in *A Short History of Linguistics*, Abingdon, 1997 (1967). For a more in-depth account, see the magisterial Anna Morpurgo Davies, *History of Linguistics*, vol. 4, *Nineteenth Century Linguistics*, Abingdon, 1999.

Proto-Indo-European. This fell to August Schleicher (1821–1868), the Lachmann of nineteenth-century linguistics. In fact, the link of this family tree method of historical reconstruction was direct: Schleicher had learned the system of manuscript classification from his university teacher Friedrich Wilhelm Ritschl (1806–1876), one of the unsung heroes of the stemmatic method about whom Timpanaro wrote in *La genesi*. Of course, there were also limitations to this method applied in historical linguistics, as much as there were in philology – just as manuscripts could be 'contaminated', so language evolution was not quite as neat as a branching tree, involving all kinds of push-and-pull, back-and-forth, and complex processes of influence. But Schleicher was a systematiser, a creature of his age. In order to reconstruct the elusive original language, he also drew inspiration from the emerging developments in the natural sciences, particularly after Darwin's *On the Origin of Species*.

While the scientific gains here were considerable, inflecting (as it were) the entire future history of linguistics, there were also some darker currents at play. Schleicher and his predecessors were by no means immune from the jingoistic German nationalism calcifying at this historical moment. The otherwise helpful categorisations Schleicher made, such as dividing language into three types – isolating, agglutinating, and inflexional – were mapped onto analogies from biology and thought to represent different historical stages of evolution, as if these kinds of language were, like fish, reptiles, birds, and mammals, all occupying the same world at different levels of 'development'. It was a short step from this sense of biological difference to thinking of these language types as hierarchically *ranked* – the agglutinating more simple and primitive, tied to the inferior East, the inflexional more complex and linked to the superior West. So was another string added to the grim bow of an emergent, shameful racial science.

The last phase of nineteenth-century German linguistics is relevant not because Timpanaro wrote about it in depth but because it led indirectly to the structuralism which partly motivated Timpanaro's linguistic explorations in the first place. In the late nineteenth century, a new, even more 'scientific' school of linguists inherited the torch: the neogrammarians. While the previous generation snatched from the playbook of biology, these scholars were yet more hard-headed, looking to geology and physics to set the pace. Their contribution, again, was in studying the historical development of language, particularly sound changes in language over time – but they argued that these changes were absolutely mechanical processes that occurred in accordance with predictable laws, and that, importantly, there were no exceptions. Even systematising predecessors like Grimm, Bopp, and Schleicher had allowed for some exceptions. But the neogrammarians, keying their arguments even more to empirical data over theory, bedded down into the absolute regularity of sound changes. Their research also led to a new focus on dialects – a relatively new field of study in which Rudolf Meringer (see chapter 5) also specialised. The neogrammarian emphasis on iron laws of sound change and pure mechanistic development raised the same kind of objections from the more idealist next generation linguists, as German scientific philology had done for the idealist philologists in Florence before Pasquali (a subject on which I shall expand below). Karl Vossler (1872–1949), for example, a devotee of Crocean idealism, reactively stressed not the mechanical and unconscious aspects of language, but the creativity of individual speakers, as if each speaker were their own language artist. He also pushed the contribution of great authors such as Dante to language itself. If the excesses of the neogrammarians prompted a flurry of idealist reaction, it also provoked the emergence of the twentieth century's most influential school of linguistics: structuralism. The Swiss linguist Ferdinand de Saussure (1857–1913), the pioneer of structuralism, reoriented linguistics away from the historical and evolutionary aims of the nineteenth century in favour of synchronic analysis. Language became less an object of historical study, more a system of signs.

Timpanaro's attitude towards structuralism should be kept in mind as the blot on the horizon inflecting his entire historiography of nineteenth-century linguistics. As with Freud, so with structuralism: Timpanaro was deeply aware of this theoretical system's creep into his intellectual world, and its reach was, arguably, becoming ever greater on both home fronts of philology and the left.[7] What were Timpanaro's objections to the structuralist school? Timpanaro saw idealism bound to it, in a couple of different ways: first, in structuralism's aforementioned indifference to history and the genesis of human institutions 'from below';[8] and, second, in structuralism's neglect of the important

---

7   Especially Pisan philology: see S.T. to Maurizio Bettini, 14 December 1978.
8   S.T. to Cesare Luporini, 31 August 1966.

connection between signs and reality. Contemporary structuralism, according to Timpanaro, treated language as an artificial snapshot of horizontal relations between signifiers, divorced from true considerations of the signified reality behind the signifier. Structuralism was, in fact, being skewed from its roots in Saussure, whom Timpanaro thought to be just as attentive to the relationship between signs and reality as he was to that between signs themselves.[9] For Timpanaro, structuralism, at its worst, was an irritatingly formalistic enterprise which made culture into a closed system of signs. This was the very antithesis of Marxism, a philosophy explicitly tasked with negating this kind of self-sufficiency.[10] Indeed, structuralism had become a way of denying the importance of reality, a sort of Platonising epistemology and metaphysics which again idealistically reduced experience purely to a matter of the knowing subject.[11] An ideal Timpanaran linguistics, on the other hand, would be fundamentally materialist, strictly maintaining a sense of the conditioning reality beyond and prior to language.[12] There was none of this in structuralism; it was an inheritance of the French existentialist tradition, not the Enlightenment.[13] In short, it ticked all the boxes for a harsh Timpanaran dismissal: anti-historical, anti-materialist, not Enlightenment. Like Freud, it had to be discredited as a partner of contemporary Marxism. This is largely the implicit project in the background behind all Timpanaran work on the history of linguistics.

But Timpanaro's attraction to language itself as an object of study ran even deeper than this local need to make an ideological intervention against structuralism, and to rescue the history of linguistics from its stranglehold. As we have seen, Timpanaro had an abiding interest in the limit cases of a given theory or methodology: the points beyond which that theory struggled to make sense of the world. Marx needed Leopardi

---

9   S.T. to Franco Lo Piparo, 15 October 1971.

10   S.T. to Adriano Pennacini, 13 November 1966.

11   S.T. to Gianni Sofri, 10 April 1969? (year unclear; numbered 1 in Timpanaro archive); cf. S.T. to Scevola Mariotti, 23 January 1971; S.T. to Franco Lo Piparo, 15 October 1971; S.T. to Pietro Montani, 24 January 1973. Timpanaro also took issue with Chomsky for his romantic view of language as poiesis: *OM*, 205. On these and other Timpanaran gripes with structuralism, see also Luca Bufarale, *Sebastiano Timpanaro: L'inquietudine della ricerca*, Pistoia, 2022, 88.

12   S.T. to Tullio De Mauro, 27 June 1974.

13   *OM*, 188.

because Marxism alone could not account for our permanent and irreparable biological frailty. We saw in chapter 2 that one of the ways philology remains difficult to reconcile with Marxism is its non-revolutionary pattern of evolution, proceeding in modest little shudders forward rather than revolutionary vaults. For Timpanaro, language itself was like philology in this respect: it was a sphere of human activity and culture which was markedly *out of phase* with politics.[14] It was emphatically *not* part of the cultural superstructure which followed the jumps of the economic base.[15] When it came to the evolution of language, the dialectic need not apply. Unlike various other 'institutions' – economic, legal, religious, cultural – the realm of language was relatively autonomous from the motor of class conflict.[16] Timpanaro essentially agreed with one of his main focal points in the history of linguistics, the pioneering Indo-European linguist Franz Bopp, whose contribution was partly to show that language was the most *unconscious* of human institutions, the least chained to socio-economic structures, and finally, what was more, the closest to the biological or animal part of humanity.[17] So we can see, again, how Timpanaro's materialist sensibilities drew him to a realm apparently governed more by the limited mechanical capacities of the human tongue to change sounds, than by the class struggle.[18] Language was another test case, and an opportunity for a worthwhile Marxism to be up front about the limits of its explanatory power. Again, Marxism could be nothing but enhanced by the ability to see clearly beyond its purview.

Timpanaro's work on the history of linguistics is inseparable from his fixation on the cultural history of nineteenth-century Italy, and it is in that context that we find his first substantial contribution: a long piece

14   Emanuele Narducci, 'Sebastiano Timpanaro', *Belfagor* 40, no. 3 (1985): 295; Umberto Carpi 'Timpanaro e il problema del romanticismo', in Di Donato, *Il filologo materialista*, 153; S.T. to Sergio Landucci, July 1962 (numbered 7 in the Timpanaro archive).

15   *SLO*, 146, 246. See De Mauro, 'Timpanaro e la linguistica', 99, 101.

16   *SLO*, 246.

17   On the linguists of the mid-nineteenth century becoming aware of the unconscious regularity of linguistic change: *CI*, 304. On the autonomy of language: *SLO*, 101. Cf. Timpanaro on Giordani's similar view of the autonomy of language: *AF*, 174.

18   *CI*, 326. On Ascoli's generally more naturalistic and historical conception of language: *SLO*, 244.

on the relationship between Carlo Cattaneo and Graziadio Ascoli.[19] Cattaneo was a Milanese philosopher, politician, linguist, and writer heavily involved in the Italian Republican movement; Ascoli was a glottologist and linguist, a professor at the Royal Scientific-Literary Academy of Milan, famous for his studies of regional dialect (indeed, considered a founder of formal, scientific dialectology). Ascoli was particularly well known for elaborating the concept of the 'substrate' – that is, the assimilatory force of the native language of a 'conquered' people, which tugs at the imposed language of the conquerors and transforms it in ways that bring it closer (especially in pronunciation) to the native language. This is perhaps not too dissimilar from the process of banalisation (chapter 5) which makes copyists pull acquired languages more towards their second-nature vernacular. For Ascoli, the presence of a deep substrate – a kind of linguistic layer beneath the conquering language – accounted for many quirks of Italian dialects, and more.[20] The accommodation of new sounds in the mouths of non-native speakers led to phonetic change on a grand scale: if the Gauls, for example, could not pronounce the *u* in the Latin *durus* except as *dürus*, then a large-scale change in vowel sound was on the cards.[21]

The substrate was no new concept in European or Italian linguistics. One of the earlier adopters of it had been Carlo Cattaneo.[22] But there was a prehistory of its use long before Cattaneo, too.[23] Timpanaro's chapter on Cattaneo and Ascoli in *Classicismo e illuminismo*, then, reads like a parallel project to do for the substrate (and a few other key concepts in the history of nineteenth-century linguistics) what *La genesi* did for 'Lachmann's' method: namely, to tease out, once more with the finest-grained analysis, precisely who came up with what. Timpanaro's story of Cattaneo and Ascoli was at once a story of a later, more sophisticated linguist rediscovering late in his career a concept found in a predecessor and fully adopting it, as well as the story of this delayed act of acknowledgement and intellectual reparation. Ascoli ignored Cattaneo's

---

19   *CI*, 229–357.

20   The history is more complex, of course: Ascoli gradually warmed to the concept of the substrate over time (*CI*, 290–357), but it was the study of Italian dialects that pushed him to revalue it positively after initial scepticism.

21   *CI*, 324.

22   *CI*, 230.

23   *CI*, 230, 248; *SLO*, 238.

contribution until he eventually recognised it as critical to his own, a process, as we have seen, closely modelling Timpanaro's own ignorance and belated enlightenment on Meringer.[24] Timpanaro loved a good story of ceded priority and acknowledgement thereof. Ascoli did this not only with Cattaneo; he was also engaged in the very Timpanaran activity of pulling up false priority claims in intellectual history, for instance, the neogrammarians claiming to have come up with the principle of the *ineccepibilità* (lack of exceptions) of phonetic laws, in reality already formulated in the work of Ascoli and the 'Italian school'.[25] In Ascoli, Timpanaro found an admired model for how to dust off a still-relevant old idea, and a vigilant eye against those who would present old ideas as their own new ones.

There are a couple of wider observable reasons for Timpanaro's attraction to this story of the substrate from Cattaneo to Ascoli. The first, I think, is the very idea of the substrate as a concept that shows the ongoing residence and relevance of the past in the present. The substrate is the technical linguistics manifestation of the philological principle mentioned in chapter 2: that residue of the past obtains in the present.[26] This is equally true of language and the history of ideas. Just as Ascoli could salvage the substrate as an old concept still relevant, so the concept itself was a kind of linguistic proof of how certain parts of human institutions conserve themselves even in the midst of vast change: language's presence in the biological sphere gave it an endurance over time, just like the evergreen discoveries of philology or the still- (or again-) contemporary resonance of Leopardi. Secondly, Timpanaro was drawn to Ascoli's version of the substrate precisely because it was bound up with the biological sphere he took so seriously.[27] Timpanaro pointed out that Cattaneo and others had understood the substrate as a kind of acquired oral 'habit' changing the conquering language on the lips of the conquered speakers. But for Ascoli, the substrate was not just a habit; it was a kind of mechanical phenomenon rooted in the very anatomy of a people.[28] Whereas Cattaneo had made a strict separation between

---

24   On Ascoli's eventual breaking of his silence towards Cattaneo: *CI*, 335.
25   *SLO*, 242–3.
26   See chapter 2.
27   On the distinctly social-biological character of language for Timpanaro: De Mauro, 'Timpanaro e la linguistica', 99.
28   *CI*, 326.

language and race, Ascoli allowed the connection back in: native speakers of certain languages could not articulate certain sounds because, biologically speaking, their word-forming infrastructure simply was not capable. Humans were, yet again, made subject to hard biological limits – and to the Leopardian Timpanaro, that rang true.

There was, however, a dark twist to such investment in the materialism of language. Ascoli's putting of the substrate back on an anatomical foot, rather than an acquired one, meant a dangerous flirtation with racial essentialism.[29] And the interpenetration of linguistic theories with ideologies of race was one of the most important topics in Timpanaro's studies of nineteenth-century linguistics. In fact, Timpanaro saw in both Cattaneo and Ascoli two very staunch exceptions to the rule of linguistics providing a breeding ground for European white supremacy, and this was made evident in both of their respective relations to a particularly thorny issue: the question of monogenesis versus polygenesis of language, that is, the problem of whether all known languages derive from a single language as their origin (monogenesis), or whether different languages emerged at different times and different places, separately and parthenogenetically as it were (polygenesis). Catholic believers in the binding brotherhood of humanity tended to opt for monogenesis, and Ascoli instinctively headed there too – if for the slightly different reason that, as an assimilated and cosmopolitan Jew, he was invested in a common origin to Jews and European gentiles.[30] The problem was that monogenesis was incompatible with the concept of the substrate, which posited multiple origins of language in many different geographical locations.[31] Ascoli ended up abandoning monogenesis for polygenesis – but, though a belief in polygenesis could pave the way for theories of essential racial difference and hence superiority of one linguistic-racial pairing over another, it did not necessarily *have* to end that way.[32] Plurality and difference at the origins of language *could* fall into a ranked hierarchy of languages and ethnicities, but not without a push. In fact, there was a whole tradition of non-racist belief in polygenesis, stretching back to Rousseau, heading through Cattaneo, and culminating in Ascoli himself.[33] It was part of

29   *CI*, 327.
30   *CI*, 346; *SLO*, 230.
31   *SLO*, 249.
32   *SLO*, 229.
33   *SLO*, 32.

Timpanaro's brief in this earlier chapter to quarantine his Enlightenment thinkers from the spun-out racial implications of polygenesis, with which they became associated through a process of *retrospective* suspicion and condemnation. The other linguistic thinkers treated by Timpanaro struggled to retain the same innocence. The story of the conflation of race and language in nineteenth-century linguistics and philology is a complex one, but much recent work (including Edward Said's famous *Orientalism*) has shown their widespread interpenetration.[34] Timpanaro took it upon himself to perform the difficult task of sorting the precise intellectual history from the rebarbative ideology infusing much of it. It was a fine line to walk.

The Cattaneo–Ascoli connection was Timpanaro's first foray into the history of linguistics, and, for obvious reasons, he stayed in Italy for it – the chapter, after all, was part of a book on nineteenth-century Italian culture. But, over the course of the 1970s, Timpanaro pushed himself to widen the angle to Germany, which was in the mid- to late nineteenth century a European pacesetter for linguistics (though Italy was not exactly lagging behind, as it was in philology).[35] The five essays collected in *Sulla linguistica dell'Ottocento* together form a way of filling in the blanks on the nineteenth-century history of linguistics, and on the issues raised by the Cattaneo–Ascoli chapter. In chronological order of original publication, we start with three 1972 essays: one on Friedrich Schlegel and the first beginnings of Indo-European linguistics in Germany (*Sulla linguistica*, chapter 1); another minute intellectual biography of Ascoli (chapter 4); then a piece (chapter 5) back on the familiar terrain of the history of philology, detailing the first fifty years of the *Rivista di filologia e di istruzione classica* (Journal of philology and classical education), one of Italy's first proper journals of philology, established in 1872. Reprinted in the *Sulla linguistica* collection was also a characteristically punctilious analysis (1973) of the relationship between

---

34   Edward Said, *Orientalism: Western Conceptions of the Orient*, New York, 1978. See also Ivan Hannaford, *Race: The History of an Idea in the West*, Baltimore, 1996; Christopher Hutton, *Linguistics and the Third Reich*, London, 1999; Ann Morning, *The Nature of Race: How Scientists Think and Teach about Human Difference*, Berkeley, CA, 2011; and for a nuanced recent view, Will Abberley, 'Race and Species Essentialism in Nineteenth-Century Philology', *Critical Quarterly* 53, no. 4 (2011): 45–60.

35   *SLO*, 261–70.

Friedrich Schlegel, his brother August Wilhelm, and Franz Bopp, concerning the structure and genesis of European languages (chapter 2), a kind of follow-up to the 1972 essay on Friedrich Schlegel. Timpanaro then finally reeled it back to Italy, with a 1979 piece on the little known linguist Giacomo Lignana and the wider intellectual synergies between philology, philosophy, linguistics and Darwinism in mid- to late nineteenth-century Italy (chapter 3). Between them, the chapters cover German and Italian linguistics through various prisms of individual thinkers, over most of the nineteenth century. What had begun with Cattaneo and Ascoli in 1965 was, by the 1970s, fanning out to a consideration of Germany too. Below I treat these chapters in the order in which they appear in *Sulla linguistica*, rather than the chronological order of their original publication. I have opted to follow this order because it shows Timpanaro's project of narrating the development of nineteenth-century linguistics as a unified intellectual history.

Cattaneo and Ascoli together formed a very Timpanaran paradigm of intellectual history, which went roughly as follows: earlier underappreciated thinker contains something of real truth value, gets neglected by later thinker, then is finally given the attention they deserve. The first two chapters of *Sulla linguistica* bear the hallmarks of a different (but no less familiar) Timpanaran pattern: the move from an idealist-spiritualist-romantic orientation to a materialist-rationalist one. The mystifications of Friedrich Schlegel at the beginning of the nineteenth century are partially cleaned up by his more rationalising brother August Wilhelm, and these romantic elements are truly rooted out by Franz Bopp, one of the 'inventors' of comparative grammar.[36] Timpanaro's eye for detail teases out the precise contributions of each link in the chain, exactly as it did in the *La genesi*, spotlighting the slow and steady progress from darkness to (partial) light. In this way, the story of nineteenth-century linguistics provides a source of hope for the present: we have dug ourselves out of idealism before; we can do it again now.

Timpanaro first gave a long account of the linguistic contributions of Friedrich Schlegel: the connection between Schlegelian linguistics and the natural sciences; the identification of Sanskrit as the root of all

---

36   Timpanaro traced the first use of the term 'comparative grammar' to Vater, writing three years before Schlegel: *SLO*, 45.

European languages, which are bound by the presence of inflection; and the almost-obsessive investment in a two-part system of languages, with the European based on inflection (the change in word form to express different grammatical categories such as tense and person, e.g., in English 'I jump' but 'she jumps') and everything else on agglutination (the stringing together of morphemes, or basic constituents of linguistic meaning, into very long words, e.g., in Uralic languages like Finnish or Hungarian).[37] It is this unshakeable conviction in a human linguistic binary that made Schlegel weigh in on the polygenesis side of the long debate: monogenesis for Schlegel became a patent impossibility due to the complete and utter difference, the uncrossable strait between inflected Sanskrit-based languages and the non-inflected rest.[38] This Schlegelian binary was then anchored to another very Timpanaran one: Schlegel assigned a *spiritual* origin to the inflected languages and an *animal* origin to the uninflected, producing a two-track system reserving the heights of idealism and romanticism for the European soul, and ghettoising a base materialism within the non-inflecting part of humanity (in whose languages Schlegel was, according to Timpanaro, fairly uninterested).[39] While Schlegel himself never fully worked out the racist ramifications of this two-track model, positing this irreconcilable linguistic difference between the West and the Rest was taken up fully in contexts looking to scaffold racial theories with whatever science or pseudo-science they could get their hands on.[40] So Timpanaro was ultimately concerned with the prehistory, as it were, of how linguistics helped ground white supremacy.[41]

Although we are in dangerous territory and will remain there – Timpanaro dealt directly with the scourge of racism affecting nineteenth-century linguistics – things got a little better temporarily with the afterlife of Schlegel's ideas in his brother A. W. Schlegel and Franz Bopp, the main focal point of chapter 2 of *Sulla linguistica*.[42] This was a double revaluation of two linguistic thinkers who had tended to be swallowed up by the

---

37   *SLO*, 27–31.
38   *SLO*, 33.
39   *SLO*, 34.
40   *SLO*, 55–6.
41   *SLO*, 95; cf. Lepschy, introduction to *SLO*, 12.
42   For racism in nineteenth-century linguistics, see, for example, *SLO*, 51, 95; *CI*, 254–5.

reputation of their more famous predecessor – the inverse, if you will, of what had happened with Lachmann's fame drowning out his precursors. Timpanaro's investigations again demonstrated the minor advancements made by August Wilhelm on his brother, which were more in tone and accent than substance: A. W. played the populariser and clarifier to his brother's mystic elements, and even when A. W. defended the most vulnerable parts of his brother's thought system, such as the gulf between agglutination and inflection, Timpanaro judged him a vast improvement in his attempt to base the claims on empirical fact rather than infer them based on metaphysical first principles.[43] To Timpanaro, these modal advancements did constitute real progress, because clarity and empiricism shifted thought into the realm of the actually contestable. It is interesting, too, that Timpanaro singled out A. W.'s role as a *populariser* of his brother's thought – a form of knowledge contribution Timpanaro himself took just as seriously as any attempt to generate 'new' ideas.[44]

But the real step forward came with Franz Bopp. Timpanaro painstakingly showed how Bopp, in his classic *Vergleichende Grammatik* (*Comparative Grammar*), critically discussed Friedrich Schlegel's concept of inflection and the relationship between inflected and non-inflected languages. Bopp tossed out the hard and fast binary – for him, Indo-European languages represented a mid-point between languages without grammar, such as Chinese, and Semitic languages.[45] This opened the gates again to the possibility that the Indo-European branch could have derived from an originally monosyllabic language – and, in general, the important conclusion was that there were no languages whose structures were totally, unrecognisably different from the others, and therefore that none were worthy of special treatment. Even if Bopp steered clear of pursuing this to its logical conclusion, monogenesis was again back in play. It was, at least, not an a priori absurdity, as it was in the rigid dualism of Friedrich Schlegel's system.[46] Bopp continued to espouse polygenesis because of a deep-seated, shared conviction about

---

43   *SLO*, 57, 66–8. However, A. W. Schlegel developed a tripartite division between monosyllabic, affix-based and inflected languages, rather than a straight bipartite inflected-non-inflected division: *SLO*, 62.

44   *SLO*, 57.

45   *SLO*, 77.

46   *SLO*, 78.

the inherent superiority of Indo-European peoples.[47] But one of his central merits, according to Timpanaro, was to reopen the space to say that this was not a necessary or natural conclusion based on linguistic genealogies. Other gains chalked up to Bopp's ledger were equally modest.[48] But, to Timpanaro, the expert creditor of small things, these acknowledgements mattered.

The next major–minor protagonist of *Sulla linguistica* (chapter 3) was Giacomo Lignana (1827–1891), to whom Timpanaro devoted well over a hundred pages in a miniature masterpiece of intellectual historicism. Even though Lignana's scientific contributions were not exactly of the highest order – and Timpanaro, as always, was quick to admit it – his value was rather in his typicalness: he embodied a certain tracking space to study the relationships between philology, linguistics, and Darwinism in mid- to late nineteenth-century Italy.[49] Timpanaro sympathised with Lignana for his early restless interdisciplinarity; he was no doubt drawn to Lignana's politics, as an anticlerical and secular force within the university (but here, too, 'typical' of the Risorgimento bourgeois left); but his real concerns were with Lignana the linguist in an intellectual context, particularly at the interface with Darwin's advances in biology and its implications for linguistics.[50] Timpanaro returned to the problem of monogenesis versus polygenesis, showing how Lignana processed this issue in the wake of Darwin, whose insights had caused problems for both hardcore monogenetic and polygenetic thinkers.[51] Lignana stuck to his polygenesis guns by a sort of selective incorporation of evolution into language systems: inflected languages went through an isolating first phase, and an agglutinating second phase, but then developed much more than non-inflected languages, which remained more or less static. And this was because inflected languages had a kind of embryonic capacity for evolution in them from the beginning.[52] Timpanaro

---

47   *SLO*, 94–5.

48   *SLO*, 95–6.

49   *SLO*, 219.

50   Interdisciplinarity: *SLO*, 122. Timpanaro compared his own 'dispersivity' to Lignana's at S.T. to Francesca Dovetto, 8 October 1988. Politics: *SLO*, 209–13. Intellectual context: *SLO*, 189–97.

51   *SLO*, 189–91.

52   *SLO*, 195.

thus showed how Lignana ingeniously propped the two-track system up; but also foreshadowed how the question of the genesis of language became redundant in the next generations of linguistic thought, represented by the neogrammarians and, ultimately, the structuralists.[53] Timpanaro always had that future traumatic loss of diachrony, the forfeiture of history, in the back of his very Pasqualian, very materialist mind.

The final coda to this problem of the genesis of language comes in *Sulla linguistica*, chapter 4, where Timpanaro treated Graziadio Ascoli's linguistic contributions in more sustained depth than he had done in *Classicismo e illuminismo*. As we saw above, Ascoli was drawn to monogenesis through a deep-seated belief in the commonality between Semitic and Indo-European peoples/languages – but the concept of the substrate threw a spanner in the works. New languages forming through intermingling implied an originary state of diverse languages.[54] Ascoli manoeuvred round the problem by positing an original phase of language that was super creative and fast moving: a monogenetic origin, then, but a very accelerated split into different linguistic types along with different human tribes.[55] The idea was to save monogenesis and reconcile the precious link between linguistics and contemporary biology. At a moment in which monogenesis was mainly defended by spiritualist cranks, and polygenesis was acquiring the taints of justifying racism and colonialism, one of Ascoli's biggest virtues, for Timpanaro, was in shoring up a secular and egalitarian defence of monogenesis.[56] Ascoli became the Enlightenment, anti-racist lifeboat to hold on to, adrift in a sea of religious zealots and rationalising racists. He even came in for high praise, towards the end of the chapter, for being sympathetic to socialists in the last phase of his life.[57] For many reasons, he came as close as possible to an ideal Timpanaran linguist.

Why did Timpanaro keep circling back to the question of the origins of language, especially given that – as above – it fell into irrelevance in the next generations? Of course, the question was an

53   *SLO*, 200.
54   *SLO*, 249.
55   *SLO*, 249–50.
56   *SLO*, 250, 39.
57   *SLO*, 250–1.

important one at that historical moment, so it deserved an intellectual genealogy. But it was also, I think, that shadow of neglect on the horizon that prompted Timpanaro to give it so much airtime. As he writes at the end of the Ascoli piece, Ascoli's approach to linguistics had nothing to do with the structuralism that would come later.[58] He adds that Ascoli should still have relevance for a linguistics that does not write off as unscientific anything beyond a strict, mathematical, synchronic-focussed system.[59] Just as Ascoli represented an alternative to the future in the past, so did this question of monogenesis versus polygenesis: it was a sign of an intellectual moment which cared about the *history* of language, about language as a phenomenon *in time*. Even if that question did not prove particularly generative in the long run, it was a sign of a linguistic tradition that went beyond language as an abstract object of theory. This tradition, whether in speculation on origins or in packing the traces of origins into the concept of a substrate, cared about how things first came about. Nineteenth-century linguistics may have sabotaged that project by using it to scaffold repugnant ideologies of race. But that did not mean that the principle of the historical study of language could not be salvaged from these ideologies and reinvigorated in more responsible ways. To Timpanaro the materialist philologist and intellectual historian, there could be nothing more important than putting objects of study back into historical time.

Timpanaran nostalgia there was, then, for a linguistics that considered the history of its object of study; more akin, in other words, to Pasqualian philology. In fact, the final essay in *Sulla linguistica* tackled the proximity, but also vexed relationship of classical philology to linguistics in the later nineteenth century very directly. Arguably, Timpanaro's intellectual history was almost always about the excavation of his own predecessors and adjacent or obliquely angled figures – but in this last chapter of *Sulla linguistica*, he really brought it home. This history of the first fifty years of the *Rivista di filologia e di istruzione classica* – Italy's first serious journal of philology in the German sense – is a way of curating the back story of Timpanaro's own philological coming-to-be. In it, we

---

58   *SLO*, 255. On Ascoli's interest in diachrony over synchrony: *SLO*, 241.
59   *SLO*, 256.

see philology grow alongside linguistics, as well as in its shadow. We also see the discipline weather other storms, a pathologically precarious and minor field. It is at once a story of the solidification and professionalisation of Italian philology, as well as a tale of its exposure to the elements. In some ways, it is a history of the minor and marginal crucible in which Timpanaro himself was formed.

In the Lignana piece (originally appearing in 1979, seven years after the original article on the *Rivista*: *Sulla linguistica*, chapter 5), Timpanaro examined the relationship between philology and linguistics in mid- to late nineteenth-century Italy as little to bigger brother. Lignana's conviction that philology should simply be swallowed up into the more capacious, cutting-edge and scientifically rigorous field of Indo-European linguistics was symbolic of the relative strength of each during that period.[60] Timpanaro productively pitted these disciplinary situations together at the beginning of this fifth piece in *Sulla linguistica*: the foundation of the *Rivista* was more or less synchronised with the foundation of Ascoli's *Archivio glottologico italiano* (the former in 1872, the latter in 1873), but the relative health of the disciplines they sought to capture could not have been more different.[61] Both journals looked to Germany as a model for proper scholarship, but linguistics in Italy was much more confident and flourishing at the time. In philology, by contrast, there had been a mid-century lull, compounding the general eighteenth- and early nineteenth-century failure to produce 'true philologists' (in the German or Timpanaran sense) that left Leopardi a relatively isolated figure in *La filologia*.[62] But Timpanaro was much more scathing about the tumbleweeds of Italian philology between 1840 and 1860, whose abysmal nadir meant that the field essentially had to be reinvented all over again.[63] So, with the founding of the *Rivista*, Italian philology, according to Timpanaro, had to teach itself the German way – to expunge the old aestheticising traditions of Greek and Latin studies, stripping out the dead-end spirit of Latin prose composition, and making history and science the watchwords of disciplinary practice.[64] Linguistics, on the other hand, had a much more robust recent tradition

60   *SLO*, 108–9.
61   *SLO*, 266–7.
62   *SLO*, 109–10.
63   *SLO*, 268–9.
64   *SLO*, 270, 274–5.

to rely on, to guard against a too 'subaltern' and deferential position towards German scholarship.[65] Italian philology was thus reborn in its very founding constitution as the attentive pupil to its stern school-masters north of the Alps.

Philology was not just performing an apprenticeship vis-à-vis Italy's northern neighbor; it was in abeyance also to the soaring field of glottology or linguistics, and the signs were in the composition of the *Rivista* itself. Lignana was not the only one pushing for an absorption of philology by glottology. Just as Indo-European linguistics had shown Greek and Latin to be mere modest parts of a huge systematic unity, so the general feeling was that the super-field of glottology would eventually swallow the subfield of philology. The *Rivista* featured many more pieces on Romance language glottology than a Greek and Latin journal should, in principle, accommodate. But in practice, this merger turned out much harder to broker than foreseen. These tracks in the *Rivista* – glottological and philological – tended to remain parallel, without much intellectual traffic moving between them.[66] Ascoli himself noted the barriers to their fusion, with the very different disciplinary priorities of philology – a 'hermeneutic micrology' – making it tough to reconcile with the more scientific ambitions of glottology.[67] We can see overtones here of a very Timpanaran story of formal philology's pathological sequestration: just as for Leopardi and Timpanaro philology represents an activity of little relation to the rest of their intellectual lives, so in the early *Rivista* there could be no communication channel between the small and the big.

How did Italian philology find its true feet again? Timpanaro portrayed as the crucial step the editorship of Girolamo Vitelli (1849–1935) and Enea Piccolomini (1844–1910), two practitioners trained in Germany and impeccably skilled in the arts of the Hermannian version of the discipline. This more scientific approach to philology – particularly from Piccolomini, usually regarded as the lesser partner but, in Timpanaro's revisionist scheme, comparing well against the conjecture-happy practice of Vitelli – was a big boost for classical studies in Italy.

---

65 The problem in philology: *SLO*, 276.
66 *SLO*, 286.
67 *SLO*, 289–90.

But this robust phase was also short lived.[68] Around the turn of the century, science and history – once saviours of philology – came back to bite it, amid calls for the abolition of Greek in the *licei* (grammar schools) to focus more on 'relevant' disciplines like science, history, and modern literature.[69] The discipline survived, as did the journal – but its directions in the first twenty years of the twentieth century became less and less agreeable to a Timpanaran palate.[70] In tune with the general complexion of the period's dominant idealism – this was never one of Timpanaro's favourite periods of intellectual history – the *Rivista* started featuring the work of Giuseppe Fraccaroli (1849–1918), whose growing aestheticism was at the expense of socio-political and cultural history.[71] Fraccaroli's aestheticism – more or less chronologically aligned with Croce's – then turned into the more fully fledged idealism of the journal under the Fascist-era editorship of Gaetano De Sanctis (1870–1957) and Augusto Rostagni (1892–1961).[72] Just as structuralism became the spectre on the horizon haunting Ascoli, so our story of the early days of one of Italy's most important journals in philology ends with a descent into philosophical darkness right at the start of the Fascist *ventennio*. Timpanaran intellectual history – especially when it touches events so relevant for his own formation – is always aware of the enemy knocking at the gates.

What this brief account of Italian philology between 1872 and 1922 does is furnish a partisan historiography for Timpanaro's primary field with a clear message similar to the forays into the history of linguistics – but with a temporal delay appropriate to the different states of the respective disciplines at the time. Just as linguistics underwent a mid- to late nineteenth-century Enlightenment, sending it into the arms of history, science, materialism, and the secular (à la Ascoli) and away from the residual romanticism and mysticism of a Schlegel, so Italian philology finally escaped its mid-century slump, and its antiquarian and rhetorical tradition, with a floruit in which the lessons of Hermannian philology were learned, and finally became

---

68   *SLO*, 291–2. On Vitelli's conjecturalism in Timpanaro, see Vincenzo Di Benedetto, 'La filologia di Sebastiano Timpanaro', in Di Donato, *Il filologo materialista*, 71.

69   *SLO*, 303.

70   *SLO*, 297–314.

71   *SLO*, 304–5.

72   *SLO*, 314.

the order of the day. But just as linguistics was susceptible to a dive towards idealism culminating in the latter-day horror that was structuralism, so philology would stumble into a Crocean and Gentilian nightmare. The solution to both was simple: the materialist philology of Sebastiano Timpanaro.

7

'Literary Criticism'

Timpanaro's Tuscan intellectual culture, defined by the academic perimeters of the *liceo* and the university, found a shared language in Marxism. But another major frame of reference was *literature*: classical, German, French, Italian. Of the vast reams of correspondence surviving in the Timpanaro archive, I have only found a single trip to the cinema mentioned, in a period where Italian film was undergoing a genuine, golden floruit.[1] Instead of engaging with the popular medium of the century, these liceo-trained Marxists remained resolutely *textual*, and their written knowledge spanned the history of European literature – with a bias, in Timpanaro's case, towards the poetry and novel of the nineteenth and early twentieth centuries. Rarely a page of Timpanaro, published or unpublished, goes by without a debate about the value of this or that author. Beyond his Leopardi, several of his books are devoted either in whole or in part to works of literature, with a focus on Italian and Latin: the *Primo Maggio* of the late nineteenth-century novelist, journalist, and poet Edmondo De Amicis (1846–1908); the *Manoscritto* and *Forte della stella* of the Livornese writer and translator Carlo Bini (1806–1842); or the eighteenth- and nineteenth-century reception of the first-century CE Roman poet Lucan.[2]

---

1 S.T. to Eugenio Grassi, 6 April 1953.
2 De Amicis: *SED*. Bini: *AN*, 199–285. Lucan: *AF*, 1–79.

But Timpanaro could also discuss Brecht and Balzac with the best of them.[3]

Was this ever, and could this ever be called, *literary criticism*? If you asked Timpanaro, it was not. The correspondence is full of protestations and retractions about doing literary criticism, which for the heavily historicist Timpanaro meant a focus on the woollier elements of literature: things like form, style, and tone, features which are notoriously difficult to pin down, and which generate a lot of noise and heat in their theorisation without (in Timpanaro's view) much gain.[4] Timpanaro kept pointing out that his closest relationship with a literary author – undoubtedly the intense, ongoing act of love, identification, and projection that formed his bond with Leopardi – was actually a strange evasion of the poetry of the poet, *as poetry*.[5] Reacting to a Crocean system of aesthetics seeking to keep the poet sacred in a holy sanctuary, ears stopped to everything but poetry, Timpanaro was, once again, more concerned with showing how Italy's national poet was also a lot more than *just* that: he was a proper philologist and philosopher too.[6] Of course, Timpanaro did engage with the poetry, but it was more as a vehicle of philosophical thought than as a site of aesthetic encounter. He also apologised for lack of attention to literary form in *Classicismo e illuminismo*, which he called more a work of 'literary sociology'.[7] As a self-proclaimed *contenutista* – 'content guy' – Timpanaro was interested in the hard stuff, the extractable core, the *message* that went beyond the vagaries of medium.[8] It was not quite Marxist criticism, at least not in

---

3   Brecht: S.T. to Cesare Cases, 5 January 1963; Balzac, S.T. to Cesare Cases, 14 September 1974.

4   See, for example, S.T. to Luigi Blasucci, 25 June 1979. Timpanaro's views on 'sterile' formalism: S.T. to Adriano Pennacini, 13 November 1966.

5   S.T. to Franco Fortini, 13 April 1967; S.T. to Alberto Brambilla, 6 April 1995; cf. S.T. to Alceste Angelini, 26 April 1963; S.T. to Vittorio Landucci, 25 May 1967; S.T. to Walter Binni, 6 August 1973.

6   Paolo Mastandrea, 'La filologia di Giacomo Leopardi (1955)', in Enrico Ghidetti and Alessandro Pagnini (eds), *Sebastiano Timpanaro e la cultura del Secondo Novecento*, Rome, 2005, 266.

7   S.T. to Fausto Curi, 15 September 1971.

8   Timpanaro as contenutista: S.T. to Giorgio Voghera, 12 November 1966, 19 November 1967; S.T. to Adriano Pennacini, 13 November 1966; S.T. to Scevola Mariotti, 1 April 1977; Ermanno Circeo, 8 March 1980; S.T. to Gian Paolo Marchi, 25 October 1985. Ironically, Timpanaro accused Crocean literary criticism of being too *contenutistica* at Sebastiano Timpanaro, 'Giorgio Pasquali', *Belfagor* 28, no. 2 (1973): 191.

any of the incarnations we might understand to be under the shade of that umbrella. But it was certainly a *materialist* way of reading. If Timpanaro had come across the new critical principle of 'the heresy of paraphrase', which sought to shore up the importance of poetry's particular formal features, he would have blinked blankly and moved right on to constructing his paraphrase. Of course, poetry could be paraphrased. As a mode of philosophical thought to be understood, assimilated, rejected, debated, and engaged, paraphrase was where poetry had to end up.[9]

Why did Timpanaro repeatedly pull back from the precipice of doing literary criticism? He did profess himself incapable of it – and there must have been an element of truth to this.[10] Technical philology and intellectual history are not exactly natural training grounds for close reading attentive to form and aesthetics, although master Pasquali himself did comment on those things at some length.[11] But Timpanaro's brain and interests were oriented elsewhere. As we saw of Timpanaro's abstention from the university, so in the case of literary criticism: we should be wary of making an act of necessity (not being able to teach due to neurosis) into a deed of virtue (conscientious objection to a compromised institution). But Timpanaro did also come out with more principled justifications of his decision not to do literary criticism, apart from bare inability.[12] Predictably, it is his suspicion of any scholarly work which, like Freud, failed to hold itself accountable to objective and articulable limits, a system of verification that can help tell true claims from false.[13] For Timpanaro, a materialist aesthetics was something that

---

9   Timpanaro was certainly always reacting, perhaps sometimes overreacting, to the Crocean separation of poet from politics: see, for instance, on Aristophanes, S.T. to Scevola Mariotti, 20 August 1957.

10   Timpanaro called himself 'illiterate' in literary criticism at S.T. to Luigi Blasucci, 25 June 1979; cf. S.T. to Sergio Solmi, 24 December 1972; *AN* 233; S.T. to Alfonso Traina, 23 March 1995, 25 November 1996.

11   See, for instance, Giorgio Pasquali, *Orazio lirico*, Florence, 1920; and 'Arte allusiva', *Italia che scrive* 25 (1942): 185–7. Timpanaro showed how Pasquali's interests in poetic allusion were still a long way from the aestheticism of Italian idealism: Timpanaro, 'Giorgio Pasquali', 190–1. But we should perhaps beware Timpanaro's tendency to artificially shrink the literary critic side of Pasquali.

12   Timpanaro also talked of literary criticism's stagnation pushing him more towards philology and cultural history (S.T. to Francesco Orlando, 26 October 1973).

13   On the inherent subjectivity of literary criticism: S.T. to Silvia Rizzo, 4 June 1979.

had not yet been invented, partly because the objectivity of materialism was irreconcilable with the subjective judgements of literary criticism.[14] There was no way to prevent the critic from arbitrarily injecting ego into their object of study, or superimposing a priori theoretical commitments onto an object to make it conform to those very theoretical commitments, as Timpanaro was always quick to call out regarding Freudian or structuralist readings of literature.[15] Literary criticism was suspicious because it was a dangerous vector of human subjectivity – and, for a materialist, this 'I' was not something worth dwelling on.

In Timpanaro's refusal to be a critic, it is not only the ego of the latter that he sought to constrain. He also admitted to a deep discomfort with the ego of the *artist* themselves. Timpanaro's rejection of the artist figure was bound to two models in the parental sphere. Firstly, as mentioned in the introduction, his mother's life provided a paradigm of art's renunciation in favour of *content*: her juvenile ventures in the Neapolitan avant-garde poetry scene were completely disavowed for a turn to the more 'serious' work of scholarship on early Greek mathematics she did later in her career.[16] Timpanaro inherited narrow-eyed reservations towards artistic sensibility and self-indulgence from his mother. But his father also played a part. Luca Bufarale points to Timpanaro Sr's intensifying literary and artistic interests, particularly his correspondence with many active poets (including Eugenio Montale).[17] In the letters, Timpanaro talks of early experiences with irritating, self-obsessed artist types among his father's connections making him suspicious of the human context in which creativity took place. He scorned the way his father took the bait and gave these people a free pass, no doubt an extension to the social realm of the sanctity of art tied to his idealist background. To Timpanaro the younger, the paradigmatic aura of 'the artist's artist' was the sense that it was *only them* in the world.[18] Timpanaro despised this sort of display of egoism or unfettered subjectivity. It was

14   S.T. to Emilio Peruzzi, 23 September 1966; Robert Dombroski, 'Timpanaro's Materialism: An Introduction', *Journal of the History of Ideas* 44, no. 2 (1983): 347–8; Emanuele Narducci, 'Sebastiano Timpanaro', *Belfagor* 40, no. 3 (1985): 310n4; Pietro Cataldi, 'Il metodo di Timpanaro', *Allegoria* 2, no. 4 (1990): 143–68.

15   S.T. to Giorgio Voghera, 7 October 1967; S.T. to Silvia Rizzo, 4 June 1979.

16   S.T. to Carlo De Matteis, 29 October 1977; S.T. to Giovanni Lista, 1983.

17   Luca Bufarale, *Sebastiano Timpanaro: L'inquietudine della ricerca*, Pistoia, 2022, 20.

18   S.T. to Giorgio Voghera, 3 September 1967.

no coincidence that his eye affixed best to a poet emphasising the limits of that subjectivity within the wider frame of an overwhelmingly powerful and destructive nature dwarfing humanity in its grip. The materialist was in the strange position of having to play down the human agent behind creative acts, with hands pointing to all the other things in the world constraining that creativity.[19] The general flight from anthropocentrism, which was a central conviction of his entire intellectual project, made Timpanaro uncomfortable with the very human-focussed and self-centred production of art itself.[20]

Timpanaro tended to be routinely dismissive of all the attempts at *en vogue* literary criticism taking place on all flanks. He scoffed at farfetched arguments aiming to connect completely random textual phenomena to bigger patterns, such as an attempt to link Ugo Foscolo's use of vowels followed by nasals or liquids to grand historical currents.[21] His reaction to the romance literature criticism of Gianfranco Contini (1912–1990; a professor of Romance philology at the University of Florence) was nothing short of total disgust, a literal regurgitative response to perceived exhibitionism, superficiality, and meaninglessness.[22] Timpanaro often used his favourite dismissive word, *civetteria* – 'coquetry' – to dismiss literary critics. His critique, in fact, will be familiar to anyone with a vague knowledge of the 'theory wars' dogging anglophone literary criticism in the latter part of the twentieth century. There is an assumption that any foreign theoretical framework brought to a text is a kind of overwriting of the thing itself: a Lacanian or Shlovskian study of Ugo Foscolo turns in to a Lacan or Shlovsky appreciation society, losing sight of Foscolo.[23] The second-century BCE Roman poet Lucilius gets lost under a thick cloud of the Latinist Adriano Pennacini's structuralist interpretation, turning the poet into something else entirely.[24] As we saw in chapter 2's discussion of unbridled conjecture in philology, there is a concern that these methods actually eat into

---

19 Timpanaro must have also absorbed this from Pasquali, who always emphasised the elements tying the creative author's hands: metrical and linguistic laws, cultural traditions, and institutions, etc. (Timpanaro, 'Giorgio Pasquali', 189).

20 For Timpanaro on anthropocentrism, see chapter 4.

21 S.T. to Marco Cerrutti, 2 May 1969.

22 S.T. to Daniele Ponchiroli, 19 May 1968? (year unclear; numbered 13 in the Timpanaro archive).

23 S.T. to Emilio Bigi, 28 May 1979.

24 S.T. to Adriano Pennacini, 13 November 1966.

the object of study, changing it and existentially threatening it, rather than observing and commenting on it. It is a question of upending an ontological hierarchy: instead of working with the text/reality that is given, literary criticism seeks to change it according to whim and will. We have been here before. By now, we know the drill.

That leads us to the final reason why Timpanaro was programmed to avoid literary criticism. He was also reserved because his training in formal philology equipped him with a very clear order of operations for treating evidence – and literary critical evidence always came last.[25] When Timpanaro discussed a textual problem, such as the phrase *arma relinquit* ('he left his arms', *Aeneid* 11.830), he only brought in literary critical reasoning as a kind of cherry on top, to cap a case already made with more 'solid' philological argumentation.[26] In Timpanaro's brilliant piece on Leopardian forgeries, his first reasons for spotting literary falsification were actually ideological: the passage of a draft of Leopardi's famous poem *L'infinito* seemed suspicious because it made use of a completely different discourse on the notorious hedge and its view.[27] This kind of ideological or philosophical inconsistency was more of a giveaway than the bad style, which is mentioned only later, shunted back as a secondary piece of evidence.[28] As a philologist interested in local textual problems, Timpanaro rarely had recourse to literary critical modes of argument, because they were considered lesser forms of argument in that particular discursive system. In fact, he claimed that formal philology explicitly forged him to be indifferent to matters of artistic value.[29] The ideal philologist was simply built not to care.

Nevertheless, even if we follow Timpanaro in his refusal to call his engagement with literature literary criticism, engage with literature he

---

25   Cf. Luigi Blasucci, 'Sugli studi Leopardiani di Timpanaro', in Riccardo Di Donato (ed.), *Il filologo materialista*, Pisa, 2003, 117, who thinks Timpanaro did wield his fair share of literary sensitivity but deliberately held literary comment back unless it was useful to the philological argument.

26   Piergiorgio Parroni, 'Timpanaro e la filologia', in Nuccio Ordine (ed.), *La lezione di un maestro: Omaggio a Sebastiano Timpanaro*, Naples, 2010, 68.

27   *AF*, 316.

28   *AF*, 317.

29   Giuseppina Magnaldi, 'Questioni di metodo: Plauto e Lucrezio', in Ghidetti and Pagnini, *Sebastiano Timpanaro*, 242.

did. Some interesting consequences follow from the way the materialist reads – consequences which feel a little heretical and counterintuitive to anyone familiar with the habits of modern literary criticism. One of the deep assumptions behind our critical encounters with literature, ranging from those led by the most committed Marxist critic to those of the most cutting-edge neoformalist, is that content and form are an inseparable unity. While different theoretical systems may privilege one over the other, or make one or the other more 'determining', most critics would acknowledge a kind of sacred bond between them. Timpanaro – ever suspicious of this brand of vague dialectical argument ramming binaries into unities – disagreed. Quite the opposite actually: form and content *are* separable.[30] One does not have to be an admirer of the one to appreciate the other. Even if the form, style, or language of a literary text reads as annoying or outmoded or aesthetically flawed in some way, one can still get something out of the ideas.[31] Indeed, Timpanaro was attracted precisely to the kind of text where these two elements feel out of phase – as if giving him a chance to say: Who cares about style, so long as the message is good and *true*? Content is the thing that *matters*.[32]

The Timpanaran canon is full of figures in literary history whose ideas were solid, but whose form and expression put people off. Leopardi and Giordani were singled out for their ability to look beyond this problem with a controversial writer like the first-century CE Roman poet Lucan, whose bombastic and sapping rhetorical style was making intellectuals write him off, to the detriment of his perfectly solid anti-Caesarism.[33] Giordani had a particularly deep appreciation of Lucan, based fundamentally on the content of his ideas, and thought people wrong to dimiss him on account of a few stylistic defects.[34] And there was a resonance here with the reception of Giordani himself. Here, the same sort of formal evaluation happened at the expense of content: readers would write off his ideas merely because they did not much care

---

30 For instance, with Leopardi on Plato: see below and S.T. to Silvano Piccoli, 28 April 1989.
31 See chapter 3.
32 S.T. to Giorgio Voghera, 22 June 1968.
33 *AF*, 6–7, 44, 53.
34 *AF*, 63.

for his archaic style.[35] But it was precisely the mismatch between back-ward-looking style and forward-looking content that characterised the contribution of Timpanaro's beloved Enlightenment classicists, includ-ing Giordani and Leopardi. And this was a pattern inaugurated much earlier, for example the first-century BCE Roman poet Lucretius making use of an archaic style for a completely radical and unprecedented 'enlightenment' (*ante litteram*) project.[36] Timpanaro set himself firmly against the tradition of Crocean aesthetics sounding off about style and form, to definitively separate this from the question of literary value. Reading was about extracting ideas. As long as the ideas contained within literature had continuing value, well, so did the literature itself: Timpanaro agreed wholeheartedly with Giorgio Fano's affirmation that a work of art needed serious and important *contents* to be truly great.[37] Conversely, bad ideas would always overrule decent aesthetic form, as the example of Giosuè Carducci's praise poetry showed.[38] What was more, the opposite arrangement might even arise. Style and content were so unhooked from each other that it was also perfectly possible to appreciate the former while hating the latter: Leopardi was anti-Platon-ist, philosophically speaking, but he still loved Plato's style.[39] Whichever way you looked at it, Timpanaro the splitter reinforced the separability of these phenomena. Once again, there was no dialectical synthesis or higher unity here. Timpanaro liked authors who were out of joint with themselves.

If there is a style to which Timpanaro was most drawn, it was the one that most efficiently enabled the readerly absorption of content, and the direct understanding of ideas: clarity. Timpanaro waxed lyrical (or perhaps crystalline) about the limpidness of style in one of his favourite works (to be discussed shortly), the historically underappreciated *Primo Maggio* of Edmondo De Amicis.[40] It was no coincidence that Timpanaro's eye settled on this work. It is an unpublished and unapologetic novel of ideas which many critics would describe as wooden and/or gelid – something which posed no issue for Timpanaro because the ideas and

---

35   *CI*, 64–5, 122–3; see chapter 3.
36   *CI*, 25.
37   S.T. to Giorgio Voghera, 22 June 1968.
38   S.T. to Roberto Tissoni, 5 July 1974.
39   *CI*, 211–15; S.T. to Silvano Piccoli, 28 April 1989.
40   *SED*, 178.

debates come across with simplicity, and they are there for us to pick up and debate as we might in a political meeting. We have seen, too, that many of Timpanaro's works were committed to the idea of widespread divulgation, and that he was attracted to works themselves designed as unoriginal 'diffusers' of particular ideas, such as Holbach's *Good Sense* (*Il buon senso*). The 'style' common to these, again, is a kind of Enlightenment packaging tailored to the full, unhampered transmission of content from page to readerly mind.[41] Even when it came to poetry, that most abstruse and remote mode of discourse, Timpanaro declared a preference for intelligible verse with propositional content.[42] Anything tending towards pure sound, which eschewed too boldly the task of sense-making in language, was not worth the time.[43] He wanted us to be able to *get it*.

These statements sometimes read like a slightly more sophisticated version of a drunken uncle at Christmas wilfully declaring the failure of poetry, simply because he refuses to understand it. Having nothing else to say about it except 'it's unintelligible', that is all he can and does end up saying. These Timpanaran aesthetics of content, we might call them, go against the deepest-held teachings of the literature industry and the academy underwriting it. But, then again, who has not sat through a poetry reading (or ploughed through an academic article for that matter) and emerged dismayed at the irritating disregard for how the ideas might actually get from author to audience? Who has not found themselves precisely attracted to the poems or works they can understand at the level of content, in part because they are understandable? As usual, the contenutista, putting forth his content in a language of roughness and bluntness we cannot help but understand, may have had a nagging point.[44]

Despite Timpanaro's ongoing resistance to performing literary criticism, and his attraction to literature as an expression of philosophical

---

41   Clarity of *Il buon senso*: BS, xviii.

42   S.T. to Alceste Angelini, 15 May 1963; S.T. to Luca Baranelli, 6 September 1967? (year unclear; numbered 15 in the Timpanaro archive); S.T. to Romano Luperini, 14 May 1968. Cf. S.T. to Romano Luperini, 29 April 1968, where Timpanaro expresses a need for the cognitive content in art.

43   S.T. to Alceste Angelini, 15 May 1963.

44   Timpanaro's programmatic 'roughness' (*rozzezza*): S.T. to Alfonso Traina, 23 March 1995, 25 November 1996.

and political ideas, he sometimes came close to lapsing into it.[45] And he came especially close in the later phase of his career.[46] Ironically, one of his most sustained efforts at a reading of a literary text focussed on an author who was writing only for himself at a moment of state-enforced solitude: Carlo Bini, the Livornese writer, translator, and revolutionary who went to prison on Elba for links with the politician and national unification figurehead Giuseppe Mazzini and the pro-unification revolutionary group Giovine Italia. Timpanaro's job in this piece – an appendix of his *Antileopardiani*, almost as long as a short book in itself – was to save the revolutionary materialism and atheism of Bini, as well as isolate him from the political project of the Tuscan moderates.[47] This was a rescue job parallel to Timpanaro's salvage of Leopardi, who had suffered in the exaltation of the group around the Florence-based *Antologia* as the ultimate organic intellectuals of the pre-Risorgimento period.[48] Timpanaro's account of Bini, as Perry Anderson has noted, is one of his most personal, most sympathetic, and most autobiographical in its resonance.[49] And one major feature of Bini by which Timpanaro was most quickened, I think, is how a writer without a public, a revolutionary in a non-revolutionary period, can communicate across time.[50] Within the Timpanaran system, writing for the self is permissible so long as that self is organically bound to a future time of which it has proved to be all too far ahead – and as long as it is not all about oneself.

Timpanaro was invested in figures whose thought shifted gear after a big experiential break. What we will see happen, below, with the artistic fallout of De Amicis's socialist conversion also happened, in a sense, for

---

45   Luca Baranelli thinks Timpanaro came close to a taste of sustained literary criticism in his exchange with Cases on Heinrich and Thomas Mann – Luca Baranelli, introduction to *Cesare Cases – Sebastiano Timpanaro: Un lapsus di Marx; Carteggio 1956–1990*, Pisa, 2015, viii.

46   Emiliano Narducci groups in this late literary burst Timpanaro's work on Senecan tragedy, the appendix on Bini, the book on De Amicis, and also the emphasis on the connection between form and content in the Holbach *Il buon senso* edition (Narducci, 'Sebastiano Timpanaro', 310).

47   Bini's *Manoscritto* as emblem of Leopardi-style materialism, anti-providentialism, and pessimism: *AN*, 86. The evolution of Bini's pessimism: *AN*, 258.

48   Leopardian materialism, according to Timpanaro, was way too advanced for the *Antologia* crowd: *AN*, 171.

49   Perry Anderson, 'On Sebastiano Timpanaro', *London Review of Books* 23, no. 9 (May 2001).

50   *AN*, 271.

Carlo Bini. Bini had an early life far more embedded among the Livornese plebs than Giuseppe Mazzini among the Genovese, and Timpanaro showed Bini's sympathy for the poor as an outgrowth of greater direct experience among them.[51] But his writing was blocked because he could not find an audience among these people, who were largely illiterate. When Mazzini asked why Bini was not writing, he replied: 'Whom to write for'?[52] It took Bini's imprisonment on Elba in 1833 for his relationship to Mazzini and Giovine Italia to get his energies properly flowing. As Timpanaro put it, it was the new impossibility of a public, from the solitude of prison, that gave Bini the excuse to write for himself.[53] And what he wrote was something new, in content as well as style. The shift, in other words, stemmed from a material change in the conditions of Bini's life.

These new departures – the *Manoscritto*, and the *Forte della Stella* – were literary-philosophical dialogues featuring a Bini-style character and an anonymous interlocutor. (The literary form of the dialogue, incidentally, was clearly one of Timpanaro's favourites, from Cicero's *On Divination* to the heavily dialogic sections of *Primo Maggio*). But it was not, in Timpanaro's view, Bini's discourse on himself. The work treated the very different carceral fates of rich and poor. There was a political commitment constantly folding out to the world beyond the author.[54] Timpanaro singled out a series of praiseworthy items of political content in this text: the merchant as a thief; the noble an idiot of leisure; the foreshadowing of the time of proletarian revolution; the denaturalisation and fierce lack of resignation to poverty as a given; the Catholic Church as a structure deeply allied with the ruling class against the proletariat; the mild pessimism that set up a post-revolutionary future as something only mildly less unhappy than the present day, still shot through with inequality, oppression, superstition, and the precarity of one's individual existence; this non-negotiable precarity making the ultimate disappearance of religion pretty unlikely; in other words, religion appears as a false consolation.[55] This is a kind of inventory, in miniature, of the Timpanaran worldview, located in a Livornese thinker

---

51 *AN*, 215.
52 *AN*, 218.
53 *AN*, 219.
54 *AN*, 220.
55 *AN*, 226–7, 232, 235–6.

in the first part of the nineteenth century. If Bini struggled to find a literate proletarian audience for his work in his own day, he certainly found a twentieth-century revolutionary who would devour him.

The contenutista was certainly at it again here, hooking on to Bini for the substance coursing through him. But there is also a short section – no more than a few pages – in which Timpanaro indulged himself the opportunity of talking about one of the most striking features of the *Manoscritto*: an oscillation between wildly different *tones*, identified as vehement, ironic, or stringently reasoning.[56] Timpanaro saw the influence of an author like the eighteenth-century satirical novelist Laurence Sterne (1713–1768) here, and possibly even a touch of Leopardi.[57] To be certain, this quick, jarring swing between tones materialised the desirable Timpanaran trait of juxtaposition and conflict without reconciliation, except here transplanted from the level of content to that of tone. But it also allowed Timpanaro a rare opportunity to comment on the function of this sort of tonal diversity, which he chalked up to a complex, constant process of 'rebalancing': if sentimentalism was about to take the upper hand, suddenly the irony came in to 'rescale' (*ridimensionare*) it, and vice versa.[58] Timpanaro thought that these swings were more extreme than anything in Sterne. They allowed for a kind of restless discomfort, an unsettling exercise in constant self-revision.[59] It is hard not to read them as the tonal equivalent of the endless thinkings and rethinkings of Timpanaran philology: a constant scrutiny of the ego to test it against the world, a state of deep unhappiness and un-compromise permitting neither an accommodation with that world nor a settled relation to it. Materialism requires constant recalibration, correction. In Bini, Timpanaro found a perfect tonal expression thereof.

After these few pages, though, Timpanaro again called himself back to earth with the usual declaration that stylistic criticism was simply not his calling. And, a few pages later, there is even a warning about excessive attentiveness to tone as a kind of distraction from content. Even those who appreciate Bini, Timpanaro wrote, seem to just appreciate

---

56   *AN*, 228.
57   *AN*, 207, 224, 228, 242.
58   *AN*, 229.
59   On Timpanaran self-revision, see chapter 2.

him for an ironic-melancholic tone similar to (and derivative from) those of Sterne and Foscolo.[60] But what about that content? Timpanaro ran straight back to contenutista-redeemer mode, arguing that engagement with Bini's social and political ideas had not included any care for the materialist and anti-providentialist components of his thought in the *Manoscritto*.[61] According to Timpanaro, Bini formed yet another chapter in the long (Italian, but also international) history of the marginalisation of materialism, the philosophical purging of the substance from thinkers who had it in their blood.[62] This process of sidelining materialism – begun straightaway in Bini's case, with Mazzini's foreword to the first edition – was part of a historical pattern which Timpanaro saw as self-repeating: wherever there was materialism (everywhere, at every moment), there were always attempts to melt it into air, to 'respiritualise' it.[63] Bini's fate happened also to Leopardi. When Timpanaro wrote the Bini piece, he saw Marxism undergoing the same process. This is why reading for content – *all of it* – mattered. For Timpanaro, content was the vehicle of materialism, and it was always under threat.

Timpanaro had already had the argument about tone versus content with Cesare Cases in 1963.[64] Cases claimed that Timpanaro's contenutista ways always made him emphasise the non-superstructural parts of art and philosophy: Timpanaro's basic materialist eye would always land on commonalities across content in time, such as the idea, present in every historical epoch, that it was good to be young and bad to be old. Cases thought that historical difference was actually contained in the tone of art, however – and tone was where the superstructure could be found and tracked. Timpanaro rebutted this with scepticism: 'tone makes the song' was one step away from an all-out idealist elevation of form over content. We can see that his reading of Bini made the same move: it gave comments on tone a mere few pages, making sure to move right along to the heart of the matter.

There are a few more strands to Bini which make him a particularly Timpanaran figure. The first is that the content of his ideas is not just

60   *AN*, 242.
61   *AN*, 243.
62   *AN*, 243–4.
63   *AN*, 243–4, 278–9.
64   Cesare Cases to S.T., 10 February 1963.

met with the seal of approval (atheism, materialism, anti-providentialism . . . Bini's ideological CV reads like a carbon copy of Timpanaro's); it
is that this content is *not particularly original*. We have seen the value
Timpanaro puts on unoriginality, and we noted his gravitation to more
derivative and divulgative texts such as *Il buon senso*.[65] Here, again,
Bini's lack of originality bumped him down in Timpanaro's estimation
not one jot: 'Until certain battles are won, striking and striking again is
necessary.'[66] We might think back to Holbach's repetitive style as a peda-
gogical tool of turning the screw on the reader: *battere e ribattere*,
ramming the point home.[67] Again, the formal awkwardness of repetition did not matter if the ideas were good and the fight righteous. (We
will return to this point in the conclusion.) Secondly, as hinted above,
there is a pathos-ridden resonance to Bini's status as a revolutionary
unable to see his plans come off because he was living in a non-revolutionary moment. As Timpanaro described Bini's bind – maintaining his
ideas, but surrendering to a loss of heart at their practicability in the
short term and uninterested in their fulfilment in the long term – the
language he uses (*a breve termine*) is hauntingly reminiscent of his own
political disillusionment. In Timpanaro's own lifetime, socialism had
gone from a real prospect, to a goal unlikely to be realised in the short
term, to a remote aspiration even in the long view.[68] It is perhaps the
bind of living in the wrong time that united Timpanaro to this Livornese
Carbonaro, as it did to Leopardi. But at least they could enjoy each
other's virtual company.

Bini's time in prison ironically liberated him from the problem of a
reading public. But after this, he never produced work of this kind again.
The rest of his written contributions were translations.[69] He was
confronted, once more, by the lack of readership. And his reception was
plagued from the start by people who have not actually read him.[70]
Mazzini's first Bini edition omitted the choice cuts of the *Manoscritto*,

65 See chapter 3.
66 'Ma finché certe battaglie non vengano vinte, battere e ribattere è necessario'
(*AN*, 245). See conclusion.
67 *BS*, lxvi; see also conclusion.
68 *AN*, 271. Timpanaro in 1971 was already critical of Lotta Continua's faith in
revolution *a breve termine* (S.T. to Grazia Cherchi, 3 March 1971), and had certainly lost
any such himself by 1981 (S.T. to Umberto Carpi, 10 June 1981).
69 *AN*, 258.
70 *AN*, 259–60, 279–81.

and the entirety of the *Forte della stella*. In Timpanaro's view, publication of those controversial works would have taken a sympathetic group of communists and materialists to be viable.[71] Instead, Mazzini's edition inaugurated a completely wrong-headed, skewed image of a radical thinker, which would then pass into another non-reader of Bini in the misprision of the literary critic Francesco De Sanctis.[72] Timpanaro's appendix corrected for this deliberate unknowing of the real Bini. When content has been erased, sometimes you need the contenutista to put it back in place.

If the early editorial interventions into Bini's corpus completely doctored his image and put his reception on the wrong track, Timpanaro was not about to let a parallel fate befall an important work of true socialist literature from the late nineteenth century, the reception of which had only just begun: the *Primo Maggio* of Edmondo De Amicis. Begun in 1891 but shelved by its author, the novel was only published almost a hundred years later, in 1980.[73] That did not mean there had not already been ample time for its critical tradition to go astray. As with Bini's first edition, so in the case of the *Primo Maggio*: the text was handled by an editor, Giorgio Bertone, who did not really grasp its author, politically speaking.[74] To make matters worse, the editor made a bit of a philological meal of it, introducing a careless mass of errors into the text. Timpanaro did not want another Bini on our hands. The only way forward was early corrective intervention – an intercession that emerged as one of Timpanaro's most beautiful and engaged books: *Il socialismo di Edmondo de Amicis*.

Why was Timpanaro interested in saving De Amicis's novel from political and philological assassination by a thousand cuts? The *Primo Maggio* is the story of a young bourgeois socialist in late nineteenth-century Turin, and the inner struggles and outer conflicts he confronts as he works and talks and agitates to actuate socialism. It is a novel of ideas, with large swathes of it devoted to political dialogue seriously

---

71 *AN*, 278–9.
72 *AN*, 280–1.
73 *SED*, 17.
74 *SED*, 18–19; on the general undeserved attacks on De Amicis in scholarship, see Luciano Tamburini, 'Cuore's progress: De Amicis socialista', in Ghidetti and Pagnini, *Sebastiano Timpanaro*, 295.

treating the contemporary issues facing the socialist movement of the Second International era: the problems of a bourgeois converting to socialism and working for the elimination of their class (*Il socialismo*, chapters 2 and 3); the difference between bourgeois and proletarian revolution (chapter 4); the necessity of scientific socialism (chapter 5); the ideological hollowing out of bourgeois values like fatherland, school, army, religion, and the family (chapters 6, 7, 8); socialism and the question of women (chapter 8); the refutation of capitalist remedies to capitalist problems (chapter 9); the unavoidable nature of class struggle (chapter 10); the problem of when the revolution would or could come (chapter 11); what the post-revolutionary world would look like, and how it should be run (chapter 12); the role of emotion and sentiment in socialist politics (chapter 13); and the relationship of anarchism to socialism, and the possibility of their cooperation (chapter 14). All of these themes come in for serious treatment in the novel. Their resonance with a socialist of Timpanaro's brand and calibre is easy to appreciate.[75] So there was again an attraction to the salvage and divulgation of content here, rather than an emphasis on form. Timpanaro agreed that, as a work of art, this unpublished novel was quite rough around the edges. Indeed, it was definitely *not* a masterpiece.[76] But it contained political material which has shown itself to be extremely valuable, particularly in the context of the rapid retreat of revolutionary politics in 1980s Italy.[77] More than ever, during this historical slump of the left, the tradition of these ideas needed philological care.

But there was also something spicier prompting this fit of Timpanaran pique, which ended up generating not only one of his best books and closest engagements with literature, but nothing short of a late-phase reassertion, with full militancy, of revolutionary socialism *itself*. Timpanaro was annoyed that the critics had got this book so *wrong*. They had made, in his view, a classic mistake of a priori automatism: because the book shared some tonal and structural elements with previous works of De Amicis, the critics had written *Primo Maggio* off as a cringeworthy text in the same vein of saccharine sentimentalism as

---

75   On the resonance of all of these issues for the contemporary socialist, see also Bufarale, *Sebastiano Timpanaro*, 51–2.

76   See S.T. to Enrico Ghidetti, 28 April 1984.

77   *SED*, 11.

Cuore, De Amicis's patriotic children's novel set in Turin during Italian unification.[78] The preconceived notion of De Amicis's style made everyone read this creative tract of De Amicisian socialism as equally kitsch and pathos ridden, a pure tear-jerker, a simplistic advocate of love and humanity and charity.[79] But that was to completely underestimate the foundations of the book in a deep scientific socialism responsibly informed by a Second International programme.[80] The fact that the critics had got the book so wrong was yet another textbook display of the failure of criticism to hold back its superimposition of ideas decided in advance. Instead, to do the book justice and to extract its value, one needed a kind of scientific and materialist criticism which attended to the specific contours of the object at hand and recalibrated the general theory of De Amicis from there. Not: De Amicis is maudlin, hence *Primo Maggio* is too. Rather: this book's newness must make us rewrite the history of De Amicisian political commitment and the history of what socialism can do. It was a classic act of radical Timpanaran empiricism: taking a singular object of study and using it as a spanner not just to jam the works but to get them working differently.

At stake here was the significant question of the very possibility of socialist 'conversion' at the individual level, and what this meant for the prospects of socialism as a collective movement. The critics who pushed for continuity in reading the *Primo Maggio* – contending that this was just the same old pre-socialist De Amicis ploughing his furrow, and that nothing had really changed – were not politically neutral. They were effectively pushing the cynical line that an individual's commitment to socialism was ultimately token and superficial. Change a person's politics and nothing happened; the aesthetic substance and identity of the text remained the same, and this aesthetic element constituted the proper object of literary analysis. With revolutionary prospects in retreat, these literary critics gave up on the very idea that a writer might convert to a deeply held, 'authentic' socialism. Timpanaro was combatting many things in this book, but perhaps above all, he was battling this contemporary disenchantment, the spirit of historic compromise, which

78   *SED*, 10.
79   Ironically, *Primo Maggio* goes out of its way to discredit the very idea of charity; a stretch, then, to call it (as Graf did) *caritativo* (*SED*, 69); cf. Tamburini, '*Cuore*'s progress', 294.
80   *SED*, 49, 59, 119.

had given up on the possibility of a revolutionary break, and retreated from the very idea of conversion to the cause. But the battleground was rescaled to the personal and individual level. Timpanaro asserted, in no uncertain terms, that De Amicis did indeed convert properly to socialism; he thought about it, debated it, internalised it deeply; and the evidence was there in the care with which this (admittedly aesthetically inchoate) text presented a live socialism in the making. No, just because we have given up on socialism in the present should not make us purge individuals of their socialism in the past. De Amicis was serious. While he may only have joined the PSI in 1896, five years after starting *Primo Maggio*, the novel could almost be considered the working draft of his conversion to true socialist.

What made this book of Timpanaran 'criticism' so charged, so interesting to read, is the convergence of these high stakes – the possibility of authentic socialist commitment – on three levels. First, there was the way this question played out internal to *Primo Maggio* itself. The novel's protagonist, Alberto, is constantly navigating the tensions of his class position: born into the bourgeoisie, he has decided to actively renounce his wealth and privilege to become a teacher – and the direct experience of want seals his radicalisation.[81] There are residual moments of wavering commitment, for instance, when Alberto finds himself siding with the police as a kind of instinctual reaction to riot. But they pass. And Alberto's commitment to socialism is ultimately proven strong enough to offer the ultimate sacrifice. Nevertheless, the problem of the paradoxical position of the bourgeois socialist is real, and there is an obvious synchronicity between Alberto's committed conversion (with lapses) and the conversion at the second level – namely, De Amicis's own navigation of his class position within his new politics.[82] If Alberto stands in for De Amicis, indeed guarantees him in the fictional universe the practicability of being a bourgeois socialist in the real one, there must also be a sympathy-chain operative at the next 'autobiographical' level – that of Timpanaro himself. While not strictly 'bourgeois' in the technical sense of coming from a family with ownership over the means of production and in the position of directly exploiting workers, Timpanaro was deeply

---

81   *SED*, 27–8.
82   Though Timpanaro points out the differences between protagonist and author too: *SED*, 72.

aware of his intelligentsia roots. He had the feeling of a sad distance from the core of the working class in Italy (who tended to cluster in the PCI),[83] and the sense that he was, at base, a bad militant: someone who had avowed revolutionary politics but lacked the gumption to fight on the front lines, were revolution actually to arrive.[84] So, for the intellectual socialist who had struggled for much of his life in a militant party without a large proletarian base (such as the PCI could boast), there was a redemptive story to hold on to here. Even if the revolutionary cause was doomed, as it proved in the historical conditions encompassing Alberto, De Amicis, and Timpanaro himself, the important thing was to commit. And, while one's non-working-class background made the 'authenticity' of that commitment harder, more fraught with doubts and contradictions, authentic commitment it still was.

Primo Maggio also underlines the astonishing difficulty of this kind of conversion when the entire power of bourgeois property and ideology are lined up against it – and it is precisely on this issue that Timpanaro reached greatest sensitivity as a 'literary critic' attentive to the function of form. The book had come in for criticism over its fairly stagnant patches of dialogue pitting mouthpieces of conflicting ideological orientations together: socialist versus capitalist, socialist versus anarchist, socialist versus advocate of family and charity. There are some particularly wooden interactions between Alberto and his wife, Giulia, who responds to Alberto's reasoning with prefabricated apothegms like 'But, dear Alberto, the mission of the woman is the family!' These oscillations of objection and reply do risk coming across as stilted, not to mention the unfortunate and predictable gender politics of placing the argument for immobile domesticity in the mouth of a woman. But Timpanaro encourages us to give these features a chance. There is a good political reason for this formal stiffness: it shows the intransigence of the bourgeoisie, the significant armoury of fixed ideas which enables them to keep batting back, with a kind of deadheaded automatism, the compelling arguments for socialism.[85] There is a pointlessness to these conversations, a frozen inflexibility to all these interlocutors of the socialist,

---

83   Timpanaro admitted he was not under any delusions that any party other than the PCI was capable of making revolution by the late '70s (S.T. to Girolamo De Liguori, 4 November 1979) – an acknowledgement of his isolation from the masses.

84   Cf. introduction.

85   *SED*, 70–1.

which must have resonated deeply with Timpanaro's participation in difficult recruitment drives for the cause over the years. The bourgeoisie's class interests block their ears. They are constitutionally deaf to the calls of socialism. And, as above, it is only Alberto's direct experience of injustice and material deprivation – not arguments – that allowed him to convert. *Primo Maggio* shows debates at deadlock.

So, the novel flags the gargantuan difficulty of actuating socialism, and that in itself gave it a lot of purchase in the world of Timpanaro's later career. But there were also upbeat elements in Timpanaro's reading of *Primo Maggio* – a sign of energy drawn from this act of 'literary criticism' doubling as a recommitment to socialism and an affirmation of authenticity. In one of the most moving chapters of *Il socialismo*, called 'the reasons of the heart', Timpanaro discussed De Amicis's realisation that socialism needed a solid grounding of reasoned theory but could not be based on that alone. It also required the resources of *feeling*: the gut disgust towards injustice and inequality, a real 'participation' at an emotional level in the suffering of the oppressed.[86] In the midst of this discussion, Timpanaro allowed himself a defence of the basics of Marxism. Marxism could never disappear, because the need and suffering created by capitalism had not yet disappeared; but there was a continual need to anchor it in the basic sentiment of the intolerability of an unjust society.[87] Through the mouthpiece of Ernesta, Alberto's sister, De Amicisian sentiment is finally given a political function: 'Sentiment gives colour to reasons', she says, 'like the sun does with things.'[88] But the telling moment arrives when Timpanaro reconciles all of this sentimental socialism with the scientific brand to which he has devoted his life. He confronted the problem of the rigidity of Marxist doctrine and the idea, often thrown against it, that if one part of it falls, the rest has to follow. But to Timpanaro, what science gave to Marxism was a kind of flexibility and animation, the very stuff of life, the organic ability to change: 'It's a matter of recognising also in Marxism those characteristics of problematic-ness, of correctability, of the possibility of

---

86   *SED*, 144–5. Bufarale, *Sebastiano Timpanaro*, 52–3, is also drawn to this crucial passage.
87   *SED*, 149.
88   *SED*, 154.

refoundation that are recognised in any science, and recognising that it is never, however, a case of "starting from scratch".[89]

What science imparts to Marxism, as a science itself, is the possibility of endless self-problematisation, self-revision, self-correction, a constant toggle without ever being wiped in reset.[90] It would be hard to find, I think, a better articulation of Timpanaro's Marxism: its status as science is not the thing that desiccates it into bloodless reason, but the thing that keeps it alive, with its eye always on the world.

We have talked of the blocks of the bourgeoisie that render socialism difficult to push in argument form and, hence, risk making the ideological content of the book come off as a bit stiff. But Timpanaro also saw in the *Primo Maggio* the kind of vibrant, contested, self-correcting socialism he spent his life trying to bring into being – and indeed living, at some level, in that very heated pose of constant critique he maintained his whole life. One of the other attractive features he located in De Amicisian socialism, as expressed in the *Primo Maggio*, was its appreciation for the value of the anarchists. Their ideas might be partly misguided, as any orthodox Marxist would think, maintaining a naive faith in the ability of humanity to bring revolution *now* as a magical and instant leap to self-governing communism without a transitional state. But if their politics raised an eyebrow as hopelessly utopian, the book also redeemed them as absolutely necessary to the healthy workings of socialism. They provide a constant force of 'revolutionary ferment', an ever-present 'goad', an oppositional force creating the proper degree of generative conflict to keep socialism on its toes – *discordia concors*, 'harmonious discord', Timpanaro called it.[91] They make life difficult, but they provide a necessary spur, a source of disagreement pushing the more 'realistic' socialists in the right aspirational direction. They are ideal vehicles of the constant correction and self-scrutiny powering any socialism worth the name.

In the end, the tireless prodding and goading of the anarchist in *Primo Maggio* is partly how Timpanaro saw his own role, as well as the role of De Amicis the socialist: pushing forward in a way that seems out

---

89   *SED*, 148.
90   Cf. chapter 2.
91   *SED*, 160. Timpanaro (not coincidentally) also described his friendship with Piero Treves – an invitation to contribute to whose Festschrift was the original prompt for the *SED* – as full of *discordia concors* (*SED*, 14).

of joint with the times. The last section of *Il socialismo* is dedicated to the honest Timpanaran task of self-updating. Timpanaro acknowledged that he had 'lost priority' on some of his points, beaten to it by the Ligurian writer and literary critic Gina Lagorio's excellent article on the socialist ideological meat of the *Primo Maggio*.[92] The piece had been published two years before the release of *Il socialismo*, but Timpanaro had been unaware of it at the time. Timpanaro was happy about this loss of priority, as he always was; he thought Lagorio, more embedded in contemporary problems, would be more effective at winning people over to the cause of *Primo Maggio* than Timpanaro himself.[93] This because he once again declared himself an irrelevance: a kind of 'nineteenth-century dinosaur' located 'by accident' in the twentieth. In posing yet again as backwards, Timpanaro wrote, as so often, of a subject too far ahead: he speculated De Amicis probably did not publish the novel initially partly because his reading public would not have been ready for it.[94] According to him, De Amicis's socialism was too advanced for his bourgeois market. If that sounds familiar, it is because it is: the same pattern held for Bini, as it did for Leopardi, as it did for many of the thinkers with whom Timpanaro sympathetically identified over the years. Again and again, the dinosaur, stuck so far behind the times he almost belongs in a different geological era, joins forces across the years with those who were ahead of him, assembles under the banner of a materialism which is constantly renewed, recommitted, and interrogated. And in the end, the contenutista finds a way of reading literature that allows those thinkers, so perennially out of step with their time, to form an ever-expanding phalanx of materialist misfits. They will reconvene with yet others, eventually – in a future they prefigured and missed, but whose content they will continue to supply, for as long as it takes.

---

92   Gina Lagorio, 'Se il cuore di De Amicis batte per il socialismo', *Resto del Carlino*, 30 April 1980.

93   *SED*, 204.

94   *SED*, 179–80.

Conclusion

Battere e Ribattere

As this study of our restless thinker draws to its close, I begin with a somewhat stressful story drawn from Timpanaro's last decade. In a chapter designed to bring some threads together, we should respect, first and foremost, that Timpanaro mostly did not *want* to be brought together. In fact, he preferred to have his various components kept apart. Nowhere is this truer than of the two main ingredients of Timpanaro's life: politics and philology.

Over the years, Timpanaro's polemical style ruffled a few feathers. Other stories of personal conflict in this book have focussed on such ruffling within two different but overlapping spheres of Timpanaro's life: the radical left and its sensitivity around Trotsky; and the politics of Leopardian cultural heritage. But Timpanaro also got snagged in conflict while engaged in the more rarefied debates of high philology. Italian philology was a sensitive world, packed with short fuses, big egos, and deep convictions. Timpanaro would always claim – though the reality must surely be more complex – that one of his oldest friends and closest leftist-philologist allies, Antonio La Penna, stopped talking to him in the mid-1980s merely because he respectfully dismissed one of his ideas about the Virgilian indirect tradition.[1] With its journal-based print culture of constant engagement, review, and response, this milieu was particularly vulnerable to the snowballing effects of statements being

---

1 S.T. to Alfonso Traina, 5 May 1997.

taken the wrong way, critiques of ideas being translated to the personal plane and heated up in the process. Mediated cultures of 'frank' debate tend to emotional volatility. And, in the world of twentieth-century Italian classical philology, the social fallout could often be real.

By far the most intense and upsetting of these erupted conflicts, for Timpanaro, was an affair with Enrico Livrea in the mid-'90s. Livrea was then a professor of classical philology at the University of Messina. The issue that came between them is a bone of contention with very low stakes (at least to a non-philologist): a reference to 'the tears of Homer' in Ennius, alluded to in the mid-first-century BCE Roman poet Lucretius's poem *On the Nature of the Universe* (1.120–26). Livrea thought that the source of these tears was meant to be pain and grief; Timpanaro, that they should be understood as tears of joy. Both scholars had their reasons, and it would not be particularly courteous to a general reader to dive too deeply into them. Nor am I particularly concerned with philological adjudication. The more interesting thing, for our purposes, is to note how acrimoniously the matter devolved into bad blood. Livrea was soon accusing Timpanaro of fascist/Stalinist/masonist tendencies of stifling debate and issuing defamatory character assassinations.[2] Timpanaro implied Livrea was psychologically unstable and depressed.[3] It got spectacularly ugly. Quite apart from the heated print exchange itself, and the evidence of Timpanaro's distress flooding his correspondence at the time, it became a matter of Timpanaro desperately rescuing himself from reputational damage. Even three years after he had vowed to say his last word on the subject, he wrote to the then editor of the UK's leading classics journal *Classical Quarterly*, Christopher Collard, with an annoyed complaint about *CQ* publishing Livrea's most recent intervention on the issue – a short article that reopened the question, as well as old wounds.[4] Timpanaro's ire in this letter was still well and truly burning. Indeed, it is one of the only times in the whole correspondence that he vented spleen through a raw display

---

2 S.T. to Siegmar Döpp, 25 July 1995? (year unclear; numbered 1 in Timpanaro archive).

3 Timpanaro explains this in 'Un'ultima risposta al prof. Livrea', *Paideia* 51 (1996): n8.

4 S.T. to Christopher Collard, 1999 (n.d. apart from year; numbered 1 in Timpanaro archive). The article was Enrico Livrea, 'A New Pythagorean Fragment and Homer's Tears in Ennius', *Classical Quarterly* 48, no. 2 (1998): 559–61.

of ego, outraged by Livrea's continuing disrespect, and making it all the more outrageous by invoking his own high standing in the philological stratosphere.[5] Timpanaro's traumatised pique over this matter clearly never subsided.

This was far from a squall in a teacup, or two litigious philologists caring too much about some silly pedantic detail. For Timpanaro, the conflict flushed out some interesting and revealing beliefs about what philology, and the intellectual ethics and politics around it, should be. The first principle Timpanaro was defending was something we have seen before, especially in the concrete episodes of conflict discussed in this book: the principle of free and *invited* dissent and debate, which he saw as a lodestone of Pasqualian philology.[6] Timpanaro was particularly offended by Livrea's overheated accusations implying he was some sort of oppressive censor of discussion, the common thread behind Livrea's scattershot critiques, by turns aligning Timpanaro with Masonry, the Mafia, Nazism, and, last but not least, Stalinism. Timpanaro had spent his life combatting all of these, and his identity was bound up in stalwart opposition to them – particularly to Stalinism, arguably his biggest opponent on the post-war left.[7] These were slights calculated to rile Timpanaro, because they called him by names he had built himself against, embodying the antithesis of the intellectual and political principles he held dearest: open critique, free debate. The move also reeked of another Timpanaran sin: lumping a person in a catch-all category that had nothing to do with them, failing to acknowledge the distinctions between the vast spectrum of positions on the left. In Livrea's careless characterisation, Timpanaro had now become the victim of his own worst nightmare: grouped unceremoniously with the Stalin apologists he despised. It is pretty clear that branding Timpanaro a Stalinist was more or less the worst thing one could have said about him: not only did it get his politics wrong, but it got the entire politics of the left equally wrong by conflating Stalinism with socialism.

So, we see how Timpanaro reacted when the accusation of suppressing discussion – which he himself had flung many a time – is on the

---

5   S.T. to Christopher Collard, 1999 (n.d. apart from year; numbered 1 in Timpanaro archive).

6   Cf. chapter 2.

7   S.T. to Siegmar Döpp, 25 July 1995? (year unclear; numbered 1 in Timpanaro archive).

other foot. But the Livrea affair was not just a menace to Timpanaro's deep-set intellectual politics. It was also so shudderingly offensive because it threatened to violate another one of Timpanaro's most hard-wired convictions: that politics should never, *ever* inflect philology. This book has tried to read against this delicate cordon sanitaire and productively breach it in its own way. But the fact is that Timpanaro policed the strictest of separations between the two spheres *insofar as philology should never get too political*. Timpanaro baldly stated the principle in his 1994 interview for *Marxismo Oggi*: 'On works of this kind [i.e., philology] the influence of Marxism is basically nothing.'[8] But nowhere was this better articulated than in the white heat of the Livrea affair. In a soul-bearing letter to German philologist Siegmar Döpp, Timpanaro complained that Livrea had broken the rules of the game in transplanting a purely philological affair into the realm of the moral-political:

> In that invective of his there was also a mention of my 'indestructible materialism' and my attachment to 'ideologies swept away by history': seeing that trouble was afoot, Prof. Livrea was trying to move the disagreement onto the political plane, while it was about a merely philological discussion.[9]

To Livrea's accusation that Timpanaro inhabited a 'Stalinist-masonic' world, our materialist philologist responded with the following proud self-definition:

> I've been a left-wing socialist, Marxist and Leninist without any particular orthodoxy, with sympathies also for the thought of Trotsky, but with clear hostility to Stalinism, which I've always considered to be a degeneration, not a continuation, of Marxism and Leninism. As regards the relationship between man and nature, I've received a great amount of the ideas of the more coherent version of French Enlightenment and of the original and (in my opinion) still relevant development that Giacomo Leopardi, a great Italian poet-thinker, has given it. As is obvious, these ideas of mine can be discussed and

8   *VR*, 219.
9   Ibid.

rejected (currently they are more than before); but I've never used these ideas of mine to interpret Greek and Latin authors in a tendentious way.[10]

Timpanaro proudly asserted that – unlike the cheap manoeuvres of Livrea – he had never let his politics intrude into his philology, to distort his interpretations of Greco-Roman literature in particular directions.[11] He claimed to have challenged Livrea purely at the level of philology; Livrea responded by shifting the goalposts, moving the discussion to political territory completely irrelevant to Homer's tears. It is almost as if a gentleman's code had been breached.

Timpanaro restated this commitment to the separation of philology and politics when he revisited the matter with the German classical scholar Hartmut Erbse (1915–2004) a few months later. Again, Timpanaro upbraided Livrea for undue code-switching: he should have replied to philological arguments with philological arguments. But this time, he also reached for a scaffolding example from the annals of philology itself. Timpanaro cited one of the major works of the legendary German philologist Ulrich von Wilamowitz-Moellendorf, *Sappho und Simonides* (Sappho and Simonides), this time to say that even if there *is* occasionally politics in philology, it can be – nay, should be – safely detached and ignored. This work was infamous for displaying signs of Wilamowitz's anti-Semitism, but for Timpanaro, from the philological point of view, that had absolutely nothing to do with anything:[12]

Wilamowitz, in *Sappho and Simonides*, wrote against the Jews, as is known, words that it would've been better not to write – but *Sappho and Simonides* nevertheless remains a work that has to be valued on the basis of its scientific worth. It's not right – if one is short for

---

10   Ibid.

11   Cf. S.T. to Silvia Rizzo, 4 June 1979 for Timpanaro's restatement of never taking 'political' approaches to antiquity. Cf. S.T. to Antonio La Penna (n.d. and unsent; numbered 61 in the Timpanaro archive).

12   Timpanaro was not necessarily consistent on this question, however: he also praised Rudolf Führer for exposing the philologist Werner's Nazism, and resented the head-in-the-sand thinking of philologists refusing to be disturbed by politics (S.T. to Rudolf Führer, 6 October 1972).

scientific arguments – to move the debate onto questions that have nothing to do with philology.

Scientifically speaking, *Sappho und Simonides* still has to be judged for its philological merits. According to Timpanaro, the question of its political flaws can be entirely divorced from this process. Even if we might disagree with this premise of a hard-line separability between politics and science sometimes used to redeem 'problematic' figures such as Wilamowitz, and can see clearly the potential fallout from its strict application, we can still appreciate the depth of Timpanaro's commitment to it. Indeed, we can view it charitably as a defence of what we might call the principle of salvageable content. As we have seen before, every thinker, for Timpanaro, is a mix of the good and bad, the useful and the discardable – and so every part of a thinker's thought should be sifted on its own terms. Just because scientific results are impregnated by ideology does not mean that ideology completely invalidates *all* the results. It is an uncomfortable, somewhat counterintuitive message in this age of high-horse moralising; but, like much of Timpanaro's thought, the echo rings true. Timpanaro's example should help us sort through the chequered legacy of European cultural history with a critical eye and an open mind, and help us reckon with the problem that the wheat and chaff of intellectual history are difficult to separate. But with attentive reading and meticulous work, we might try.

The Livrea affair, then, raised Timpanaro's guard because it got to the heart of a thread we have been following throughout this book. On the line was nothing less than his sworn oath to free and open debate; his investment in the ability of philology to escape the judgements of politics; and, perhaps, his own ability to be judged as a philologist on the terms of that science without having his status as a card-carrying socialist invoked to disqualify him. Timpanaro did not want his politics to matter for his philology. This book has argued that it was more the other way round: Timpanaro exported the techniques of philology for use on a much broader cultural and political plane. The philologist could (and should) think without Marxism, but the Marxist continued to think with philology.

Can the many branches of this thinker be reduced, like the virtual archetype at the base of a Lachmannian family tree, to certain unifying foundations? We have fired seven chapters at Timpanaro, all to capture the many strands of this eccentric philologist and heterodox Marxist. My assumption throughout this book is that there has been unity in the diversity. Through and beneath Timpanaro's singular intellectual output lie running threads, obsessions, connections, commitments. I have sketched these along the way. But, before further wrapping these up to make final claims on what energised Timpanaro – and why these things should still energise us too – I would like to briefly second-guess myself. I want to deploy Timpanaro against himself and myself. I want to take for a moment his preferred pose, to read him 'emically' as it were, on his own internal terms, in order to question the very task of unity which underlies this book.

Leftist arguments are often weighted to the assumption of connection and commonality. We are predisposed towards totality. The explanatory framework of Marxism is constitutionally built to wed the economic sphere to every other component of human life. We prefer to steer clear of individuals and talk systems, interested in the game itself rather than the player (or the ball). This bias towards unity is perhaps a remnant of that infamous Hegelian dialectic, the idealist tendency to resolve the world's contradictions into a higher principle, against which Timpanaro battled his whole life. If we are guilty of this at the level of the world in general, we also do it at the scope of the individual. I have approached Timpanaro similarly in trying to shuttle regularly between his particular interests and his overall guiding principles. In a sense, I have reduced him to the general abstraction of his very worst nightmares. In so doing, I have read Timpanaro against his own grain. I am not sure he would be happy about it.

At several points in his correspondence, Timpanaro draws attention to the conflicting parts of his intellectual identity. The lines of division are inscribed in different ways, but the main message is usually the same. To Carlo Ginzburg, Timpanaro claimed that his pedantic philologist side sat uncomfortably next to his populist-pessimist side.[13] To Luca Baranelli, Timpanaro described his life as an oscillation between his political interests and his 'library mouse' activity, without ever managing to heal the contradiction.[14] But, even before these claims, Timpanaro

---

13   S.T. to Carlo Ginzburg, 5 March 1971.
14   S.T. to Luca Baranelli, 25 May 1971.

wrote to his old friend Giorgio Voghera in 1969 and admitted the difficulty of reconciling his bigger-picture materialist-cultural work with his
philological 'little questions' (*questioncelle*):

> On the one hand I'd be tempted to dedicate my modest forces exclu-
> sively to materialism-pessimism, letting go of classical philology and
> the history of nineteenth century culture; on the other hand, I don't
> know how to detach myself from an interest – of a kind also merely
> technical – for philological little questions. Certainly an exponent of
> the non-existence (or of the not-necessary existence) of the unity of
> the human personality would have in me an ideal example: I am, in
> reality, an aggregate of different interests, to which a common denom-
> inator could only be found by sophistic argument. But the exponents
> of the opposite thesis could justly hit back that 'successful' personali-
> ties have a solid unity, and that, if some people like me have remained
> in the state of incoherent 'aggregate', there's no reason to consider
> them 'paradigmatic' and to found on them a theory of the
> non-personality.[15]

This passage sums Timpanaro's divided self on two fronts: it leaves him
as an aggregate of interests without coherence, a point chalked up for
the theory of non-integrated personalities. This self-description was
clearly important to Timpanaro, as he framed himself in strikingly similar terms in an interview with Fabio Minazzi in 1991, twenty-two years
down the track.[16] Yet, even in this early diagnosis of Timpanaro's unrec-
onciled selves, he cannot quite agree with himself, making sure to put
the opposite case (note 'hit back', *ribattere* in the original Italian): that
successful personalities have a certain unity to them, and his own lack of
coherence is not necessarily something on which to base a *general*
theory of the non-integrated personality (he is, after all, a philological
particular in his own right). If his interests do not sum to a whole, then,
is this a sign that none of us is whole? Or that Timpanaro has simply
failed to be whole? When the time comes to offer himself as empirical

---

15   S.T. to Giorgio Voghera, 20 November 1969.
16   Sebastiano Timpanaro, 'Dialogo sul materialismo' with Fabio Minazzi (1991)
(at *VR*, 207). See Cortesi, introduction to *VR*, xliv; epigraph to Bufarale, introduction to
Sebastiano Timpanaro, 19.

evidence, Timpanaro denies his representativeness and extrapolability. He is no paradigm for anything. He cannot be abstracted, cannot be theorised. Timpanaro wants to remain a singularly unresolved being, and he disapproves in advance of the whole point of this book, to draw a 'common denominator' (*un comune denominatore*) to make something more synthetic of an awkwardly meshing aggregate. We remember from the discussion of dialectic in chapter 4 that aggregates are not the only form of relation. He gives us a good hint here that were he to have read this book, he would have considered it 'sophistry' – or perhaps mere 'coquetry' (*civetteria*) – for that is what the argumentative move of superimposing unity on diversity is always about.

In the next letter to Giorgio Voghera – one of the jewels in the collection, where we catch Timpanaro prompted to perform a rare and grudging act of intellectual autobiography – he again invited consideration of his internal heterogeneity:[17] first, in the diverse roots of his initial dissatisfaction with idealism; second, in the soldering of Marx and Leopardi we have seen feature so often in this book. Here, Timpanaro implied the relationship between the two in his thought to be one of synthesis – but then, as if triggered by the very term, pulls back to a parenthetic alternative:

> Later, through Leopardi and eighteenth-century thought, my pessimism went on clarifying itself in a materialist-hedonist sense, while in the meantime I had (very late, alas!)[18] 'discovered' Marxism and undertaken those attempts at synthesis (or at eclectic juxtaposition?) between Marxism and Leopardism in which I still now dabble.

'Synthesis' might be a natural shorthand to describe Timpanaro's combination of Leopardi and Marx. But in reality, the question in parenthesis – 'eclectic juxtaposition?' – represents a better description of what Timpanaran combinations do. The editor of Timpanaro's collected political writings Luigi Cortesi nicely remarks that Timpanaro ended up preferring the elegant hendiadys *marxista e leopardiano* over the monstrous hybrid *marxista–leopardiano* – but this preference to remain

---

17   S.T. to Giorgio Voghera, 27 December 1969.
18   By 'late', Timpanaro exaggerates somewhat; he joined the PSI when he was still only twenty-three.

two-in-one persists throughout his thought.[19] Whether it be philology with Freud or nineteenth-century cultural history, or Leopardi with Marxism, or the library mouse with the engaged life, Timpanaro's mind is a series of 'eclectic juxtapositions', diagrams which struggle to overlap. But there is a point to maintaining those juxtapositions in that particular form of unresolved relationship. In a political culture of disappearing opposition, of fading antagonism, of pallid 'unity' and innocuous compromise, the Timpanaran mission is to keep the contradictions intact as a mode of powering struggle. At the highest level of history or politics, these contradictions need not be resolved – indeed *should not* be resolved – because irresolution sharpens debate and drives generative conflict. So, at the level of the individual, the forces competing within one's mind should not necessarily be spirited away into a master narrative that leaves them explained, but inert. The tensions within us are productive. They work on one another without needing to be disappeared. Our leftist habits of thought would have us lump Timpanaro. He himself would prefer to stay split.

And yet, the possibility of unity does call to Timpanaro. Why would he spend his life pushing for the combination of Marx and Leopardi if he thought they were ultimately incompatible? In the same letter to Voghera, he responded to his interlocutor's point that non-unitary personalities tended, at least, to be harmless. Does that mean unitary personalities, conversely, are necessarily harmful? Definitely not. And in the hypothetical possibility of unity, Timpanaro gives us a glimpse, I think, of some motive forces behind *him*:

> What you add is perhaps true, and can be a reason for comfort: that non-unitary personalities rarely manage to be 'harmful'. I wouldn't subscribe without doubt to the reciprocal proposition, that unitary personalities are necessarily harmful: Why couldn't unity be constituted indeed by an acute sense of the unhappiness and vanity of human affairs, or by a powerful need for justice and equality?

It is possible to conceive that a unitary personality could be found in the consciousness of the unhappiness and vanity in human affairs, or by a

---

19   Cortesi, introduction to *VR*, xii. See also Timpanaro's remarks at *VR*, 170, 173, 220.

powerful need for justice and equality. With typical Timpanaran under-statement, we have to pause a second to visualise whom he might be picturing in these prospective states of unity. He could be thinking of Leopardi, particularly in that first possibility. But in both the first and the second, 'someone' formed by an 'acute sense' (I would say formed *against* the general unhappiness and vanity in human affairs, and formed *for* justice and equality), we detect none other than Timpanaro himself. He would never make it about himself. But we glimpse here an oblique acknowledgement of what he was about.

If we were to extract the unity from Timpanaro, we could do worse than starting with the concerns hinted above. Timpanaro's self-appointed intellectual doppelganger, Leopardi, was brought together as a being by humanity's fundamental unhappiness. He also showed, as Timpanaro would always point out, that this innate miserable condition was a source of solidarity *for all*. Pessimism was a perfectly respectable way to bring coherence not just to the self but also to humans as a collective. But the more interesting place to begin our Timpanaro envoi is perhaps the second possibility: justice and equality.

The words 'justice and equality' are often to be found embedded in the bland management-speak of liberal politics nowadays. They might sound empty. But their pairing anaesthetises us to their true resonance. These principles fuelled the Timpanaran project, in what-ever he did. Their role in his political activity is obvious. The social-ism towards which Timpanaro spent his life driving and searching was nothing if not a promise of instituting those very things within human society. But they also feature in his work in a more abstract sense. As Perry Anderson has surmised, Timpanaro was constantly motivated by the need to do the work of retrospective justice in intel-lectual history – to render unto X what was X's, where X was invari-ably a little known or underappreciated bit player in the history of ideas. This broad objective would apply to countless of the figures we have encountered in this book: from the small-name philologists forming the unseen props to Lachmann's method, to lesser lights of late nineteenth-century Italian philology such as Enea Piccolomini, to obscure linguists like Giacomo Lignana, to undervalued 'Enlightenment classicist'–style figures like Pietro Giordani, Ludovico Di Breme, and Carlo Bini, to then-neglected leftist heroes like Engels and Trotsky.[20] While Timpanaro's work here is limited by the homogeneity of these agents in terms of race and gender, his careful mode of performing such acts of retrospective justice can teach us much as we strive to do the same across greater swathes of the past. Timpanaran intellectual history is nothing if not an attempt to salvage from that past the people who propped it up in an un-flashy way, the thinkers now lost and underrated, but who made their mark, and deserve a place in the credits for it. Just as Timpanaro wants to give the forgotten currents of cultural history their due – for romanticism was not all there was, and we must remember Enlightenment classicism too – so he wants acknowledgement restored to the agents of those currents. The apportioning of credit in retrospect is Timpanaro's small way of doing justice to – and in – history. It is one of his most defining habits of thought. And it helps us understand why he needed the philological eye for detail in everything he did. To recover the precise contours of history's fine grains, to work out precisely who did what, you need to pick nits.

Timpanaro was also committed to equality in evidence. As we have seen, his philological training made him remarkably indifferent to the aesthetic charms or defects of texts. All he really cared about was the philosophical or propositional content of art, and this made him singularly well placed to see things other people could not see for the blinding effects of aesthetic prejudice and distraction. Ironically, his insensitivity to the containers was also a unique sensibility for the content of ideas. Timpanaro was among the first to redeem De Amicis's *Primo Maggio*, I think, precisely because he was desensitised to questions of artistic form or style. Where everyone was busy bursting into allergic paroxysms at the badness of the *Primo Maggio*, its subpar version of annoying and saccharine Deamicisian style, Timpanaro could cut through the snag of aesthetic distraction and get to the point about why this was an interesting text – ultimately, a piece of evidence which advertised the transformative power of socialist commitment. Timpanaro had his ideological baggage, of course. But he genuinely came to texts free of the freight which disqualified many of his generation from seeing certain things merely because of the politics and fashion of artistic form. While pure judgement without

---

20   Timpanaro's recuperation of Engels is a central pillar of his materialism: see Luca Bufarale, *Sebastiano Timpanaro: L'inquietudine della ricerca*, Pistoia, 2022, 82–3.

apriorism is technically impossible, Timpanaro did have a genuine capacity to treat literary and intellectual objects on their own terms. He could weed out the mixed legacies of individual thinkers with even-handedness and honesty. And he could do it as a philologist who did not care much for 'artistry' or 'quality' or 'originality'. Timpanaro's focus remained *truth*.

If anything could be recovered as Timpanaro's big unifier, it might be just that: truth. Several thinkers familiar with Timpanaro's work have commented that urgency of truth was ever present at the back of his mind. Perry Anderson suggests Timpanaro's passion for truth is his driving force;[21] Salvatore Settis and Michele Feo agree;[22] Romano Luperini too;[23] Federico Santangelo is not far off.[24] Ted Kenney calls Timpanaro's 'a mind that never rested in its unflagging quest after the truth'.[25] They are right: the search for truth animates all of Timpanaro's work, and it is part of what makes him sound completely anachronistic in temper, a strange peal of earnestness ringing in our jaded age. As he self-deprecatingly puts it in a letter to his old friend Luigi Blasucci, this search for truth and its negative aspects, its flirtation with all-out positivism, is what makes literary critic Mario Fubini 'right' when he called Timpanaro a *fossile tardo-ottocentesco*.[26] Few of us writing and thinking in the long shadow of post-structuralism would be quick to resort to such language of naked truth. This remains for me a significant discomfort in reading Timpanaro, because I have been trained in a tradition that combines a philological respect for objectivity with a post-structuralist scepticism towards such objectivity claims. I have an unshakeable sense that the language of 'truth' always masks a closet positivism that is

---

21   Perry Anderson, 'Timpanaro among the Anglo-Saxons', in Riccardo Di Donato (ed.), *Il filologo materialista. Studi per Sebastiano Timpanaro*, Pisa, 2003, 190.

22   Salvatore Settis, script of a speech given by Settis at the Accademia Lincei in Rome (numbered 8 under 'Settis' in the Timpanaro archive). Feo: Giuseppina Magnaldi, 'Questioni di metodo: Plauto e Lucrezio', in Enrico Ghidetti and Alessandro Pagnini (eds), *Sebastiano Timpanaro e la cultura del Secondo Novecento*, Rome, 2005, 241.

23   Romano Luperini, 'Testimonianza per Timpanaro: Il dibattito sul materialismo e altri ricordi degli anni sessanta e settanta', in Ghidetti and Pagnini, *Sebastiano Timpanaro*, 372.

24   Federico Santangelo, 'Voler "capire tutto" '. Appunti sullo stile di Sebastiano Timpanaro', *Anabases* 20 (2014): 66.

25   E.J. Kenney, 'Timpanaro (S.) *The Genesis of Lachmann's Method*. Edited and translated by G.W. Most', *Classical Review* 57, no. 1 (2007): 241.

26   S.T. to Luigi Blasucci, 28 July 1978.

simply refusing to be up front about the a priori commitments it claims to disavow. But at some level, the truth continues to call.

When we regularly catch Timpanaro asking questions we have been taught to dodge or dilute, it makes for strange reading, sometimes even inducing reflexes approaching cringe. He pulls up comrades for not even discussing whether psychoanalysis is true or false, simply whether it is revolutionary or reactionary; objective truth is to them sidelined as 'false bourgeois objectivity'.[27] Likewise, on issues of free will and determinism, the question for Timpanaro is not whether a philosophy is sympathetic or antipathetic, but whether it is true or false.[28] Even of literature, Timpanaro asks the unaskable: he criticises Lukácsians for questioning not whether a work of literature is beautiful or ugly, *true or false*, but only whether it is timely, whether it responds to the epoch.[29] This basic philosophical test – owing something to a blunt positivism we in the humanities are trained to be hostile towards, because such questions never seem to end well for us – is something Timpanaro has no compunction about putting to all the material with which he comes into contact, even where it seems distinctly out of place or unproductive. This is partly what makes Timpanaro such an eccentric and compelling figure. He asks questions that may seem irrelevant or wrong headed, or are perhaps taken from a discursive system quite different from the object of study ('Is psychoanalysis true or false?' 'Is literature true or false?'), but the asking generates untimely and unnerving effects, as if we were finally listening to a long-repressed voice needling us with the important question of *what really matters*. If we no longer apply this truth test, perhaps we should. After all, the reason for our scepticism towards such language is that it has often been used to ground the dominance of history's victors, whose status is shored up by claims to the 'neutral', the 'objective', the 'true'. Timpanaro's virtue is in showing the force of the truth is not just for the winners.[30]

Timpanaro's searching philological method may feel alienating at times, but it also speaks to a very human need at the heart of all humanistic acts: to turn back to particular historical objects, to pay attention to

---

27   S.T. to Francesco Orlando, 30 June 1974; cf. Giorgio Voghera, 22 March 1969.
28   S.T. to Cesare Cases, 29 July 1966.
29   S.T. to Giorgio Voghera, 11 September 1966.
30   Thanks to Francesca Bellei for articulating this.

and care for them in all of their particularity, to know them intimately, to granulate their findings, to get to know their knowledge, to interact fully with small pieces of the world as meaningful constitutive parts of it. Philology might seem remote to many consumers and producers of culture nowadays, and it has of course come under sustained critique for its many historical sins in aiding and abetting the invention of race in the nineteenth century. But there continues to be something compelling about its practice, which keeps prompting repeated announcements of the 'return to philology' in the humanities.[31] Indeed, no lesser critic of European philology than Edward Said, Timpanaro's near contemporary, came to use this very phrase to title a defence of philology in one of his last works, the posthumously published *Humanism and Democratic Criticism*. Responding to what he saw as an increasing suspicion towards reading itself in the humanities, Said decided to defend philology as 'the abiding basis for all humanistic practice': 'That basis is at bottom what I have been calling philological, that is, a detailed, patient scrutiny of and a lifelong attentiveness to words and rhetorics by which language is used by human beings who exist in history.'[32] It is that repeatedly hailed 'return' to the fundamental building blocks of humanistic knowledge – what Said calls the 'individual particular' – which represents the best of philology in many traditions, non-Western and Western alike.[33] Timpanaro is a stunningly effective example of a thinker who expanded philology's capacity for historically attentive close reading to a restless search for truth in so many other spheres of humanistic enquiry. The philologist maintained this 'lifelong attentiveness to words', but the materialist kept turning it towards the world. It proved quite a combination.

Not only was Timpanaro himself wholly committed to the scrutiny of words in the search for truth; this was also a drive he looked for in his resonant objects of study, in every historical period of his vast expertise. As we saw in the James Zetzel debate over the ancient Virgilian

31 See Andrew Hui, 'The Many Returns of Philology: A State of the Field Report', *Journal of the History of Ideas* 78, no. 1 (2017): 137–56; Merve Emre, 'The Return to Philology', *Publications of the Modern Language Association of America* 138, no. 1 (2023): 171–7.

32 Edward Said, 'The Return to Philology', in *Humanism and Democratic Criticism*, New York, 2004, 61.

33 Ibid., 80.

commentators in chapter 2, Timpanaro hated the (to him) baseless notion that these commentators simply made things up. His assumption was, rather, the reverse: that they were basically serious scholars after the truth, studying their objects in good standing, acting in good faith.[34] The same issue was in play over Timpanaro's fallout with Antonio La Penna: whether these commentators were true or false.[35] The intensity of the rift with La Penna was perhaps reflective of the depth of Timpanaro's conviction on the issue. Fast-forwarding to Timpanaro's cherished Enlightenment, his favourite French thinker, Holbach, was character-ised by anti-conformist courage for the truth, a direct and sometimes uncomfortable truth without easy consolation, and an attempt to found a morality based on truth.[36] Leopardi and Giordani were truth-seekers in the same tradition.[37] In another but related intellectual genealogy, objective truth was also, to Timpanaro, the animation behind Lenin's *Materialism and Empiriocriticism*.[38] 'Respect for the truth' was a mate-rialist first principle connecting all of these admired thinkers to each other – and all of them to Timpanaro.[39]

Timpanaro's philosophical appetite for truth came to him largely through philology.[40] That quest for an objective truth was fundamental to Timpanaro's philological practice.[41] But he would have been the first to admit it did not come from him. We need not read much beyond Giorgio Pasquali's *Filologia e storia* (Philology and history) to get a sense of the discourse passed from older to younger philologist in Timpanaro's tender years:

> The author of the present little book is thirsty for truth, wants to know it, wants that others know the truth and persuade themselves of it.[42]

---

34 S.T. to Leopoldo Gamberale, 19 May 1984 or 1986 (year unclear; numbered 6 in the Timpanaro archive).
35 S.T. to Antonio Piromalli, 10 May 1997.
36 *BS*, xxxvii, lxxv, lvi–lvii.
37 *CL*, 104–5; *AN*, 187.
38 *OM*, 233. On Timpanaro's attraction to this particular Lenin, see Bufarale, *Sebastiano Timpanaro*, 84–5.
39 *OM*, 26.
40 On the connection: Luperini, 'Testimonianza', 372.
41 Santangelo, 'Voler "capire tutto" ', 66.
42 Giorgio Pasquali, *Filologia e storia*, Florence, 1971 (1920), 4.

> The modern human, insofar as being human, is not indifferent to beauty, but, insofar as he is modern, does not seek in the study of antiquity only gratification of his thirst for beauty. The modern human is also thirsty for knowledge, he wants to understand the past historically, he wants to obtain from it a vision as full and entire as possible. And this need, because it is a thirst for truth and truth is eternal, will remain the same whether culture is oriented towards the east, or to the west, regardless of whatever intellectual alliance is concluded.[43]

Timpanaro would sign off on all of this and more: the 'thirst' for truth as a kind of base, biological *need* (good materialist language this), a vital requirement as fundamental as food, drink, air; the eternal validity of the truth independent of historical variation; the need not only to know it oneself but to *have others know it*. And just as the body's thirst is more or less unquenchable, requiring constant upkeep and replenishment, so, for Timpanaro (and Pasquali), the philological truth was something that could be accessed but never exclusively *possessed*. Timpanaro was scathing about arrogant English philologists partly because they imply that it was they, and only they, who could arrive at the philological truth through their bold conjectures.[44] For Timpanaro, the truth could not be monopolised by any person or group on some trumped-up divine right of creative genius. It remains 'out there' to be found, by grit and graft. It is a true common good, inalienable, immune from the property claim.

A commitment to truth was not only about finding it; it was about asserting the right to express it, even among difficult or hostile circumstances. And it was about securing the right of access to it for others, so that, as Pasquali would have wanted, they too may know it. We have seen these principles in action again and again in Timpanaro's intellectual life. As discussed in the Trotsky affair, Timpanaro squirmed and thrashed at the faintest hint of ideological censorship. Open and honest debate was a sine qua non of any true Marxist culture; nothing should be ruled off the table of ideas, nothing suppressed or weaselled out of. Timpanaro was ruthless in his open critique of wrong-headed

---

43   Ibid., 44.

44   Santangelo, 'Voler "capire tutto" ', 64–5; see also Vincenzo Di Benedetto, 'Discutendo di Timpanaro e di congetture', *Rivista di cultura classica e medioevale* 47, no. 1 (2005): 168–9.

directions among both allies and foes; he always wrote his mind with a bluntness that perhaps compensated for his shyness in speech.[45] That free interchange of ideas was another version of his commitment to conflictual discussion as an end in itself – something useful for sharpening ideas across the board, even if there was no ground given or mind convinced on the other side. That Enlightenment penchant for straight-talking back-and-forth was complemented by a conviction that information should always be accessible. Leopardi's early work should long ago have been published so we can know the entire picture of this important thinker. It was down to the private interests of the old aristocracy that the unfortunate blanks in Leopardi's output remained. Sometimes the truth had to be spoken, no matter what. Sometimes, it had to be all-out expropriated from attempts to privatise it. Either way, it was always for the common good.

If philology, for Timpanaro, was one way of getting at that truth, another was science. The preponderance of empiricism and positivism in the anglophone tradition perhaps makes us deaf to how very strangely a figure like Timpanaro rang in the Italian context, where a particularly intense sundering of the 'two cultures' made figures seriously overlapping between the sciences and the humanities fairly rare indeed. The idealist spirit of humanistic education in the Italy of Timpanaro's generation translated to a serious slighting of science among large swathes of the cultural elite. Timpanaro's struggle was thus a continuation of his father's (minus the idealism), nothing short of a concerted attempt to restore respect for the sciences in Italian intellectual culture.[46] A deep historical suspicion for science had also been intensified by leftist scepticism towards it, considering it, as we have seen, nothing more than the pure expression of bourgeois ideology. Timpanaro was always pushing hard against this move. Leopardi's thought was not just ideology or false consciousness but contained real, objective knowledge of the human condition in the world: Marxism should not admit the undesirable part of Gramsci, namely the idea of science as just ideology; one should not

---

45 Timpanaro also suggested his honest polemical style arose in response to the verbal culture of beating about the bush and very mild disagreement in the political discussions of the '50s (S.T. to Attilio Chitarin, 24 June 1972).

46 See Pierpaolo Antonello, *Contro il materialismo*, Turin, 2012.

discount scientific results merely because they were intermingled with bad ideology (cf. Wilamowitz above); Karl Korsch came in for criticism for not understanding that Lenin's *Materialism and Empiriocriticism* was not an attack on science itself but its ideological misuse (and Marx and Engels made the same distinction themselves, particularly apropos of Darwin); Kepler's laws could in no sense be reduced to ideology. Over and over again, Timpanaro makes the same basic point: whether we call it science or materialism, there obtains a hard core of reality that cannot be denied by its absorption into the realm of the mind. The more general point, again, is Timpanaro's indefatigable opposition to resolution as such, by appeal to some higher principle of the spirit or the mind. The omnipresence of 'ideology' was, for Timpanaro, merely the latest land-grab phase in idealism's epistemic greed, its tendency to make the whole world into an epiphenomenon of the thing between our ears. The defence of science's core was a way of striking back, of reinscribing the limits of idealist encroachment and giving the materialist's line-in-the-sand riposte: 'Enough.'

The inscription of limits, as well as the search for and expression of truth, formed the mainstay of Timpanaro's intellectual system. All of his work was motivated by a sense of injustice and imbalance – the perception that a particular theory or method or framework has taken too much of the world, and that we need to bring it back down to size (*ridimensionare*, 'rescaling' or 'resizing', was a Timpanaran keyword). Romanticism was dominating the cultural historiography of a whole period and drowning out the complexity and counter-currents parallel to it; Gramsci's concept of the organic intellectual had become so bloated and distorted as to twist the left's estimation of anyone who did not fall into its neat category fit (even Leopardi); idealist currents such as Freud and structuralism had crept into materialism and needed to be bunted back, just as the economic sphere of Marxism was butting into biological territory and claiming deterministic ownership over something beyond its power; Trotsky had become too reduced under the anti-Leninist tendencies of contemporary Marxism and needed to be scaled back up; the dialectic could not account for every form of relationship or every kind of historical change; Freud's explanation of lapsus through recourse to unconscious repression had become too broad for its own good; linguistics' newfound feel for synchrony was crowding out the important dimension of diachrony; language needed defence as an object of study beyond the reach of the Marxist concept of superstructure; obsession with form and style in literary criticism were blinding us to the truth content of serious Enlightenment-spirit literature such as Bini and De Amicis. All of these warpings were generated by a priori commitments, another way the human mind was wilfully changing the world in the process of observing it. Timpanaro saw it as his duty to push back against all these modes of thinking, aggressive ways of lumping a reality that should by rights be split. This approach, of course, itself involved a series of a priori commitments on Timpanaro's part. His work, at least, has the merit of being up front about them.

Timpanaro tended to say the same things over and over again, and some of these things strike us as obvious. His pessimism was rooted in the conviction that in a future socialist society, there will still be catastrophic car crashes and devastating volcanic eruptions. We will still, always, get sick, get old, and die. Our mortal frames, at the mercy of nature, will keep suffering the same limits. As we saw in chapter 1, Timpanaro in fact turned towards the green later in his life as the prospect of an authentic red wave receded. His thought became more and more aware that capitalism's infinite expansion threatens to accelerate our collective demise, ultimately and ironically introducing a new natural limit beyond which we as a species (rather than as individuals) cannot go. Timpanaro fought tooth and nail his whole life to put an end to capitalism, and he tragically saw on the horizon the ever-increasing urgency (and ever-receding impracticability) of that task: put an end to it, or it will put an end to us. What he wrote to the scholar of nineteenth-century Italian literature Guido Bezzola in 1983 about atmospheric pollution today stands as yet another indictment of capital's inexorable marching of us all even closer to the brink:

Already we're paying, with respect to health, a high price for such pollution; but if the process is (as one is right to fear) ever increasing and irreversible, there will come a moment in which the state of the atmosphere will be incompatible with human life on earth.[47]

Thanks to capitalism's eternal growth and exhaust, the apocalypse was now the remit of the materialists rather than the mystics. It was

---

47   S.T. to Giuseppe Bezzola, 21 January 1983.

conceivable, and it was something Timpanaran: 'If, then, western civilisation (which has its most advanced expression, technologically speaking, in the capitalist system) proceeds in this way, the end of humanity
is assured, for reasons entirely concrete and material . . . not for mystical
exaltations.'[48] The only way of swerving from this suicidal path, according to Timpanaro, was communism. We knew he would say something
like that. It does not make it untrue.

I think it should be in that context, of resisting capitalism's exaltation
of the unlimited and its seemingly endless ability to expand and reinvent itself anew, that we should see the deliberately *limited* and *limiting*
thought of Timpanaro. If capitalism remains the driver of relentless
growth and newness, the seeker of evergreen 'innovation', Timpanaro
pushed back through assuming the role of obstinate dinosaur philologist. Philology was the art of rearticulating the unoriginal, of having the
courage to say something over and over again because it was true, so
that it would not be forgotten, and until people would get it. This has a
certain resonance with the spirit of Timpanaro's intellectual twin Carlo
Bini, who never suffered from lack of originality, because saying the
same truths in a slightly modulated way was just as good:

> Nor are those pages damaged by their 'lack of originality'.
> Enlightenment thinkers of entirely another stature and fertility than
> Bini were also, as is known, 'not very original'. But until certain battles
> are won, insisting [literally, 'bashing and bashing again', *battere e
> ribattere*] is necessary. And since the environments and epochs of the
> battles change, as well as the adversaries with whom one has to strug-
> gle, that implies a different structuring, and therefore an originality, of
> different works. Originality consists also in the different point of
> departure, in the merging of different thrusts, practical and intellec-
> tual, with individual polemicists.[49]

In politics, as in philology, everything is usually already there. We do
not need to keep reinventing the wheel endlessly. At this point, perhaps
we must simply pound and pound again until we win. From context to
context, spread across the mouths of Cicero, the ancient Virgilian

---

48   Ibid.
49   *AN*, 245.

commentators, Holbach, Bini, Leopardi, Giordani, Cattaneo, Marx, Engels, Lignana, Ascoli, Meringer, Trotsky, and Pasquali, the recovery and reiteration of *truth* against shifting targets is an originality more important than being original. It is a restless intervention, an ongoing strike and counterstrike, an uncompromising antagonism, a never-ending correction in the making and to be made. That is the materialist philology of Sebastiano Timpanaro.

Acknowledgements

This book's serpentine genesis would have stretched even Timpanaro's powers of reconstruction. It certainly has mine. The work of making *Major Corrections* has cohabited with the most epoch-shifting personal and political events. For me it will always act as a token of the transformations, displacements, disappointments, and despair that suffused it, for better or worse.

What started with my philologist mentor Frances Muecke's recommendation of *The Freudian Slip* in 2007 didn't properly amass momentum till I had a sleepless night in Somerville, Massachusetts, in 2018, my brain full of a completely different project. By some unexpected swerve, Timpanaro re-entered my skull. I buzzed with the idea of writing a book on him. I started reading around. In 2019, I managed a reconnaissance mission to test the depths of the Timpanaro archive in Pisa, and applied for a grant to do a longer stint there. Covid happened; the grant came through. I delayed the research for a year or so while we waited for a vaccine. When I finally made it to Pisa in August 2021, I began an intensive stint of rinsing through the entire letter correspondence within the archive. On a quick break back from the stacks in Australia in March 2022, my mother's cancer returned, her dementia kicked in, and in a few months, she was dead. This book was mainly written within the line spaces of her deterioration, death, and afterglow. Perhaps in order to be born, the book needed to live that most Timpanaran experience of biological finitude, to creak beneath the binding structures of old age, illness, and death. This book is mainly for my mother, its ultimate genesis.

Amid the chaos, the grief, the guilt, and the relief, I logged debts. There feels like a world to thank. There is. The art history library of the Scuola Normale Superiore in Pisa, where Timpanaro now survives as archive, enabled everything. Its archivist Barbara Allegranti got sick of me asking for folder after folder of correspondence. I thank her for the welcome and the indulgence of interruption. Though Covid took her life before I could thank her in person, I also owe a deep debt to Maria Augusta Timpanaro Morelli – herself a great scholar and archivist who took time from her own precious studies to curate her late husband's archive. This book could not have materialised without her work. At the Scuola Normale itself, Luigi Battezzato, Gianpiero Rosati, and Alessandro Schiesaro welcomed with open arms a strange Australian digging in the dungeons of their institutional and intellectual history. The graduate students of the Normale made for brilliant interlocutors, sometimes moonlighting as expert bibliography trackers (thanks to Nicolò Campodonico in particular for finding me a copy of Timpanaro's *Il socialismo di Edmondo De Amicis* at a critical time; thanks likewise to Charlie Pemberton, a PhD student at the University of Cambridge, for doing the same with Timpanaro's *Contributi*). Larisa Ficulle Santini's timely gift of the Cesare Cases – Sebastiano Timpanaro published correspondence helped me kickstart things even before I could drown in the archive. Thanks also to friends of Timpanaro – Luca Baranelli, Michele Feo, and Daniela Paccella – for sharing memories and resources. Serendipitously running into the latter over a coffee at a Pisan haunt run by a former member of Lotta Continua made me realise the deep networks of red Tuscany are still alive and kicking.

Three interlocutors were particularly important fonts of inspiration in the initial research phase. First and foremost, Henry Stead, who initially encouraged me to chase Timpanaro down, and without whose work on classical antiquity and the European left this project would've been inconceivable. I miss our freezing surfs in the North Sea after frosty mornings on the picket lines. Secondly, enthused conversations with Greg Mellen, an unexpected companion in Tuscany, gave me the illusion I had something worth saying. Thirdly, a chance overlap with Luca Bufarale in the first week of my period at the Timpanaro archive was pure providence. I thank him for giving me a first induction into the overwhelming acronyms of the Italian left, and for sharing electronic and physical versions of his book. Few better things have been written on Timpanaro's politics and philosophy.

As the ideas matured, generous audiences at Princeton, the Critical Antiquities Network, the University of Pisa, and the Australian National University gave valuable input. At draft stage, the book was transformed by the close reading of a cast of brilliant minds: Francesca Bellei, Andrew Brooks, Elena Giusti, Liam Grealy, Barney Lewer, Ramsey McGlazer, Frances Muecke, Alessandro Schiesaro, Federico Santangelo, and Henry Stead. One of the tightropes of this book was making relatively arcane subject matter legible to intelligent readers without a knowledge base in many, or any, of the disciplines in which Timpanaro worked. These readers helped pull the book outwards, towards that goal. At the last hurdle, the book benefited immeasurably from the acumen of Perry Anderson, whose large- and small-scale feedback was spot on (even if he would bristle at my irrepressible recourse to the Australian demotic, in this very sentence as elsewhere). I thank my commissioning editor at Verso, Sebastian Budgen, for shepherding the book through contract and production phases, and my production editor Jeanne Tao and copy editor Sam Smith for cleaning up the final manuscript with the keenest eyes.

In writing of a thinker so attentive to the material sphere, I must also thank the institutions that kept me fed, principally my old home the University of St Andrews, and now my new one, the Australian National University. I couldn't have invented better colleagues and comrades to bounce off, whether facing the North Sea (Ralph Anderson, Emma Buckley, Michael Carroll, Jason König, Myles Lavan, Guto Machado, Consuelo Martino, Beppe Pezzini, Roger Rees, Henry Stead, Rebecca Sweetman, Nicolas Wiater) or Lake Burley-Griffin (Tatiana Bur, Caillan Davenport, Theodore Ell, Meaghan McEvoy, Georgia Pike-Rowney, Francesco Ricatti, Estelle Strazdins). Special thanks to Rebecca Sweetman for allowing me the time and space to rove out of office – a sine qua non of this kind of research. The Leverhulme Trust was generous beyond generous in funding the project not once, not twice, but effectively three times: the first with an award of a Leverhulme Research Fellowship, the second with a six-month extension of that fellowship due to Covid delays, the third with the award of a Philip Leverhulme Prize. A teaching job in the straitened contemporary university simultaneously demands and denies the practice of deep research. I wouldn't have been able to write this book in anything resembling its current form if the Leverhulme Trust had not given me some time and space to read, write, and think all around it. Living in a world where the humanities are properly valued and their practitioners generously funded remains a fantasy, but one I refuse to think unrealisable within a different future. In the meantime, the Leverhulme Trust provides.

To the beautiful collection of oddballs and reprobates who have agreed to be my friends in Australia (Saul Bert, Zoe Blome, Andrew Brooks, Vinnie Brooks, Robert d'Apice, Ben Etherington, Jet Geaghan, Dani Gessler, Roman Gessler, Daisy Gibbs, Liam Grealy, Duncan Hilder, Taichi Hoshino, Jo Laidler, Aristea Kaydos-Nitis, Evy Kaydos-Nitis, Barney Lewer, Astrid Lorange, Meredith Medway, Elodie Murphy, Sean Murphy, Ivan Muniz Reed, James Newman, Miro Sandev, Asher Sandev-Medway, Volker Schlue, Celina Siriyos, Catherine Trundle, Camilla Wagstaff, Marty Wieczorek), Europe and the UK (Louise Benson, Clem Cheetham, Isla Cowan, Raph Cormack, Carlos Cueva, Barbara Del Giovane, Patrick Errington, Will Ferguson, Larisa Ficulle Santini, Camilla Furetta, Yuddi Gershon, Guido Giovanardi, Elena Giusti, Sam Goff, Lucy Jackson, Talitha Kearey, Aris Komporozos-Athanasiou, Adam Lecznar, Sophie Mallett, Marina Dora Martino, Ric McLauchlan, Michal Murawski, Steph O'Rourke, Giulio Pertile, Sam Rose, Miguel Santa Clara, Laura Rosella Schluderer, Henry Stead, Isobel Stott, Ellie Stedall, Katrina Zaat), and the US (Francesca Bellei, Chiara Graf, Harvey Lederman, Alex Schultz): thanks for keeping my head above water in some very hard times, and thanks for giving me so many reasons to get up in the morning. This book dovetailed with some very special new lives entering my chosen extended families: Felix came to Giules Amato and Georgia Sholl as a little brother to fascinate and annoy Teddy; and Mara eventually rocked up for Miriam Hillyard and Lotte Kühlbrandt after some long months of comical yet failed collective attempts to hasten her conception in a Livorno attic. These relationships of dona-tion have enriched my life no end, and I'd recommend everyone capable of forming sperm to give it away if you can.

In particular, my people in Sydney, Rome, Edinburgh, and Livorno humoured me by at least feigning interest in a philologist and socialist whose name they'd never heard of and would likely instantly forget. Livorno is one of the cities of my life – a bastion of leftist fun, committed open-mindedness, and anarchic energy, resolutely immune to the creeping fascism of contemporary Italy (and the world). Though I commuted to the city of the leaning tower every day to work, my heart always did and always will nest in Livorno.

While I lost my mother between the pages of this book, I am lucky to have father figures still roaming this world. My academic dad, John Henderson, may not like my philological turn, but I learned from him everything I know about reading against the grain and bringing the subject to life. He must take some responsibility for creating this monster. My biological dad, Andrew Geue, a former mathematician turned actuary, once upon a time taught me the wonder of science, and to look for how things work. May he consider this book a way of redeeming my Freudian abandonment of a science degree. Thanks for all your support, Dad. My love and admiration for you is a constant, not a variable.

I pay respects to the traditional owners of the country on which this book was finalised: the Gadigal, Ngunnawal, Ngambri, and Wangal peoples. I live and work on land expropriated by settler violence, past and present. The sovereignty of these First Nations peoples remains unceded. I acknowledge that I write as a guest on this land, and that this acknowledgement comes as an inadequate placeholder for justice still to be done.

My last words are for Rosie Short. We fell into each other's lives while we were living worlds apart. The fact that we found each other remains a miracle to me. Now I can't imagine life without you. Even a whole life with you feels a prospect too small. Thanks for letting a Latinist into your world. I love you. May this book weigh lightly on our shelves, as we lean gently on each other to build more of them.

Appendix 1: Prominent Friends and Correspondents

The following list gives an indicative (certainly not exhaustive) sense of Timpanaro's social and intellectual network. I have chosen to list only the most recognisable profiles, organised by rough field groupings. The total correspondence contained in the Timpanaro archive in Pisa lists 1,515 different correspondents and 10,738 letters in total. The full list is readily available from the Scuola Normale Superiore library website.

Classical philology

Graziano Arrighetti (1928–2017)

Ferruccio Bertini (1941–2012; medieval Latin philology)

Augusto Campana (1906–1995)

Vincenzo Di Benedetto (1934–2013)

Eduard Fraenkel (1888–1970)

Mario Geymonat (1941–2012)

Francesco Giancotti (1923–2017)

Alberto Grilli (1920–2007)

Ted Kenney (1924–2019)

Harry Jocelyn (1933–2000)

Antonio La Penna (1925–2024)

Hugh Lloyd-Jones (1922–2009)

Scevola Mariotti (1920–2000)

Arnaldo Momigliano (1908–1987)

Franco Munari (1920–1995)

Giuseppe Pacella (1920–1995)

Ettore Paratore (1907–2000)

Cesare Questa (1934–2016)

Giuseppe Ramires (1960–)

Michael Reeve (1943–)

Carlo Ferdinando Russo (1922–2013)

Giuseppe Scarpat (1920–2008)

Nino Scivoletto (1923–2008)

Otto Skutsch (1906–1990)
William Spaggiari (1948–)
Alfredo Stussi (1939–)
Alfonso Traina (1925–2019)
Vincenzo Tandoi (1929–1985)
Mario Untersteiner (1899–1981)

Creative literature
Alceste Angelini (1920–1994)
Emilio Bigi (1910–1969)
Anna Calvelli (dates unavailable)
Giorgio Voghera (1908–1999)

French literature
Francesco Orlando (1934–2010)

German literature
Cesare Cases (1920–2005)

History
Giuseppe Barbieri (dates unavailable; history of art)
Delio Cantimori (1904–1966)
Ambrogio Donini (1903–1991)
Carlo Ginzburg (1939–)
Antonio Rotondò (1929–2007)
Armando Saitta (1919–1991)
Domenico Settembrini (1929–2012)
Piero Treves (1911–1992)

Italian literature
Luca Baranelli (1936–)
Walter Binni (1913–1997)
Luigi Blasucci (1924–2021)
Umberto Bosco (1900–1987)
Umberto Carpi (1941–2013)
Mario Fubini (1900–1977)

Enrico Ghidetti (1940–)
Romano Luperini (1940–)
Carlo Alberto Madrignani (1936–2008)
Antonio Piromalli (1920–2003)

Linguistics
Tullio De Mauro (1932–2017)
Giulio Lepschy (1935–)
Paolo Ramat (1936–)

Philosophy and history of philosophy
Giuseppe Cambiano (1941–)
Girolamo De Liguori (1933–2022)
Jean Fallot (1912–1992)
Giorgio Fano (1885–1963)
Valentino Gerratana (1919–2000)
Adolf Grünbaum (1923–2018)
Sergio Landucci (1938–)

Politics
Piergiorgio Bellocchio (1931–2022)
Walter Binni (1913–1997; PSI)
Delio Cantimori (1904–1966; PCI)
Umberto Carpi (1941–2013; PCI)
Grazia Cherchi (1937–1995)
Luciano Della Mea (1924–2003; PSI and PSIUP)
Tullio De Mauro (1932–2017)
Ambrogio Donini (1903–1991; PCI)
Mario Geymonat (1941–2012; PCI)
Antonio La Penna (1925–2024; PCI)
Romano Luperini (1940–)

Appendix 2: Notes on Bibliography

References to letters in Timpanaro's correspondence are given in the form of author, addressee, and date, for example, 'S.T. to Antonio Perin, 28 March 1981'. Much of this correspondence is unpublished and housed in the Timpanaro archive at the Scuola Normale Superiore in Pisa. However, the following volumes of correspondence between Timpanaro and certain addressees have now been published:

Sebastiano Timpanaro – Francesco Orlando. Carteggio su Freud (1971–1977), Pisa, 2007.

Sebastiano Timpanaro – Giuseppe Ramires. Carteggio su Servio (1993–2000), ed. Giuseppe Ramires, Pisa, 2013.

Cesare Cases – Sebastiano Timpanaro. Un lapsus di Marx. Carteggio 1956–1990, ed. Luca Baranelli, Pisa, 2015.

'Carlo Ginzburg and Sebastiano Timpanaro, Correspondence on Freud (1971–1995)', *Psychoanalysis and History* 25, no. 2 (2023): 143–72.

Sebastiano Timpanaro – Scevola Mariotti. Carteggio (1944–1999), ed. Piergiorgio Parroni with the collaboration of Gemma Donati and Giorgio Piras, Pisa, 2023.

Below I list the major published works of Timpanaro on which I draw in the book, keyed to abbreviations used throughout. Where several editions of the book exist, I indicate to which I refer in the book by highlighting the title in bold.

FGL, *La filologia di Giacomo Leopardi* [The philology of Giacomo Leopardi], Florence, 1955.
>2nd edition: ***La filologia di Giacomo Leopardi***, revised and expanded, Rome, Bari, 1978.
>3rd edition: *La filologia di Giacomo Leopardi*, revised and expanded, Rome, Bari, 1997.

GLM: *La genesi del metodo del Lachmann* [The genesis of Lachmann's method], Florence, 1963. Contains revised articles originally published as:
>'La genesi del metodo del Lachmann I', *Studi italiani di filologia classica* 31 (1959): 182–228.
>'La genesi del metodo del Lachmann II', *Studi italiani di filologia classica* 32 (1960): 38–63.

>2nd edition: *La genesi del metodo del Lachmann*, revised and expanded, Padua, 1981.
>English translation: ***The Genesis of Lachmann's Method***, trans. Glenn Most, Chicago, 2006.

CI: *Classicismo e illuminismo nell'Ottocento italiano* [Classicism and enlightenment in the Italian nineteenth century], Pisa, 1965. Contains revised articles originally published as:
>'Le idee di Pietro Giordani', *Società* 10 (1954): 23–44, 224–54.
>'Giordani, Carducci e Chiarini', introduction to Giuseppe Chiarini (ed.), *Scritti di Giordano*, Florence, 1961.
>'Carlo Cattaneo e Graziadio Ascoli', *Rivista storica italiana* 73 (1961): 739–71, and 74 (1962): 757–802.
>'Alcune osservazioni sul pensiero del Leopardi', *Critica storica* 3 (1964): 397–431.

2nd edition: ***Classicismo e illuminismo nell'Ottocento italiano***, expanded, Pisa, 1969.
>Reprint of 2nd edition: *Classicismo e illuminismo nell'Ottocento italiano*, 1988. Contains addition of a note to xxxvi.

SF: Giacomo Leopardi, ***Scritti filologici (1817–1832)*** [Philological writings, 1817–1832], ed. Giuseppe Pacella and Sebastiano Timpanaro, Florence, 1969.

SM: *Sul materialismo* [On materialism], Pisa, 1970. Contains revised articles originally published as:

'Considerazioni sul materialismo', *Quaderni Piacentini* 5, no. 28 (1966): 76–97.

'Prassi e materialismo', *Quaderni Piacentini* 6, no. 32 (1967): 115–26.

'Engels, materialism, "libero arbitrio" ', *Quaderni Piacentini* 8, no. 39 (1969): 86–122.

2nd edition: *Sul materialismo*, revised and expanded, Pisa, 1975.

3rd edition: ***Sul materialismo***, revised and expanded, Milan, 1997.

OM: English translation: ***On Materialism***, trans. Lawrence Garner, London, 1975. Contains additional introduction.

2nd edition: *On Materialism*, 1980. Contains additional postscript.

LF: *Il lapsus freudiano. Psicanalisi e critica testuale* [The Freudian slip: Psychoanalysis and textual criticism], Florence, 1974.

Revised reprint: *Il lapsus freudiano. Psicanalisi e critica testuale*, 1975. Contains typographical corrections and the addition of a note to 203–4.

2nd edition: ***Il lapsus freudiano. Psicanalisi e critica testuale***, ed. Fabio Stok, Turin, 2002.

FS: English translation: *The Freudian Slip: Psychoanalysis and Textual Criticism*, trans. Kate Coper, London, 1976.

Translation of chapters 3 and 4 published as 'The Freudian Slip', trans. J. Matthews, *New Left Review* 91 (1975): 43–56.

Paperback reprint: ***The Freudian Slip: Psychoanalysis and Textual Criticism***, London, 1985.

CF: ***Contributi di filologia e di storia della lingua latina*** [Contributions in philology and the history of the Latin language], Rome, 1978. Contains substantially revised and updated articles originally published as:

'Il "Carmen Priami" ', *Annali della Scuola Normale Superiore di Pisa* 16 (1947): 194–200.

'Nota di latino arcaico: Livio Andronico, Odyssia fr. 24 Morel (= 24 Lenchantin)', *Paideia* 4 (1949): 400.

'Note a Livio Andronico, Ennio, Varrone, Virgilio', *Annali della Scuola Normale Superiore di Pisa* 18 (1949): 186–204.

'Note a testi latini', *La parola del passato* 6 (1951): 129–32.

'Sul testo dell'*Anthologia Latina*', *Studi italiani di filologia classica* 25 (1951): 33–48.

'Atlas cum compare gibbo', *Rinascimento* 2 (1951): 311–18.

'Delle congetture', *Atene e Roma* 4, no. 3 (1953): 95–9.

'Recensione a Frontonis Epistulae quas edidit M. P. J. van den Hout, Lugduni Batavorum 1954', *Annali della Scuola Normale Superiore di Pisa* 24 (1955): 276–82.

'Note serviane con contributi ad altri autori e a questioni di lessicografia latina', *Studi Urbinati* 31 (1957): 155–98.

'Tre noterelle', in H. Dahlmann and R. Merkelbach (eds), *Studien zur Textgeschichte und Textkritik in onore di G. Jachmann*, Köln-Opladen, 1957, 297–300.

'Lucrezio III.1', *Philologus* 104 (1960): 147–9.

'Per la storia di *ilicet*', *Rivista di filologia e di istruzione classica* 91 (1963): 323–37.

'Per la critica testuale dell'*Ephemeris* di Ditti-Settimio', in *Lanx Satura Nicolao Terzaghi oblata*, Genoa, 1963, 325–42.

'Recensione a Macrobius, ed. I. Willis', *Gnomon* 36 (1964): 784–92.

'Recensione a *Vibii Sequestris de fluminibus* ed. P. Parroni', *Atene e Roma*, series V, 11 (1966): 38–40.

'Recensione a M. Mühmelt, *Griechische Grammatik in der Vergilerklärung*, München 1965', *Rivista di filologia e di istruzione classica* 94 (1966): 336–41.

'Note a interpreti virgiliani antichi', *Rivista di filologia e di istruzione classica* 95 (1967): 428–45.

'Lucano VI.495', *Maia* 19 (1967): 370–2.

'Recensione a Macrobio, I Saturnali, a cura di N. Marinone, Torino 1967', *Rivista di filologia e di istruzione classica* 96 (1968): 473–5.

'"Positivus pro comparativo" in latino', in *Studia Florentina A. Ronconi sexagenario oblata*, Rome, 1970, 455–81.

'Alcuni casi controversi di tradizione indiretta', *Maia* 22 (1970): 351–9.

'Due noterelle al testo di storici antichi (Dion. Halic., Antiqu. XV 9; SHA IV 6, 1; IV 8, 9; VII 8, 5)', in *Studi di storiografia antica in memoria di Leonardo Ferrero*, Turin, 1971, 127–30.

'Lucrezio V.1442 (e I.314, e V.1203), *Rivista di cultura Classica e Medievale* 19 (1977), *Miscellanea di Studi in memoria di M. Barchiesi*: 725–49.

AF: *Aspetti e figure della cultura ottocentesca* [Aspects and figures of nineteenth-century culture], Pisa, 1980. Contains substantially revised and updated articles originally published as:

'Angelo Mai', *Atene e Roma*, series V, 1 (1956): 3–34.

'Due note leopardiane (1. 'A Silvia', v. 46; 2. Sul titolo delle 'Annotazioni a Eusebio')', *Giornale storico della letteratura italiana* 138 (1961): 101–5, annotated by M. Fubini, 105–6.

'Theodor Gomperz', *Critica storica* 2 (1963): 1–31.

'Recensione a P. Treves, *Lo studio dell'antichità classica nell'Ottocento*', *Critica storica* 2 (1963): 603–11.

'Di alcune falsificazioni di scritti leopardiani', *Giornale storico della letteratura italiana* 143 (1966): 88–119.

'Recensione a L. Di Breme, *Lettere*, a cura di P. Camporesi, Torino 1966', *Belfagor* 22 (1967): 240–4.

'Domenico Comparetti', in G. Grana (ed.), *Letteratura italiana. I critici*, Milan, 1969, 491–504, 508–10.

'Ancora sul Foscolo filologo', *Giornale storico della letteratura italiana* 148 (1971): 519–44.

'Il Giordani e la questione della lingua', in *Atti del Convegno di studi nel II centenario della nascita di Pietro Giordani*, Piacenza, 1974, 157–208.

'Cassi, Francesco', in *Dizionario Biografico degli Italiani*, vol. 21, 1978, 464–72.

AN: *Antileopardiani e neomoderati nella sinistra italiana* [Antileopardians and neomoderates on the Italian left], Pisa, 1982. Contains updated articles originally published as:

'Antileopardiani e neomoderati nella sinistra italiana', parts 1–2, *Belfagor* 30 (1975): 129–56, 395–428.

'Antileopardiani e neomoderati nella sinistra italiana', parts. 3–4,
    Belfagor 31 (1976): 1–32, 179–200.

SED: *Il socialismo di Edmondo De Amicis. Lettura del 'Primo Maggio'*
[The socialism of Edmondo De Amicis: A reading of 'Primo Maggio'],
Verona, 1984.

BS: Paul H. T. d'Holbach, *Il buon senso* (*Good Sense*), trans., introduced,
and annotated by Sebastiano Timpanaro, Milan, 1985.
    This book has undergone five identical reprintings, the most recent in
    2016 (which I use).

PLS: *Per la storia della filologia virgiliana antica* [Towards the history
of ancient Virgilian philology], Rome, 1986.
    2nd edition: *Per la storia della filologia virgiliana antica*, with an after-
    word by P. Parroni, Rome, 2002.

DD: Marco Tullio Cicerone, ***Della divinazione*** (*On Divination*), ed.
Sebastiano Timpanaro, Milan, 1988.
    This book has undergone eleven reprintings, the most recent in 2020
    (which I use). The only significant revisions were made in the
    edition of 1998 and carried forth in subsequent editions.

FR: **La 'fobia romana' e altri scritti su Freud e Meringer** [The 'Roman
phobia' and other writings on Freud and Meringer], Pisa, 1992.
    English translation of the first part: 'Freud's Roman Phobia', *New Left
    Review* 146 (1984): 4–31.

NC: *Nuovi contributi di filologia e storia della lingua Latina* [New
contributions in philology and the history of the Latin language], Bologna,
1994. Contains updated versions of articles originally published as:
    'Ovidio, *Amores* III. 4, 8 e le vicende del verbo *occludere*', in *Studi di
    poesia latina in onore di A. Traglia*, vol. 2, Rome, 1979, 625–32.
    'Un lapsus di Seneca?', *Giornale italiano di filologia* 31 (1979): 293–305.
    'Carm. epigr. 881 e Arnobio 1, 16', *Rivista di filologia e di istruzione
    classica* 108 (1980): 422–30.
    'Note a Lucano', in *Letterature comparate: problemi e metodo, Studi in
    onore di E. Paratore*, vol. 2, Bologna, 1981, 603–8.

'Serv. Daniel. ad Aen. IV.219', *Giornale italiano di filologia* 33 (1981): 99–105.

'Il "Praxidicus" di Accio', *Maia*, n.s., 34 (1982): 21–30.

'La tipologia delle citazioni poetiche in Seneca: Alcune considerazioni' ('Una citazione virgiliana in Seneca'), *Giornale italiano di filologia* 36 (1984): 163–82.

'Due note enniane (I. Ann. 15 sg.; 2. Ann. 502)', *Rivista di filologia e di istruzione classica* 114 (1986): 5–47.

'Alcune note all'*Anthologia Latina*, in U. J. Stache, W. Maaz, and F. Wagner (eds), *Kontinuität und Wandel. Lateinische Poesie von Naevius bis Baudelaire. Festschrift F. Munari*, Hildesheim, 1986, 298–314.

'Spigolature frontoniane', in *Studi in onore di A. Barigazzi*, vol. 2, Rome, 1986, 237–43.

'Il "ius osculi" e Frontone', *Maia*, n.s., 39 (1987): 201–11.

'Alcuni tipi di sinonimi in asindeto in latino arcaico e loro sopravvivenza in latino classico', *Rivista di filologia e di istruzione classica* 116 (1988): 257–97, 385–428.

'Virgilio, *Aen.* 10, 543-552', *Materiali e discussioni per l'analisi dei testi classici* 20–21 (1988): 91–118.

'Ancora su alcuni passi di Servio e degli scolii danielini al libro III dell'*Eneide*', *Materiali e discussioni per l'analisi dei testi classici* 22 (1989): 123–82.

'Hīc maschile plurale', in *Mnemosynum. Studi in onore di A. Ghiselli*, Bologna, 1989, 537–46.

'Il nuovo "Frontone" di van den Hout', *Rivista di filologia e di istruzione classica* 117 (1989): 365–82.

'Quanti concilii degli dèi negli *Annali* di Ennio?', *Giornale italiano di filologia* 41 (1989): 209–31.

'Servio Danielino ad Aen. 10, 8', *Annali della Scuola Normale Superiore di Pisa*, series III, 19 (1989): 1267–81.

'De ciri, tonsillis, tolibus, tonsis et quibusdam aliis rebus', *Materiali e discussioni per l'analisi dei testi classici* 26 (1991): 103–73.

NS: ***Nuovi studi sul nostro Ottocento*** [New studies on our nineteenth century], Pisa, 1995. Contains updated versions of articles originally published as:

'Cesari, Antonio', in *Dizionario Biografico degli Italiani*, vol. 24, 1980, 151–8.

'Pietro Gioia, Pietro Giordani e i tumulti piacentini del 1846', *Bollettino storico piacentino* 76 (1981): 1–31.

'Recensione di P. Giordani, *Il peccato impossibile*, ed. W. Spaggiari, Parma, 1985; P. Borsieri, *Avventure letterarie di un giorno*, ed. W. Spaggiari', *Critica storica* 24 (1987): 508–21.

'Epicuro, Lucrezio e Leopardi', *Critica storica* 25 (1988): 359–409.

'Il Leopardi e la Rivoluzione francese', in *La storia della storiografia europea sulla Rivoluzione francese* (*Relazioni tenute al Congresso dell'associazione degli storici europei*) (May 1989), vol. 2, Rome, 1990, 367–81.

'Le lettere di P. Giordani ad A. Papadopoli', *Critica storica* 27 (1990): 732–41.

'De Amicis di fronte a Manzoni e a Leopardi', in T. Iermano and T. Scappaticci (eds), *Da Carducci ai contemporanei. Studi in onore di A. Piromalli*, Naples, 1994, 17–49.

VR: Il verde e il rosso. Scritti militanti (1966–2000) [The green and the red: Militant writings 1966–2000], ed. Luigi Cortesi, Rome, 2001. Contains articles previously published as:

'Considerazioni sul materialismo', *Quaderni Piacentini* 5, no. 28 (September 1966): 76–97.

'(Intervento su) Il materialismo e la rivoluzione culturale cinese', *Nuovo Impegno* 2, nos 9–10 (August 1967 – January 1968): 54–66.

'Quel "cane morto" di Lev Davidovic' (in collaboration with F. Belgrado), *Giovane critica* (1972): 56–9.

'Karl Korsch e la filosofia di Lenin', *Belfagor* 28 (1973): 1–27.

'Recensione a A. Chitarin, *Sulla transizione*, Roma 1975', *Belfagor* 31 (1975): 715–17.

Introduction to J. Fallot, *Il piacere e la morte nella filosofia di Epicuro*, Turin: Einaudi, 1977, ix–xxxi.

'Nuova sinistra e regime autoritario', *Quaderni Piacentini* 70–71 (May 1979): 69–77.

'L'internazionalismo di Leonetti e l'europeismo di Berlinguer', *Belfagor* 34 (1979): 467–71.

Postscript from second edition of *On Materialism*, trans. Lawrence Garner, London, 1980.

'Gramsci antimaterialista?, I' (correspondence, not intended for publication, with R. M. Morano), *Ipotesi 80* 8–9 (1983): fasc. 3–4, 60–9.

'Recensione a G. Matteotti, *Scritti sul fascismo*, a cura di S. Caretti, Pisa 1983', *Belfagor* 39 (1984): 368–74.

'Il "Leopardi verde" ', *Belfagor* 42 (1987): 613–37.

'Il Verde e il Rosso: Memorie lontane e riflessioni attuali', *Giano* 1 (1989): 97–107.

Introduction to D. Paccino, *I colonnelli verdi e la fine della storia*, Rome, 1990, v–xi.

'Le idee intelligenti e combattive di un riformista d'altri tempi', *Belfagor* 45 (1990): 673–9.

'S.T. – F. Minazzi, Dialogo sul materialismo', *Marx centouno*, n.s., 7 (February 1991): 99–112.

'Risposta a un'inchiesta su intellettuali e marxismo', in 'Gli intellettuali e il marxismo', ed. G. Oldrini, special issue, *Marxismo oggi* 7, nos 2–3 (June–October 1994): 101–8.

Preface to G. Ciabatti, *Abicì d'anteguerra*, Naples, 1997, vii–xiv.

'Qualcosa si muove . . . (titolo redazionale)', *I ciompi* 6 (December 1999): 28–9.

'Ancora su sinistra e pseudo-sinistra', *Il Ponte* 56, no. 2 (Feburary 2000): 71–81.

'Lettera a Edo Cecconi del 29 agosto 1979', *Il Grande Vetro* 24–25, no. 155 (December 2000 – January/February 2001): 20–1.

VA: *Virgilianisti antichi e tradizione indiretta* [Ancient Virgilians and indirect tradition], Florence, 2001.

SLO: *Sulla linguistica dell'Ottocento* [On nineteenth-century linguistics], Bologna, 2005. Contains articles originally published as:

'Il primo cinquantennio della *Rivista di filologia e di istruzione classica*', *Rivista di filologia e di istruzione classica* 100 (1972): 387–441.

'Graziadio Ascoli', *Belfagor* 27 (1972): 149–76.

'Friedrich Schlegel e gli inizi della linguistica indeuropea in Germania', *Critica storica* 9 (1972): 72–105.

'Il contrasto tra i fratelli Schlegel e Franz Bopp sulla struttura e la genesi delle lingue indeuropee', *Critica storica* 10 (1973): 553–90.

'Giacomo Lignana e i rapporti tra filologia, filosofia, linguistica e darwinismo nell'Italia del secondo Ottocento', *Critica storica* 15 (1979): 406–503.

Index